IDW

www.IDWPublishing.com

STORY BY
ROBERTO ORCI & ALEX KURTZMAN
AND JOHN ROGERS

SCREENPLAY BY
ROBERTO ORCI & ALEX KURTZMAN

adaptation by **Kris Oprisko**

art by **Alex Milne**

colors by **Josh Perez**

color assist by **Zac Atkinson, Mark Bristow, Josh Burcham, Andrew Elder, Lisa Moore, Kieran Oats, and Rob Ruffolo**

lettering by **Robbie Robbins and Chris Mowry**

edits by **Chris Ryall**

design by **Chris Mowry**

Licensed by: Special thanks to Hasbro's Aaron Archer, Elizabeth Griffin, Sheri Lucci, Richard Zambarano, Jared Jones, Michael Provost, Michael Richie, and Michael Verrecchia for their invaluable assistance.

IDW Publishing is:
Ted Adams, Co-President
Robbie Robbins, Co-President
Chris Ryall, Publisher/Editor-in-Chief
Kris Oprisko, Vice President
Alan Payne, Vice President of Sales
Neil Uyetake, Art Director
Dan Taylor, Editor
Justin Eisinger, Editorial Assistant
Chris Mowry, Graphic Artist
Matthew Ruzicka, CPA, Controller
Alonzo Simon, Shipping Manager
Alex Garner, Creative Director
Yumiko Miyano, Business Development
Rick Privman, Business Development

ISBN: 978-1-60010-067-3
10 09 08 07   1 2 3 4 5

To discuss this issue of *Transformers*, or join the IDW Insiders, or to check out exclusive Web offers, check out our site:
www.IDWPUBLISHING.com

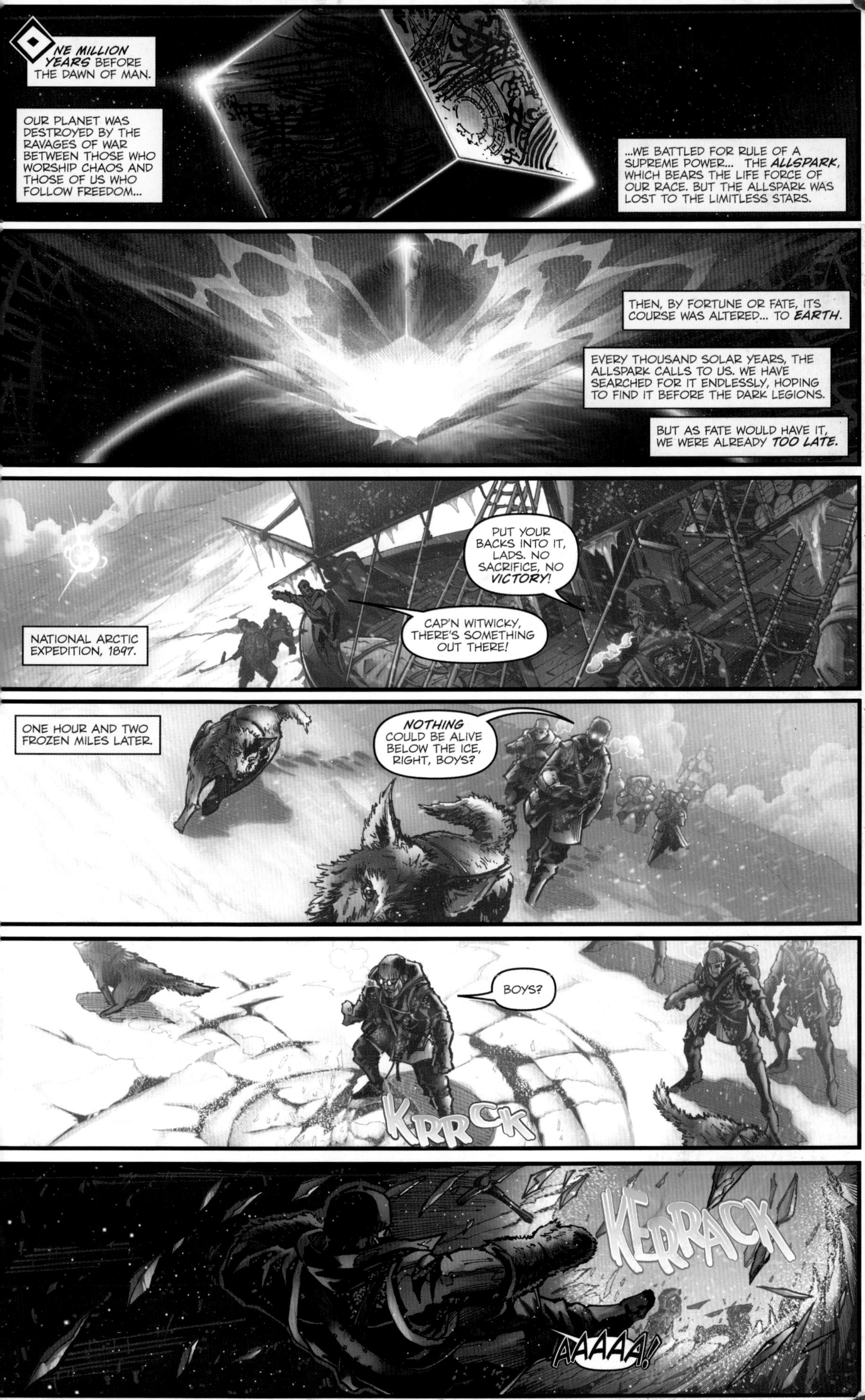
ONE MILLION YEARS BEFORE THE DAWN OF MAN.
OUR PLANET WAS DESTROYED BY THE RAVAGES OF WAR BETWEEN THOSE WHO WORSHIP CHAOS AND THOSE OF US WHO FOLLOW FREEDOM...
...WE BATTLED FOR RULE OF A SUPREME POWER... THE ALLSPARK, WHICH BEARS THE LIFE FORCE OF OUR RACE. BUT THE ALLSPARK WAS LOST TO THE LIMITLESS STARS.
THEN, BY FORTUNE OR FATE, ITS COURSE WAS ALTERED... TO EARTH.
EVERY THOUSAND SOLAR YEARS, THE ALLSPARK CALLS TO US. WE HAVE SEARCHED FOR IT ENDLESSLY, HOPING TO FIND IT BEFORE THE DARK LEGIONS.
BUT AS FATE WOULD HAVE IT, WE WERE ALREADY TOO LATE.
PUT YOUR BACKS INTO IT, LADS. NO SACRIFICE, NO VICTORY!
CAP'N WITWICKY, THERE'S SOMETHING OUT THERE!
NATIONAL ARCTIC EXPEDITION, 1897.
ONE HOUR AND TWO FROZEN MILES LATER.
NOTHING COULD BE ALIVE BELOW THE ICE, RIGHT, BOYS?
BOYS?
KRRCK
KERRACK
AAAAA!

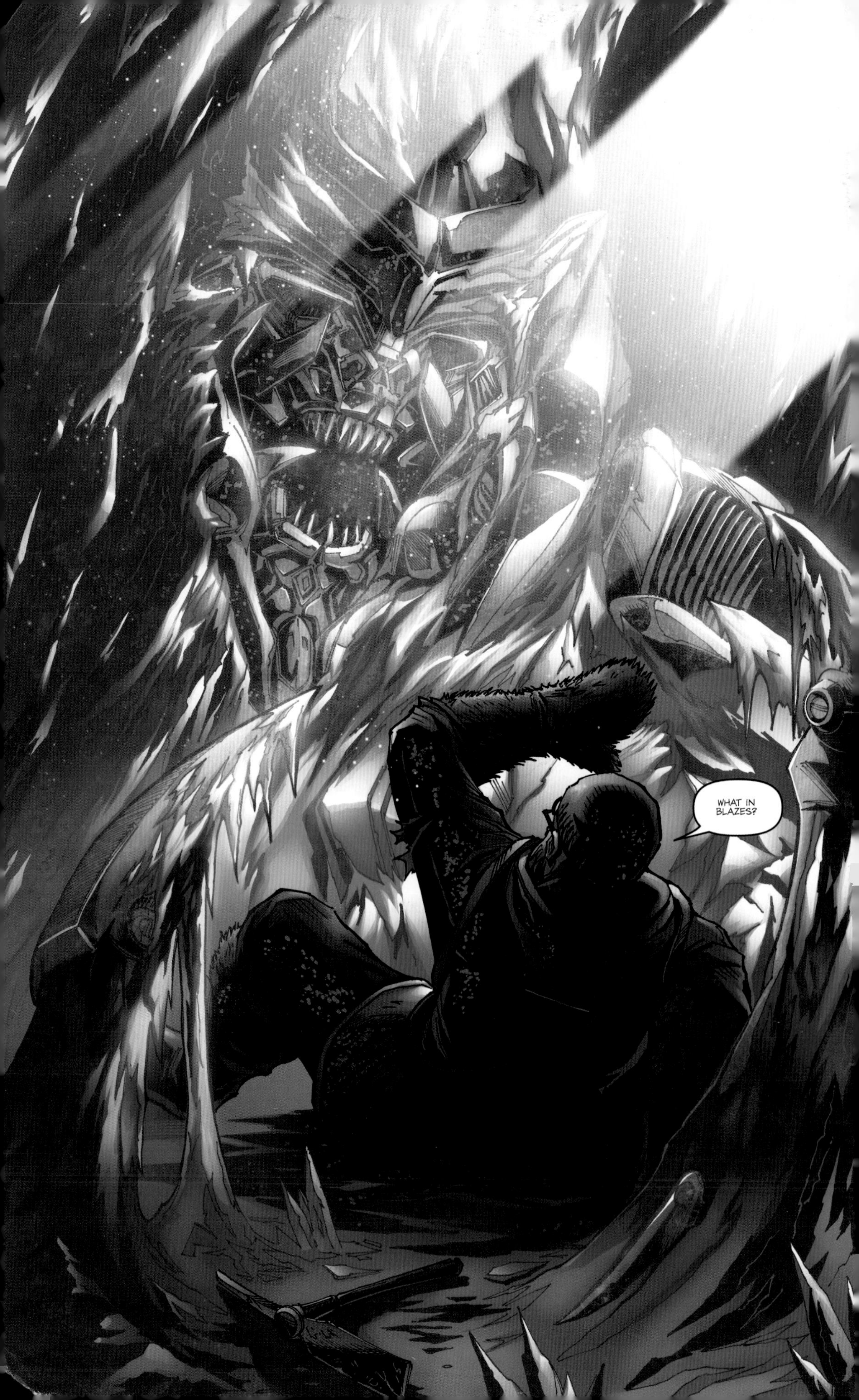
WHAT IN BLAZES?

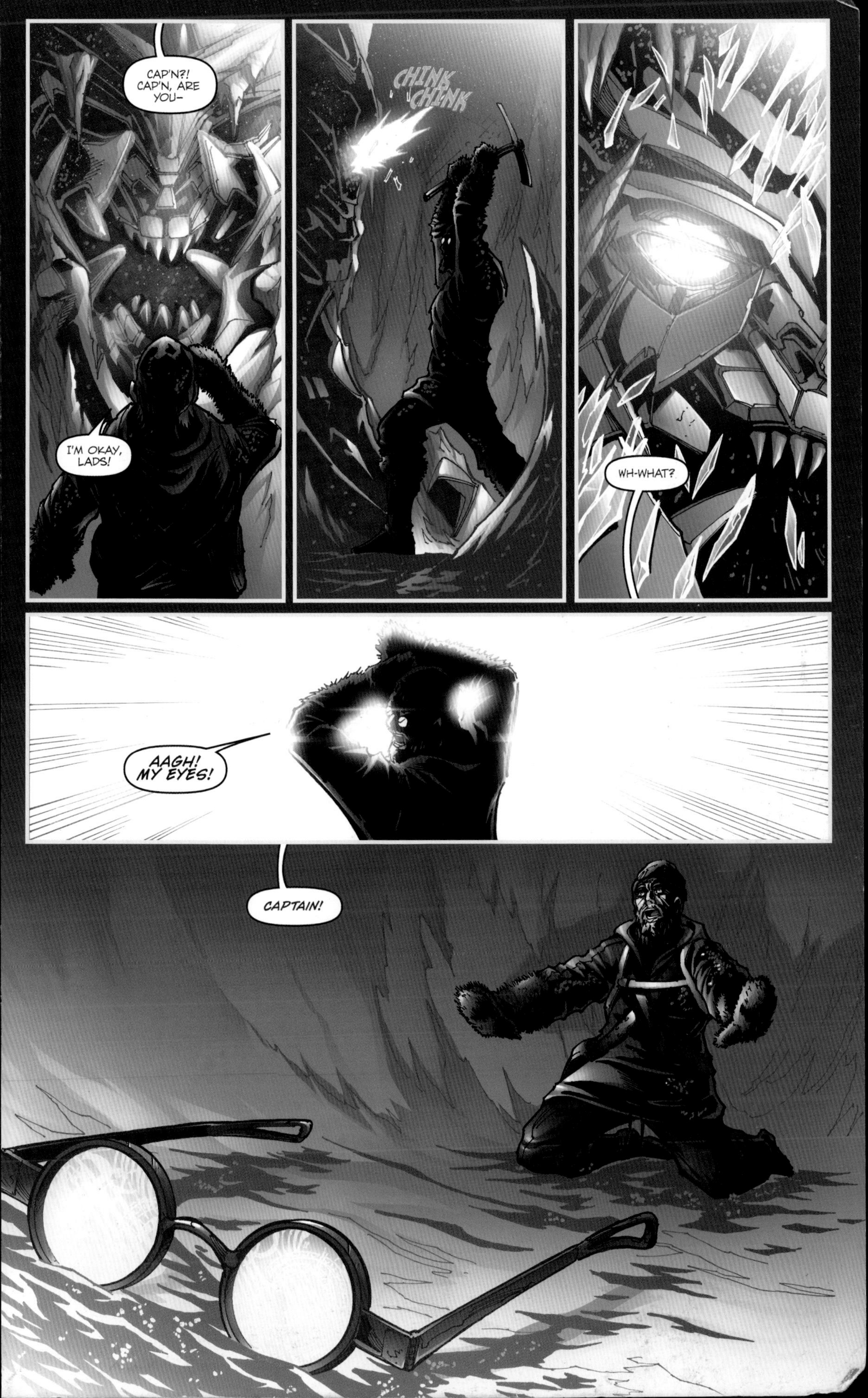
CAP'N?! CAP'N, ARE YOU–
I'M OKAY, LADS!
CHINK CHINK
WH-WHAT?
AAGH! MY EYES!
CAPTAIN!

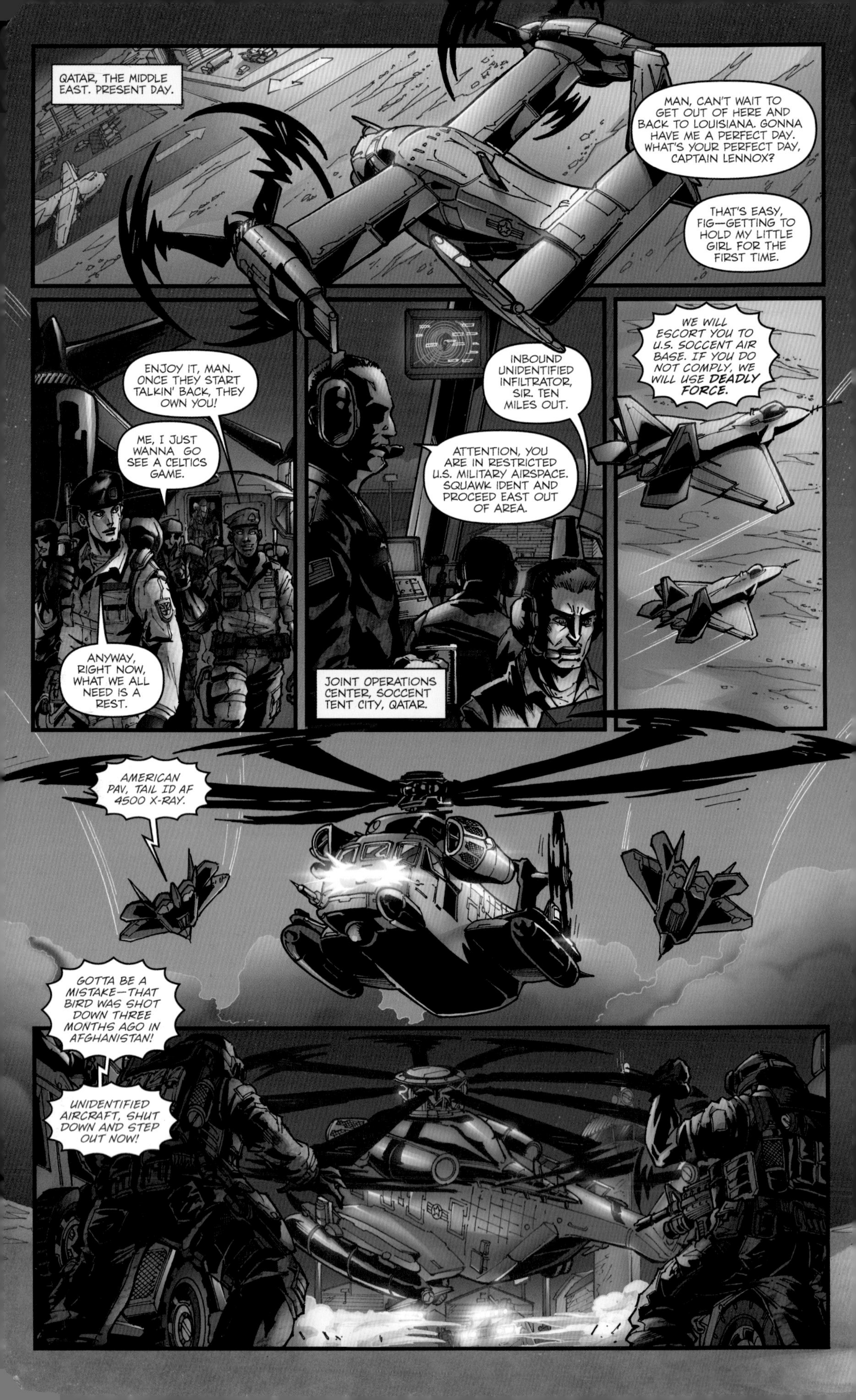
QATAR, THE MIDDLE EAST. PRESENT DAY.
MAN, CAN'T WAIT TO GET OUT OF HERE AND BACK TO LOUISIANA. GONNA HAVE ME A PERFECT DAY. WHAT'S YOUR PERFECT DAY, CAPTAIN LENNOX?
THAT'S EASY, FIG—GETTING TO HOLD MY LITTLE GIRL FOR THE FIRST TIME.
ENJOY IT, MAN. ONCE THEY START TALKIN' BACK, THEY OWN YOU!
ME, I JUST WANNA GO SEE A CELTICS GAME.
ANYWAY, RIGHT NOW, WHAT WE ALL NEED IS A REST.
INBOUND UNIDENTIFIED INFILTRATOR, SIR. TEN MILES OUT.
ATTENTION, YOU ARE IN RESTRICTED U.S. MILITARY AIRSPACE. SQUAWK IDENT AND PROCEED EAST OUT OF AREA.
JOINT OPERATIONS CENTER, SOCCENT TENT CITY, QATAR.
WE WILL ESCORT YOU TO U.S. SOCCENT AIR BASE. IF YOU DO NOT COMPLY, WE WILL USE DEADLY FORCE.
AMERICAN PAV, TAIL ID AF 4500 X-RAY.
GOTTA BE A MISTAKE—THAT BIRD WAS SHOT DOWN THREE MONTHS AGO IN AFGHANISTAN!
UNIDENTIFIED AIRCRAFT, SHUT DOWN AND STEP OUT NOW!

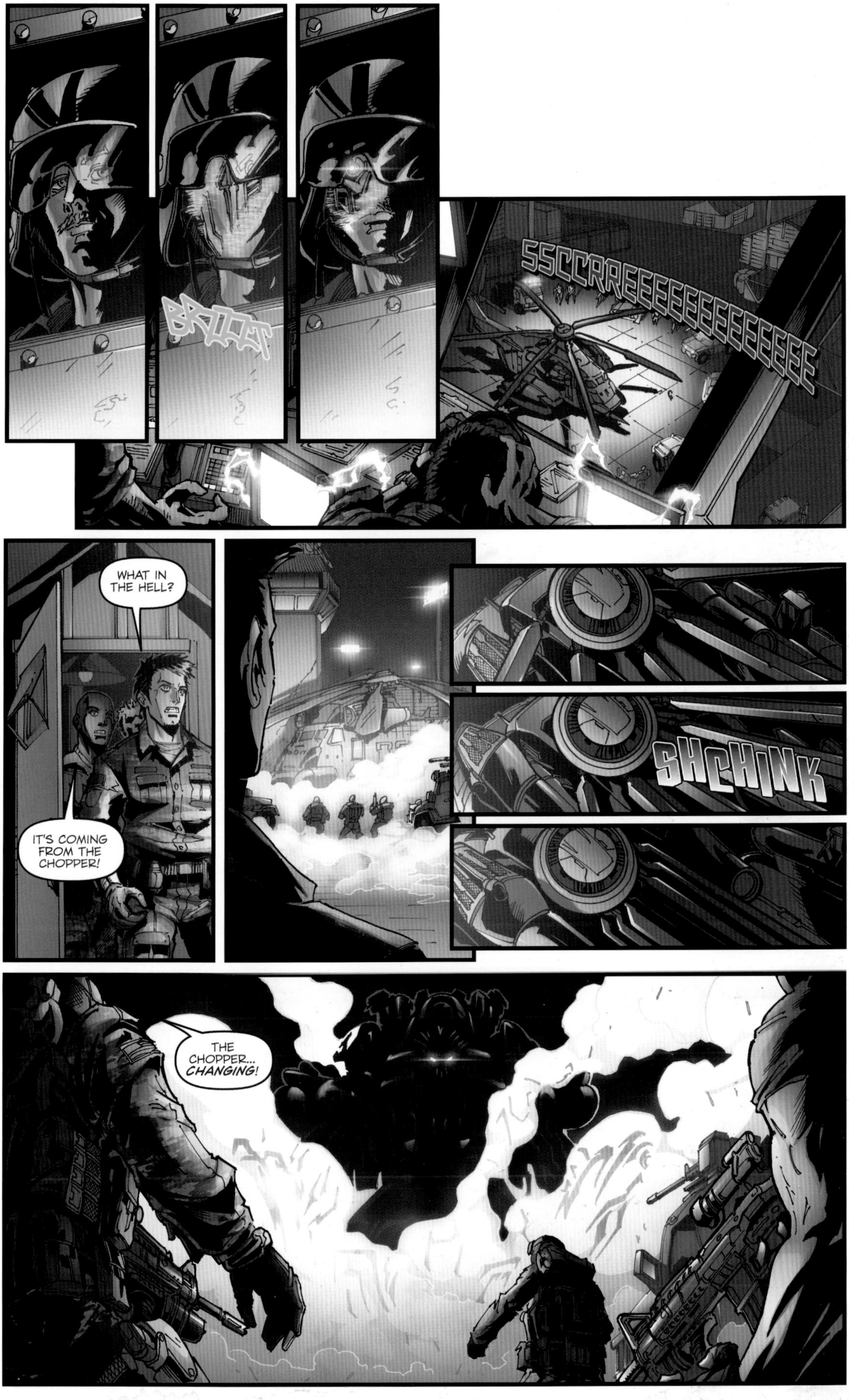
BRZZZT
SSCCRREEEEEEEEEEEEEE
WHAT IN THE HELL?
IT'S COMING FROM THE CHOPPER!
SHCHINK
THE CHOPPER... *CHANGING*!

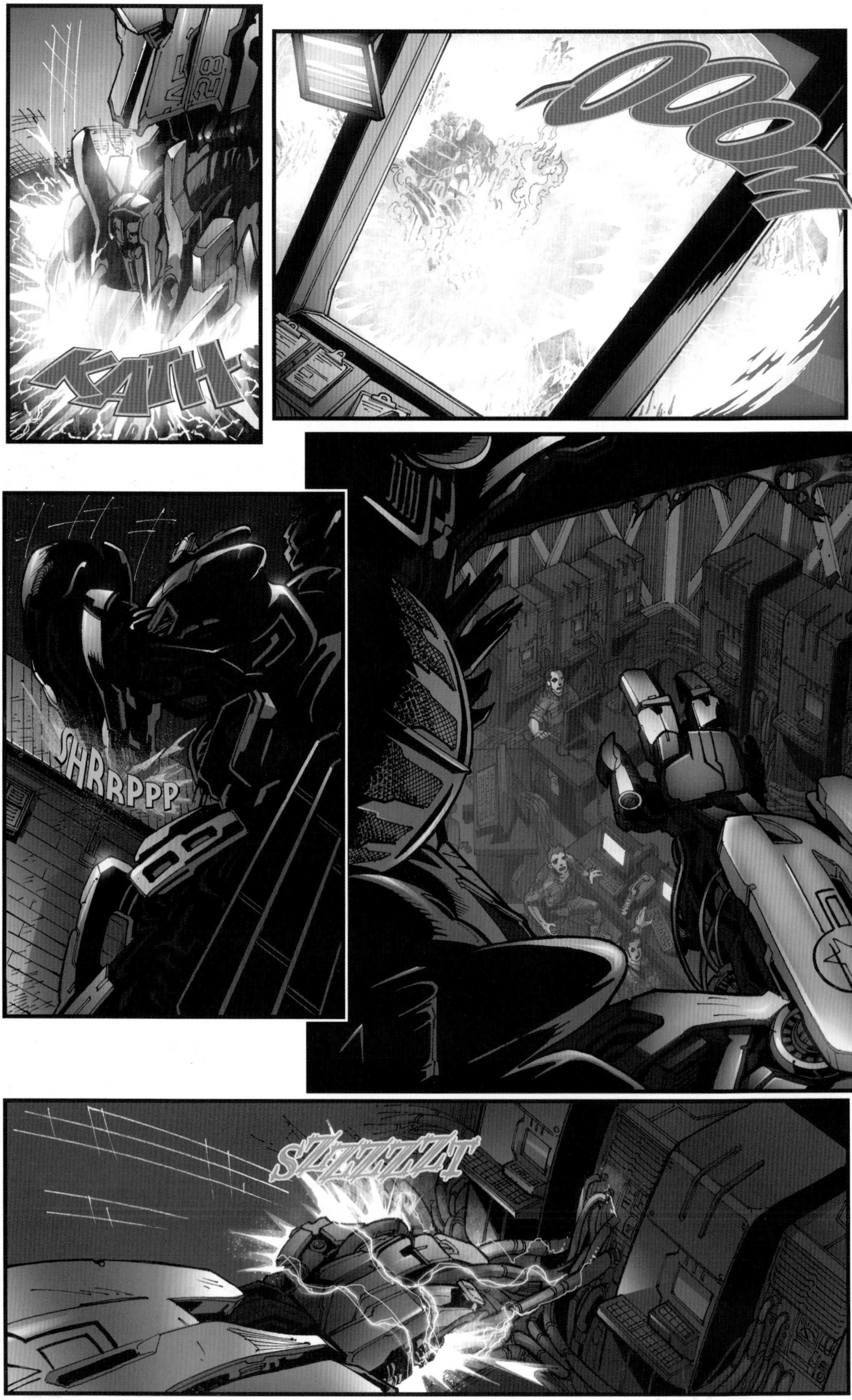

KATH!
WOOO
SHRRPPP
SZZZZZT

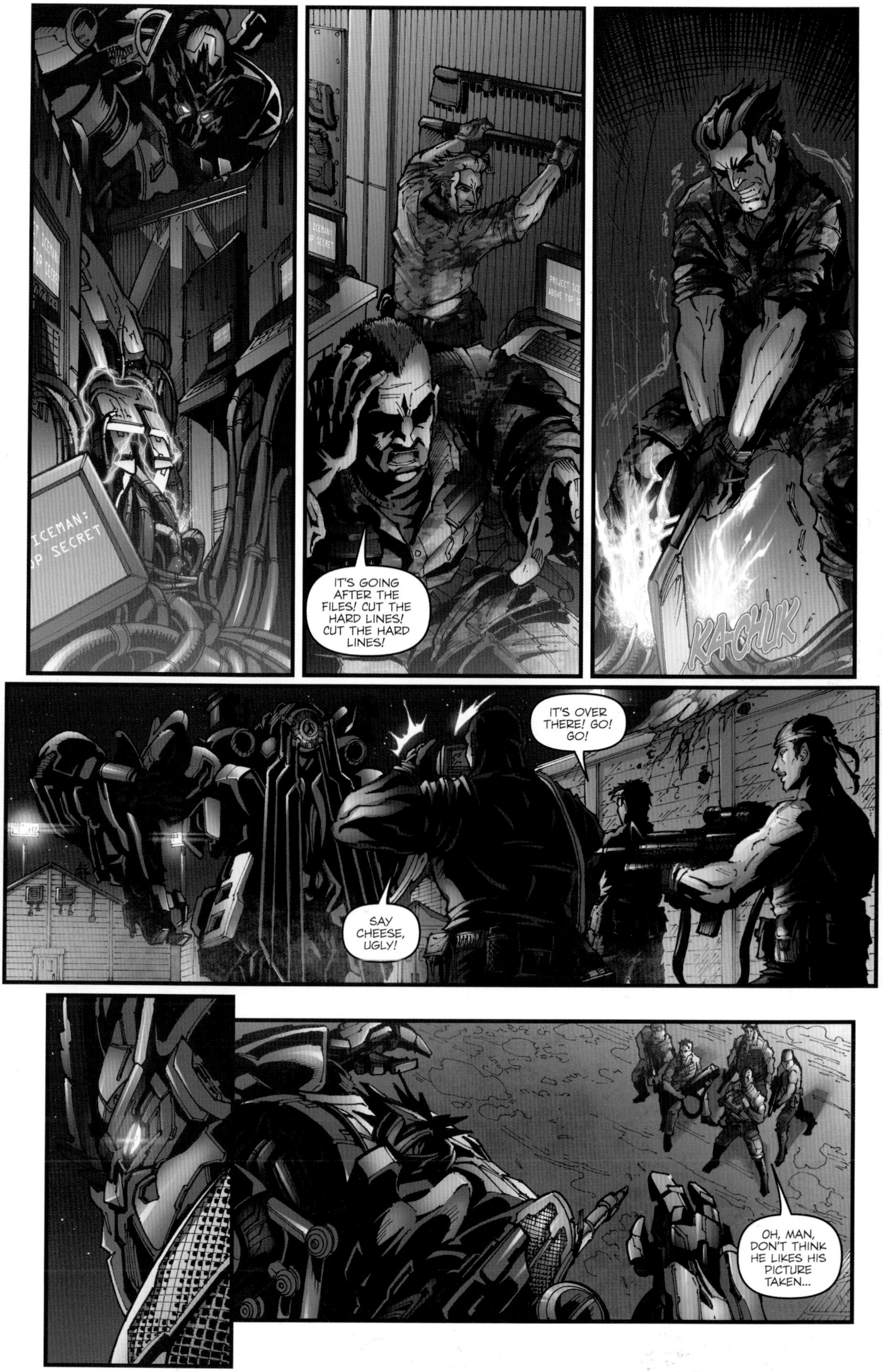
ICEMAN:
TOP SECRET
PROJECT ICEMAN:
ABOVE TOP SECRET
IT'S GOING AFTER THE FILES! CUT THE HARD LINES! CUT THE HARD LINES!
KA-CHUK
IT'S OVER THERE! GO! GO!
SAY CHEESE, UGLY!
OH, MAN, DON'T THINK HE LIKES HIS PICTURE TAKEN...

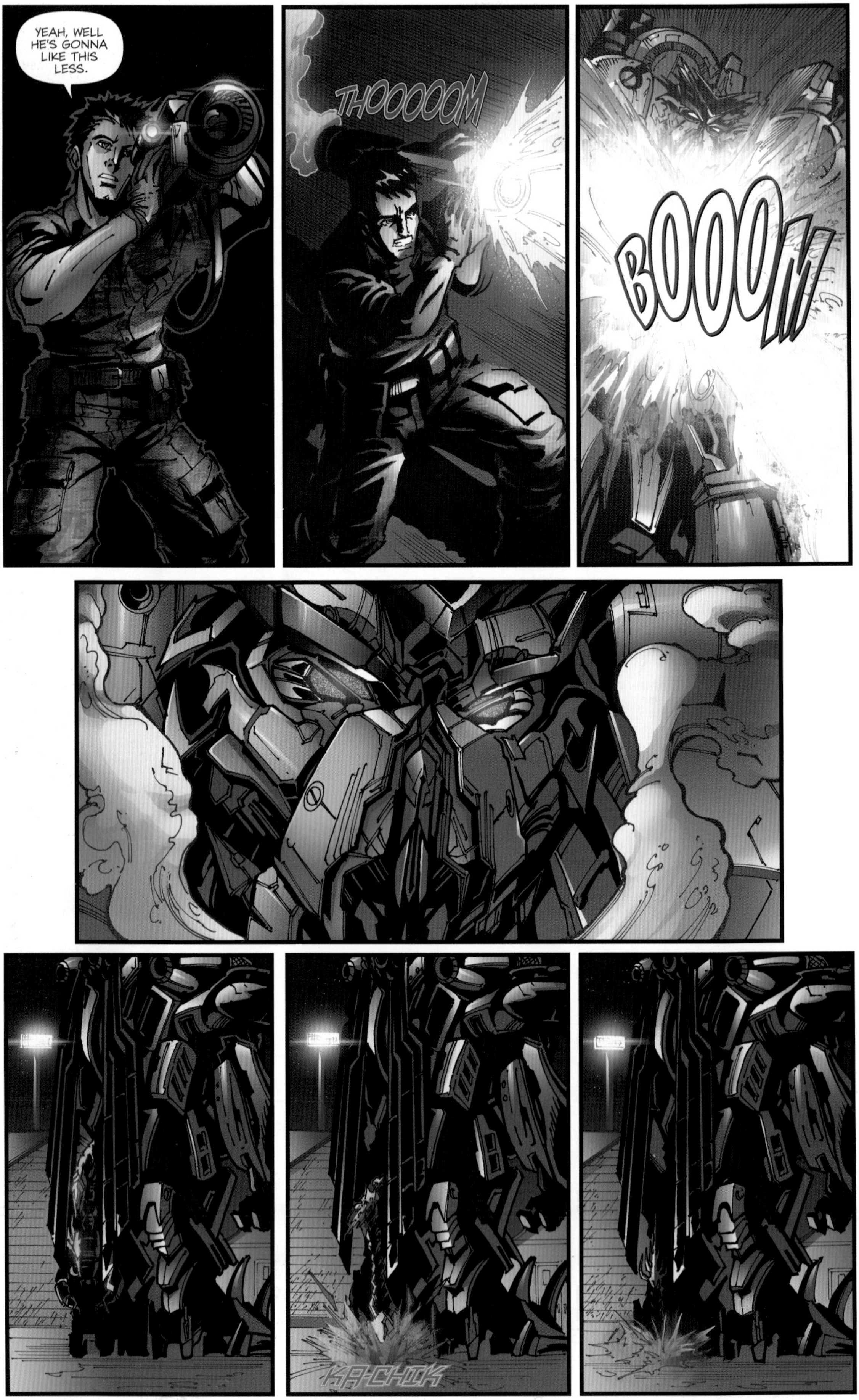
YEAH, WELL HE'S GONNA LIKE THIS LESS.
THOOOOOM
BOOOM
KA-CHIK

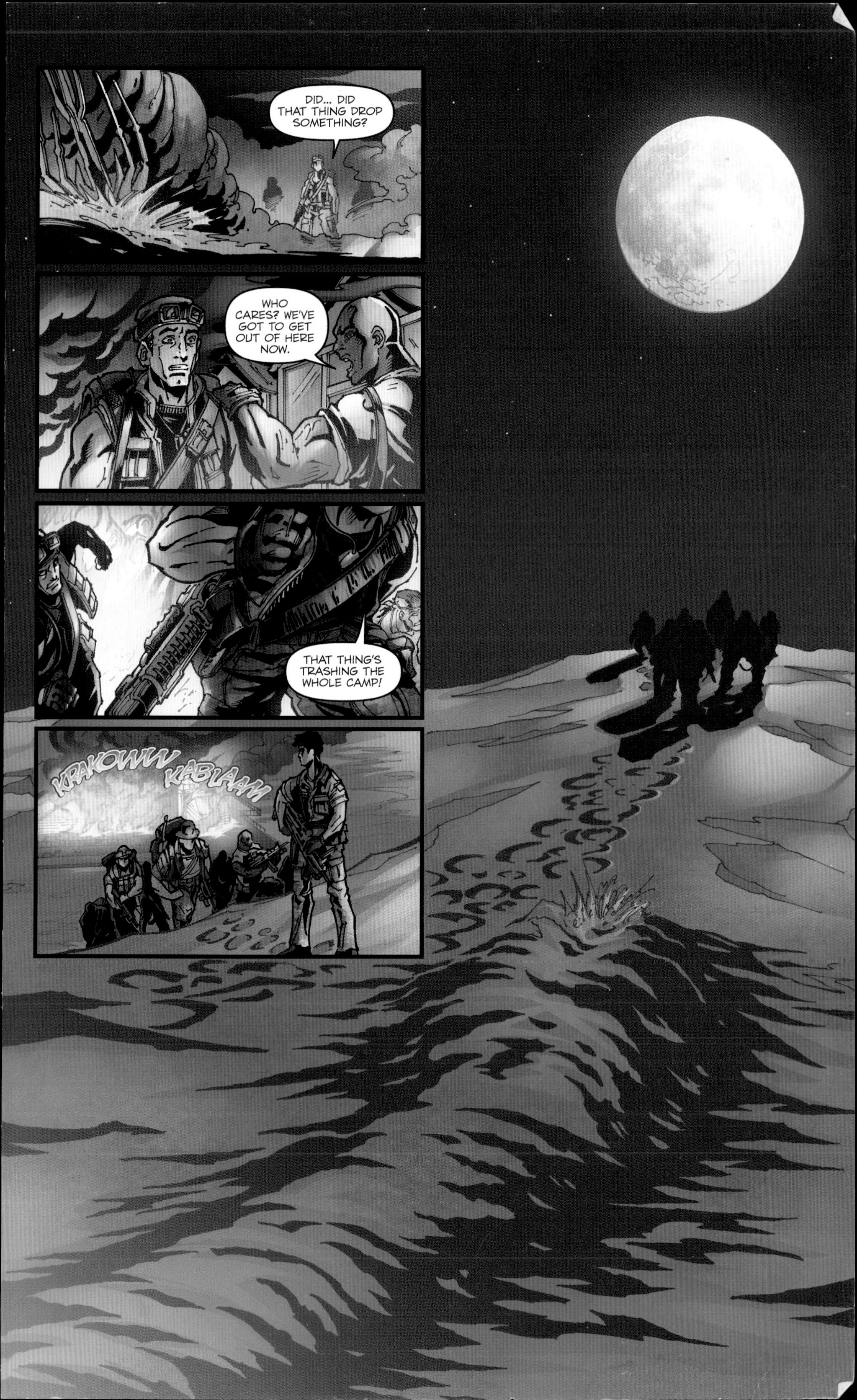
DID... DID THAT THING DROP SOMETHING?
WHO CARES? WE'VE GOT TO GET OUT OF HERE NOW.
THAT THING'S TRASHING THE WHOLE CAMP!
KRAKOWW
KABLAAM

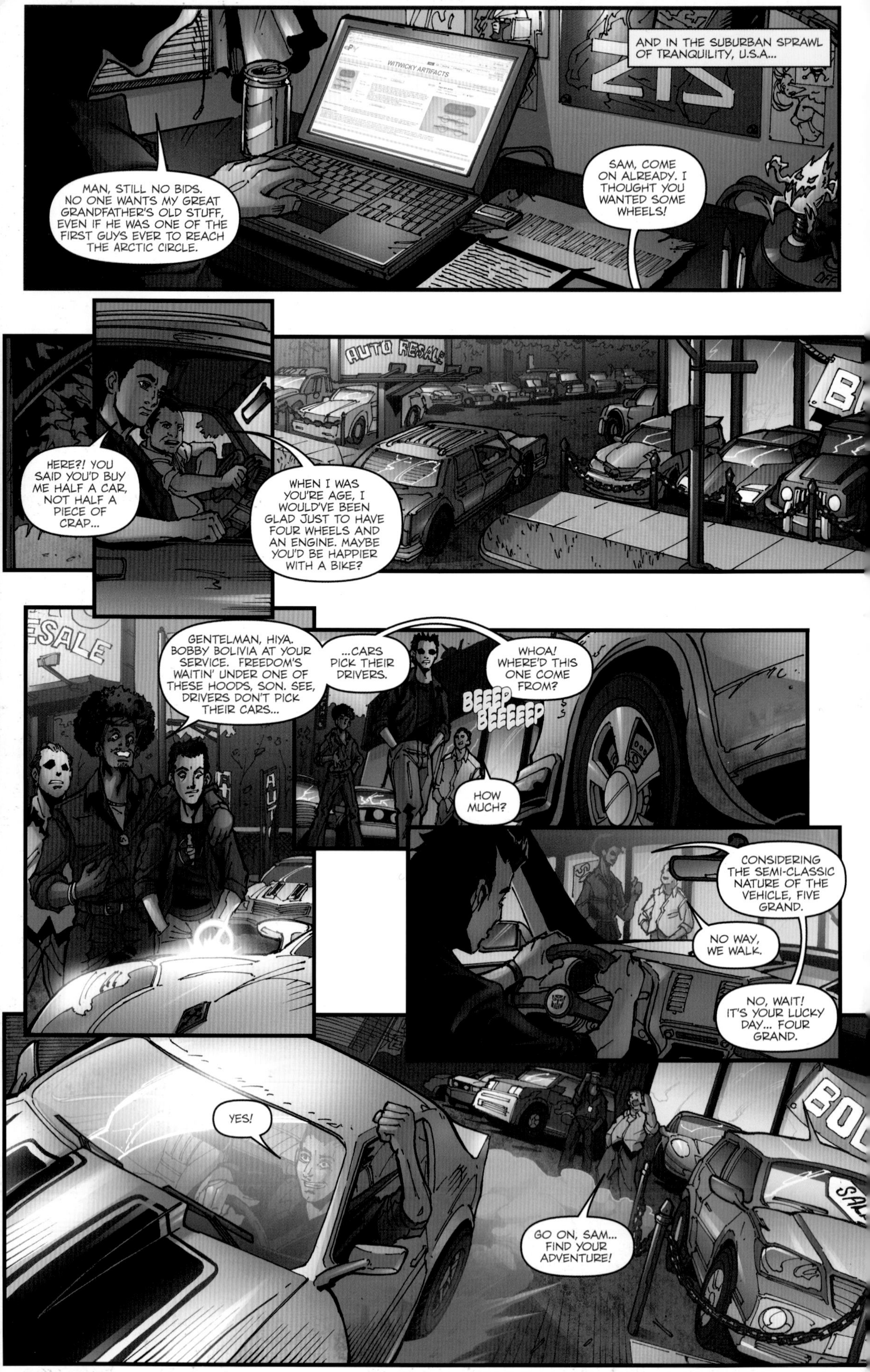
AND IN THE SUBURBAN SPRAWL OF TRANQUILITY, U.S.A...
WITWICKY ARTIFACTS
MAN, STILL NO BIDS. NO ONE WANTS MY GREAT GRANDFATHER'S OLD STUFF, EVEN IF HE WAS ONE OF THE FIRST GUYS EVER TO REACH THE ARCTIC CIRCLE.
SAM, COME ON ALREADY. I THOUGHT YOU WANTED SOME WHEELS!
AUTO RESALE
HERE?! YOU SAID YOU'D BUY ME HALF A CAR, NOT HALF A PIECE OF CRAP...
WHEN I WAS YOU'RE AGE, I WOULD'VE BEEN GLAD JUST TO HAVE FOUR WHEELS AND AN ENGINE. MAYBE YOU'D BE HAPPIER WITH A BIKE?
GENTELMAN, HIYA. BOBBY BOLIVIA AT YOUR SERVICE. FREEDOM'S WAITIN' UNDER ONE OF THESE HOODS, SON. SEE, DRIVERS DON'T PICK THEIR CARS...
...CARS PICK THEIR DRIVERS.
WHOA! WHERE'D THIS ONE COME FROM?
BEEEP BEEEEEP
HOW MUCH?
CONSIDERING THE SEMI-CLASSIC NATURE OF THE VEHICLE, FIVE GRAND.
NO WAY, WE WALK.
NO, WAIT! IT'S YOUR LUCKY DAY... FOUR GRAND.
YES!
GO ON, SAM... FIND YOUR ADVENTURE!

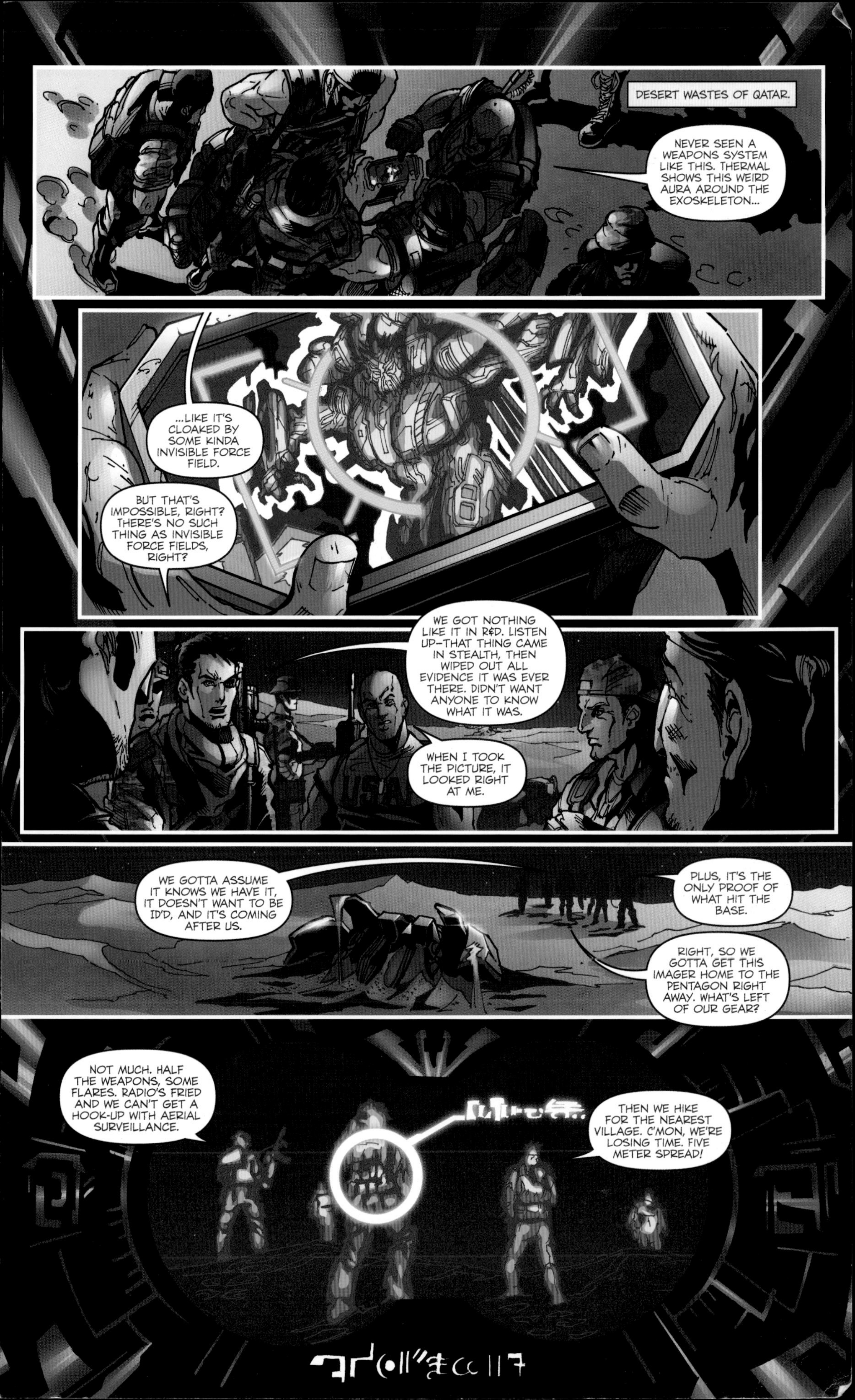
DESERT WASTES OF QATAR.
NEVER SEEN A WEAPONS SYSTEM LIKE THIS. THERMAL SHOWS THIS WEIRD AURA AROUND THE EXOSKELETON...
...LIKE IT'S CLOAKED BY SOME KINDA INVISIBLE FORCE FIELD.
BUT THAT'S IMPOSSIBLE, RIGHT? THERE'S NO SUCH THING AS INVISIBLE FORCE FIELDS, RIGHT?
WE GOT NOTHING LIKE IT IN R&D. LISTEN UP–THAT THING CAME IN STEALTH, THEN WIPED OUT ALL EVIDENCE IT WAS EVER THERE. DIDN'T WANT ANYONE TO KNOW WHAT IT WAS.
WHEN I TOOK THE PICTURE, IT LOOKED RIGHT AT ME.
WE GOTTA ASSUME IT KNOWS WE HAVE IT, IT DOESN'T WANT TO BE ID'D, AND IT'S COMING AFTER US.
PLUS, IT'S THE ONLY PROOF OF WHAT HIT THE BASE.
RIGHT, SO WE GOTTA GET THIS IMAGER HOME TO THE PENTAGON RIGHT AWAY. WHAT'S LEFT OF OUR GEAR?
NOT MUCH. HALF THE WEAPONS, SOME FLARES. RADIO'S FRIED AND WE CAN'T GET A HOOK-UP WITH AERIAL SURVEILLANCE.
THEN WE HIKE FOR THE NEAREST VILLAGE. C'MON, WE'RE LOSING TIME. FIVE METER SPREAD!

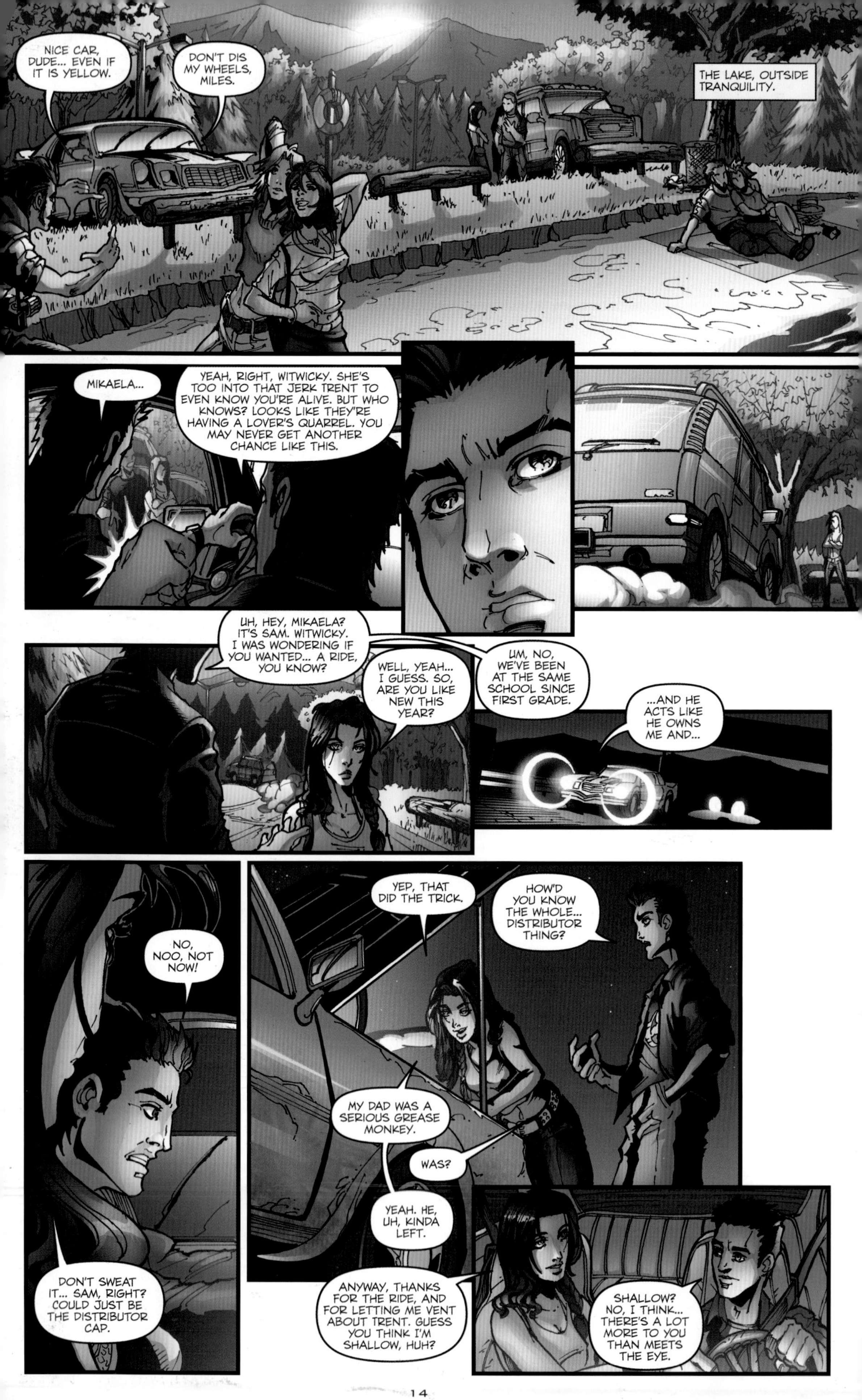

NICE CAR, DUDE... EVEN IF IT IS YELLOW.
DON'T DIS MY WHEELS, MILES.
THE LAKE, OUTSIDE TRANQUILITY.
MIKAELA...
YEAH, RIGHT, WITWICKY. SHE'S TOO INTO THAT JERK TRENT TO EVEN KNOW YOU'RE ALIVE. BUT WHO KNOWS? LOOKS LIKE THEY'RE HAVING A LOVER'S QUARREL. YOU MAY NEVER GET ANOTHER CHANCE LIKE THIS.
UH, HEY, MIKAELA? IT'S SAM. WITWICKY. I WAS WONDERING IF YOU WANTED... A RIDE, YOU KNOW?
WELL, YEAH... I GUESS. SO, ARE YOU LIKE NEW THIS YEAR?
UM, NO, WE'VE BEEN AT THE SAME SCHOOL SINCE FIRST GRADE.
...AND HE ACTS LIKE HE OWNS ME AND...
NO, NOO, NOT NOW!
DON'T SWEAT IT... SAM, RIGHT? COULD JUST BE THE DISTRIBUTOR CAP.
YEP, THAT DID THE TRICK.
HOW'D YOU KNOW THE WHOLE... DISTRIBUTOR THING?
MY DAD WAS A SERIOUS GREASE MONKEY.
WAS?
YEAH. HE, UH, KINDA LEFT.
ANYWAY, THANKS FOR THE RIDE, AND FOR LETTING ME VENT ABOUT TRENT. GUESS YOU THINK I'M SHALLOW, HUH?
SHALLOW? NO, I THINK... THERE'S A LOT MORE TO YOU THAN MEETS THE EYE.

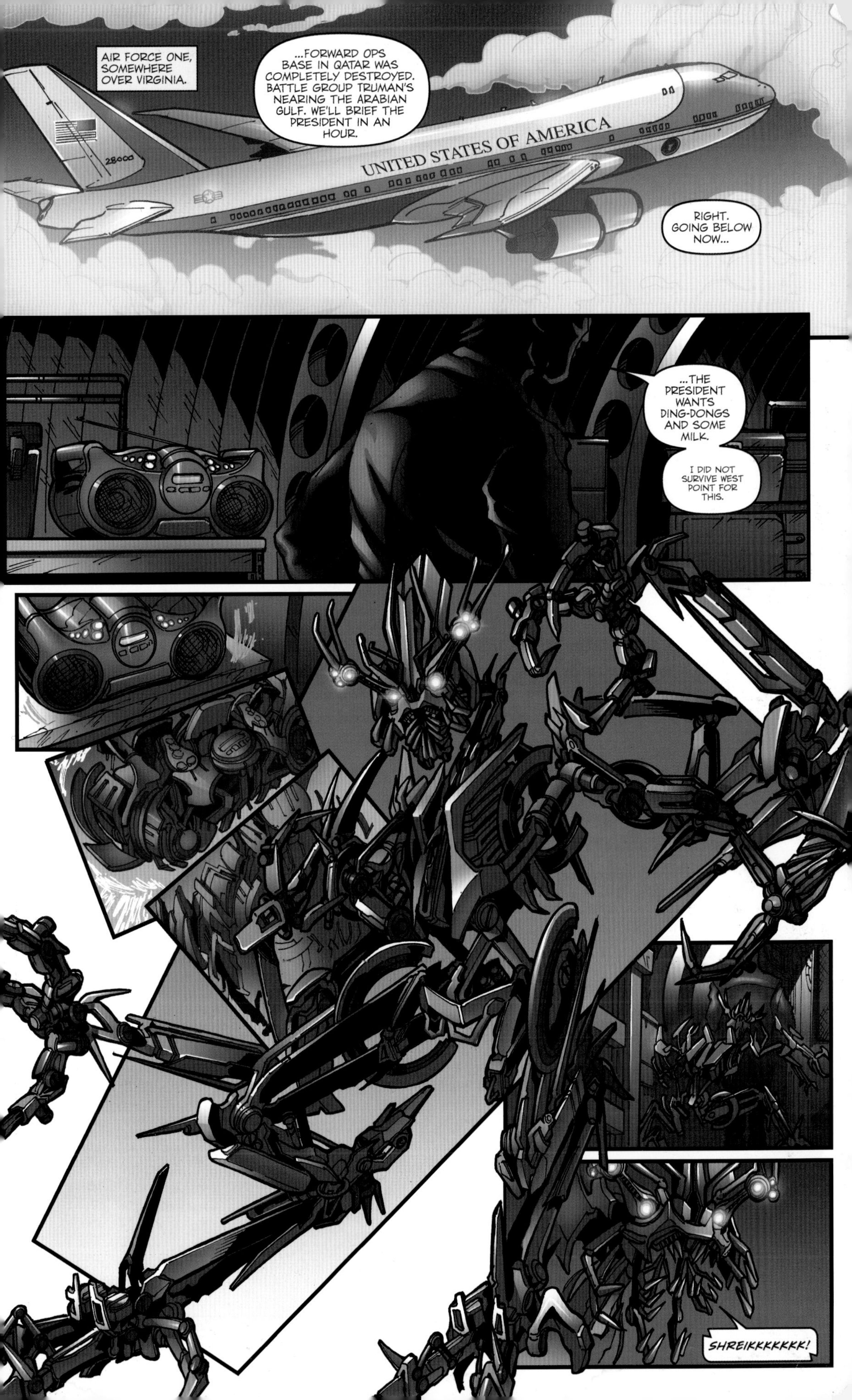
AIR FORCE ONE, SOMEWHERE OVER VIRGINIA.
...FORWARD OPS BASE IN QATAR WAS COMPLETELY DESTROYED. BATTLE GROUP TRUMAN'S NEARING THE ARABIAN GULF. WE'LL BRIEF THE PRESIDENT IN AN HOUR.
UNITED STATES OF AMERICA
28000
RIGHT. GOING BELOW NOW...
...THE PRESIDENT WANTS DING-DONGS AND SOME MILK.
I DID NOT SURVIVE WEST POINT FOR THIS.
SHREIKKKKKKK!

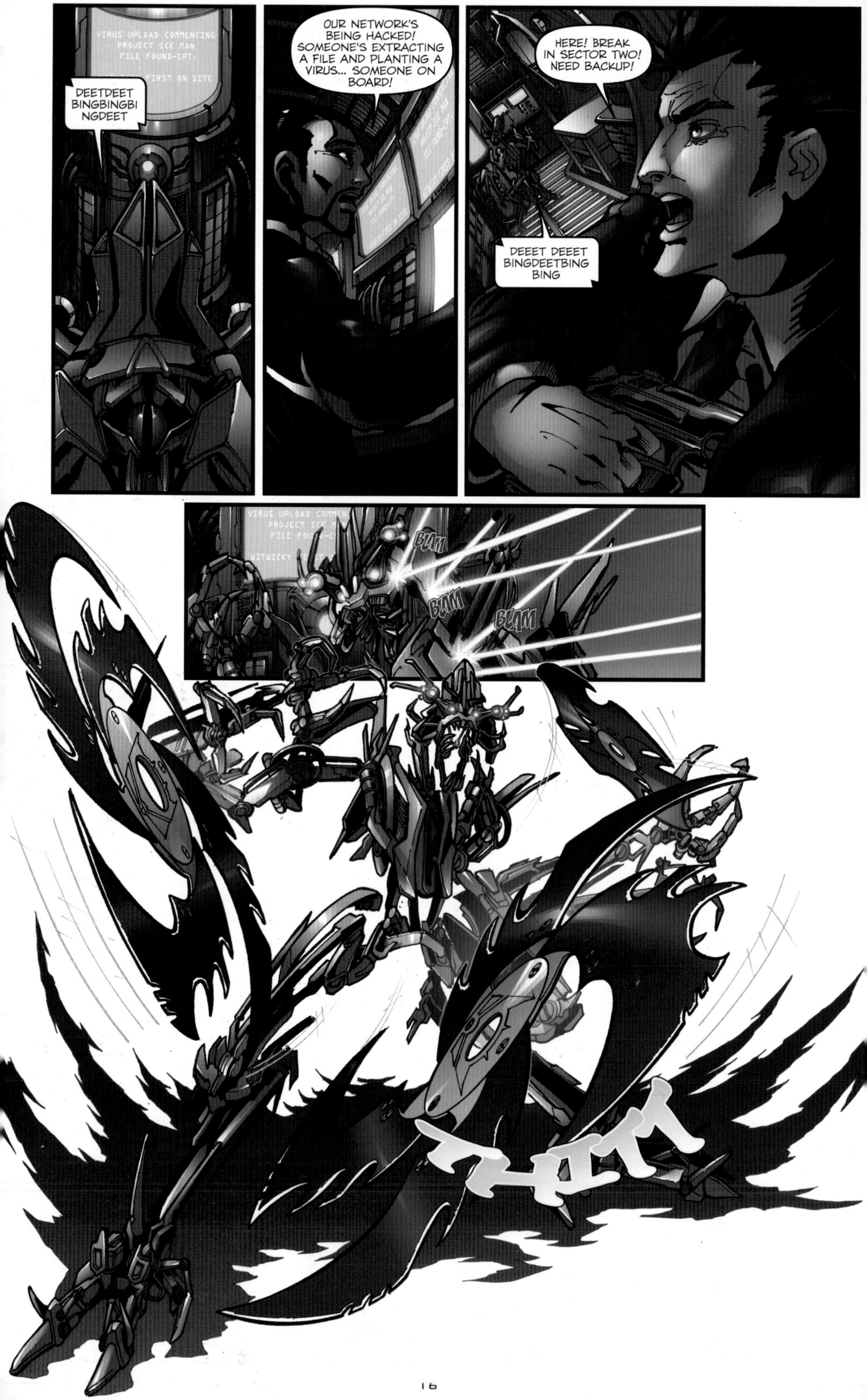

VIRUS UPLOAD COMMENCING
PROJECT ICE MAN
FILE FOUND-CPT.
DEETDEET BINGBINGBINGDEET
OUR NETWORK'S BEING HACKED! SOMEONE'S EXTRACTING A FILE AND PLANTING A VIRUS... SOMEONE ON BOARD!
HERE! BREAK IN SECTOR TWO! NEED BACKUP!
DEEET DEEET BINGDEETBING BING
BLAM
BLAM
BLAM

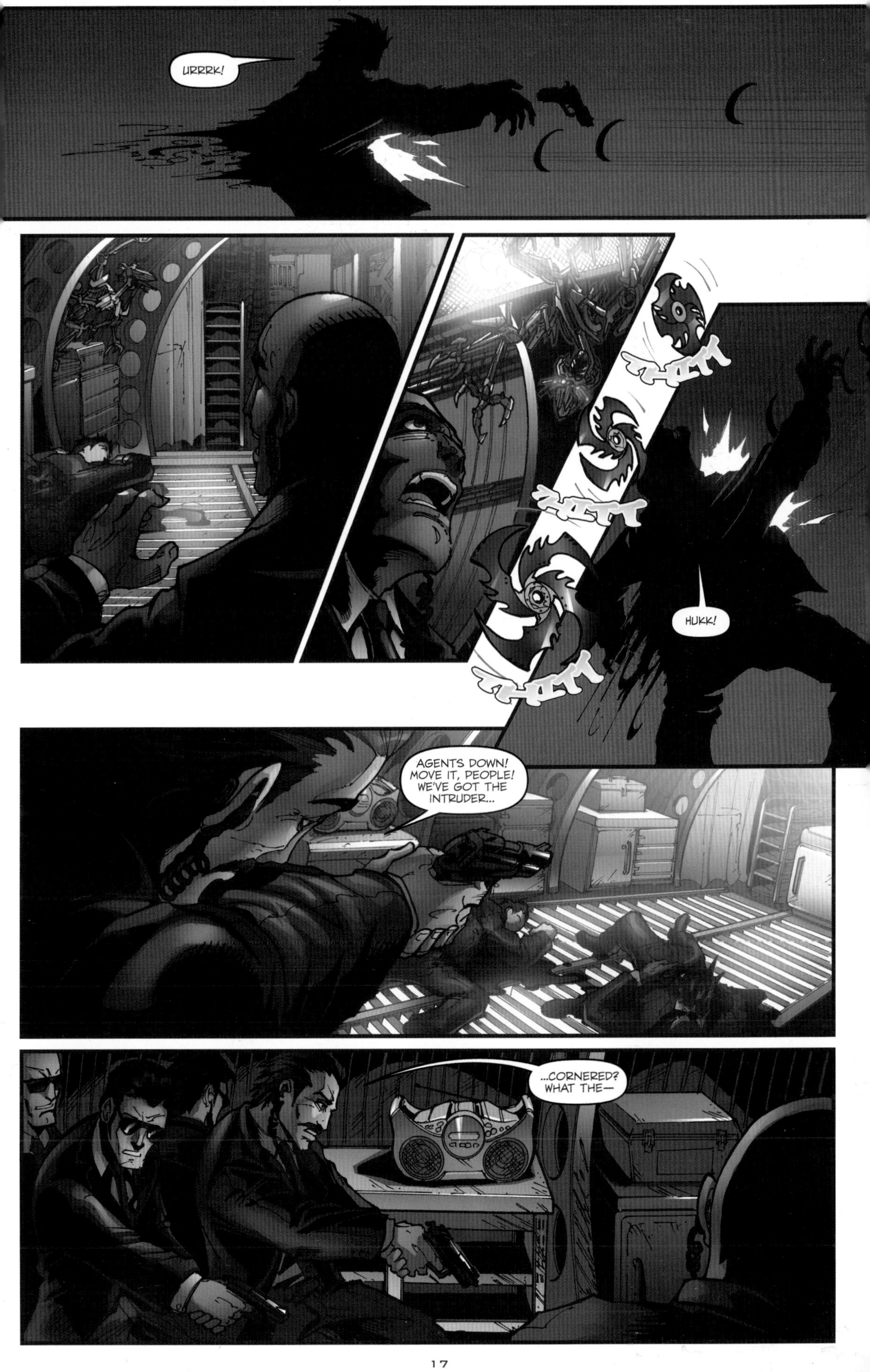
URRRK!
THTT
THTT
THTT
HUKK!
AGENTS DOWN! MOVE IT, PEOPLE! WE'VE GOT THE INTRUDER...
...CORNERED? WHAT THE—

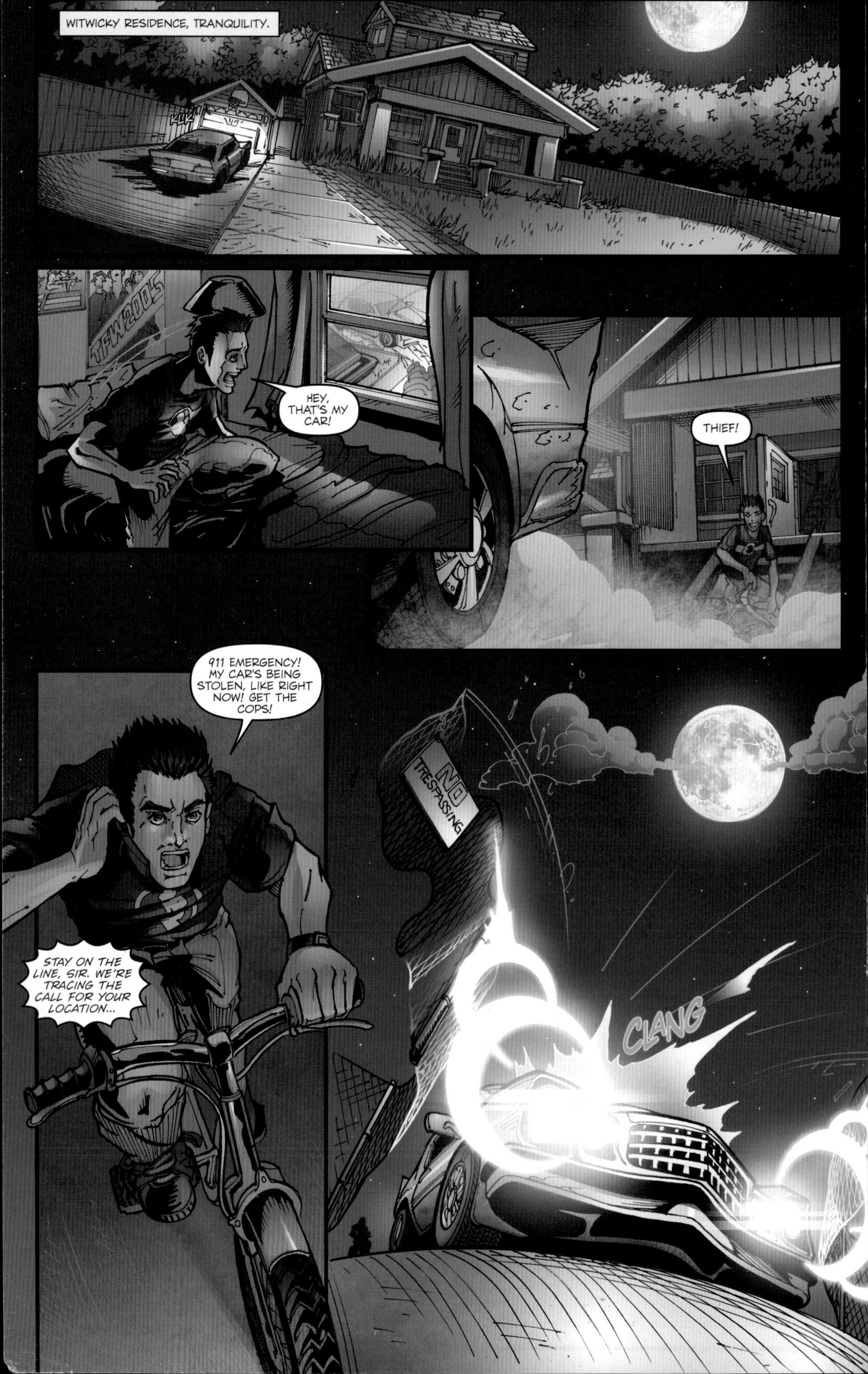
WITWICKY RESIDENCE, TRANQUILITY.
KLIK
HEY, THAT'S MY CAR!
THIEF!
911 EMERGENCY! MY CAR'S BEING STOLEN, LIKE RIGHT NOW! GET THE COPS!
STAY ON THE LINE, SIR. WE'RE TRACING THE CALL FOR YOUR LOCATION...
NO TRESPASSING
CLANG

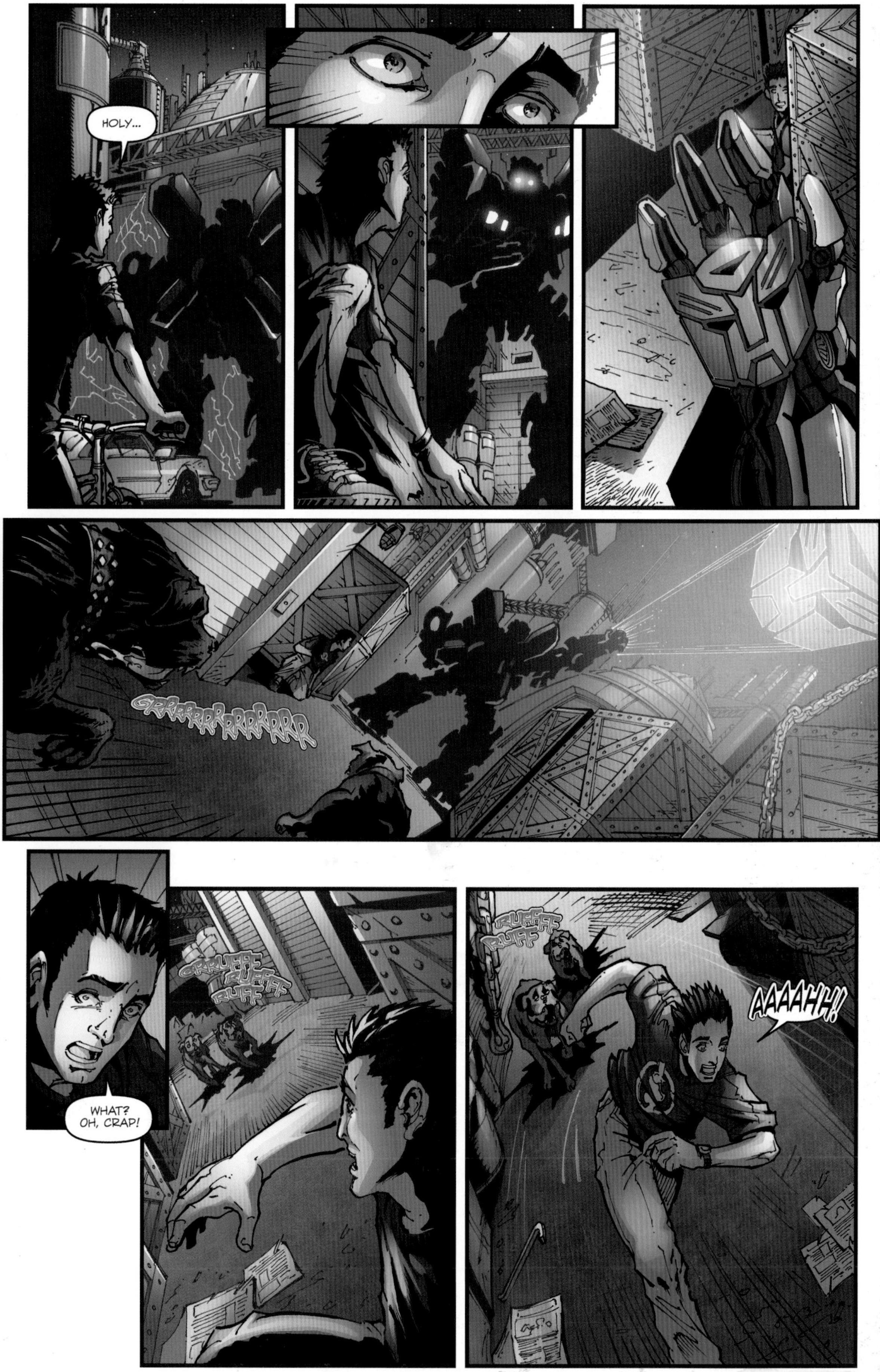
HOLY...
GRRRRRRRRRRRRRR
WHAT? OH, CRAP!
GRRUFFF RUFFF RUFF
RUFFF RUFF
AAAAHH!

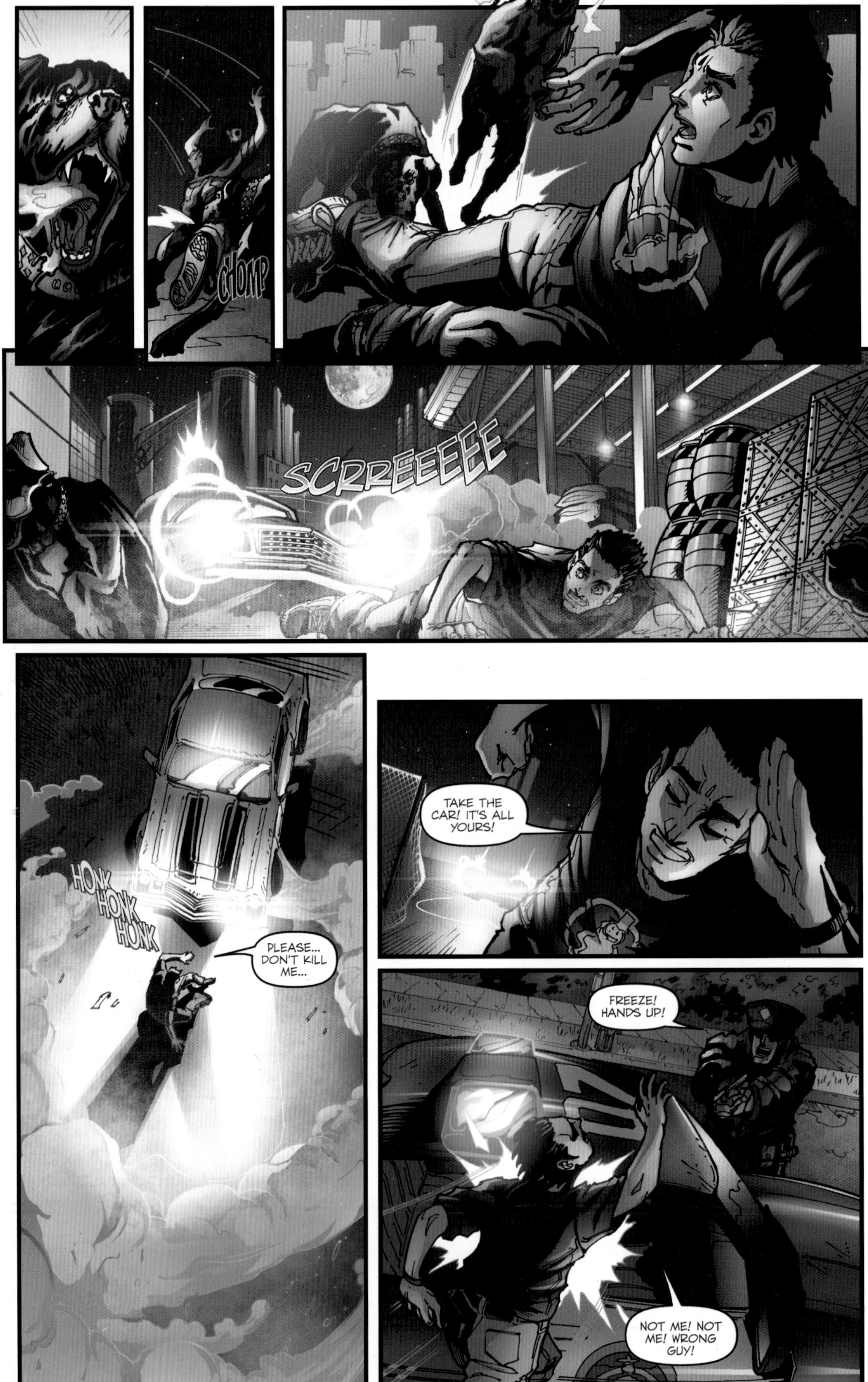
CHOMP
SCRREEEEEE
HONK HONK HONK
PLEASE... DON'T KILL ME...
TAKE THE CAR! IT'S ALL YOURS!
FREEZE! HANDS UP!
NOT ME! NOT ME! WRONG GUY!

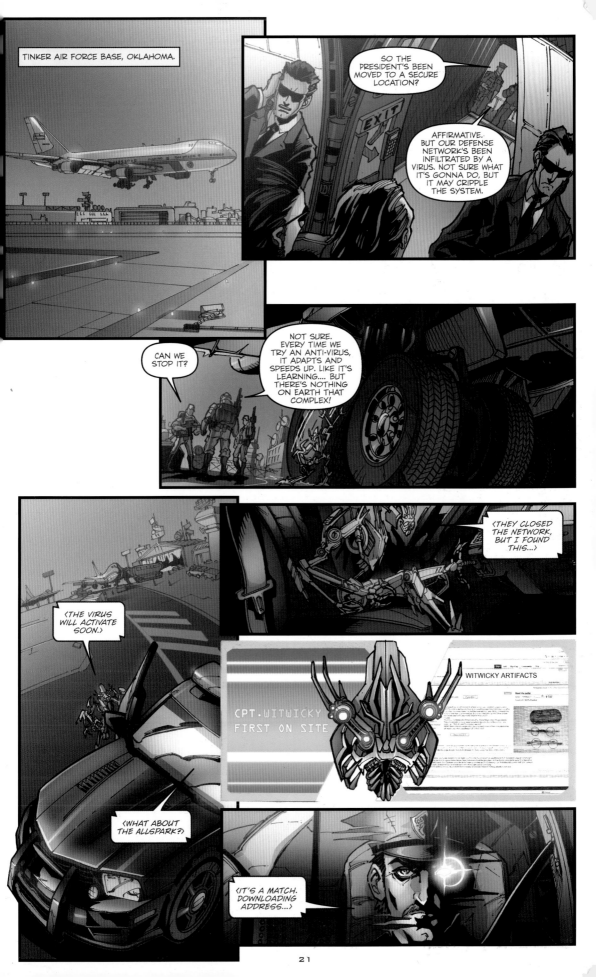

TINKER AIR FORCE BASE, OKLAHOMA.

SO THE PRESIDENT'S BEEN MOVED TO A SECURE LOCATION?

AFFIRMATIVE. BUT OUR DEFENSE NETWORK'S BEEN INFILTRATED BY A VIRUS. NOT SURE WHAT IT'S GONNA DO, BUT IT MAY CRIPPLE THE SYSTEM.

CAN WE STOP IT?

NOT SURE. EVERY TIME WE TRY AN ANTI-VIRUS, IT ADAPTS AND SPEEDS UP. LIKE IT'S LEARNING.... BUT THERE'S NOTHING ON EARTH THAT COMPLEX!

<THEY CLOSED THE NETWORK, BUT I FOUND THIS...>

<THE VIRUS WILL ACTIVATE SOON.>

WITWICKY ARTIFACTS

CPT.WITWICKY FIRST ON SITE

<WHAT ABOUT THE ALLSPARK?>

<IT'S A MATCH. DOWNLOADING ADDRESS...>

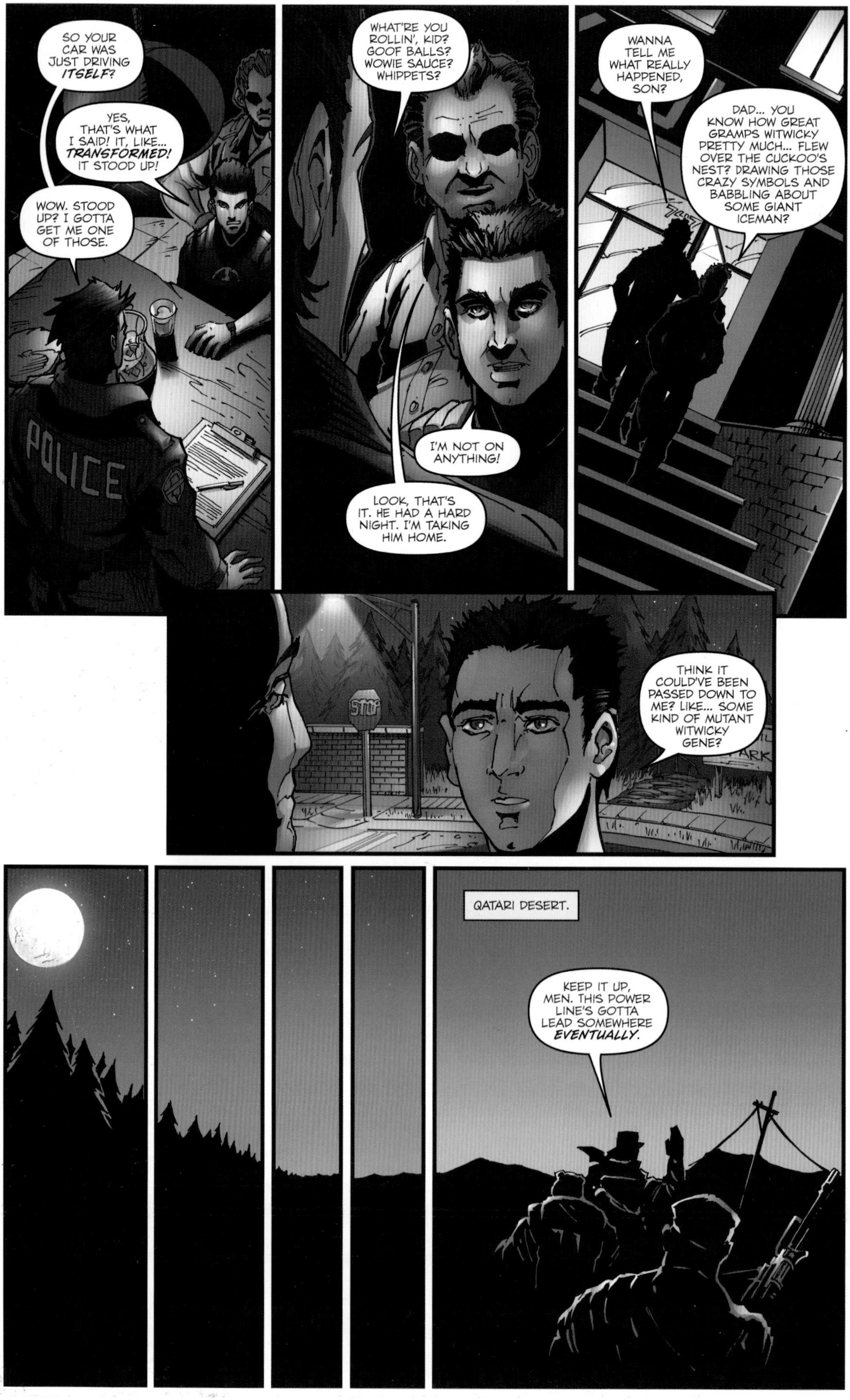
SO YOUR CAR WAS JUST DRIVING *ITSELF*?
YES, THAT'S WHAT I SAID! IT, LIKE... *TRANSFORMED!* IT STOOD UP!
WOW. STOOD UP? I GOTTA GET ME ONE OF THOSE.
POLICE
WHAT'RE YOU ROLLIN', KID? GOOF BALLS? WOWIE SAUCE? WHIPPETS?
I'M NOT ON ANYTHING!
LOOK, THAT'S IT. HE HAD A HARD NIGHT. I'M TAKING HIM HOME.
WANNA TELL ME WHAT REALLY HAPPENED, SON?
DAD... YOU KNOW HOW GREAT GRAMPS WITWICKY PRETTY MUCH... FLEW OVER THE CUCKOO'S NEST? DRAWING THOSE CRAZY SYMBOLS AND BABBLING ABOUT SOME GIANT ICEMAN?
THINK IT COULD'VE BEEN PASSED DOWN TO ME? LIKE... SOME KIND OF MUTANT WITWICKY GENE?
QATARI DESERT.
KEEP IT UP, MEN. THIS POWER LINE'S GOTTA LEAD SOMEWHERE *EVENTUALLY*.

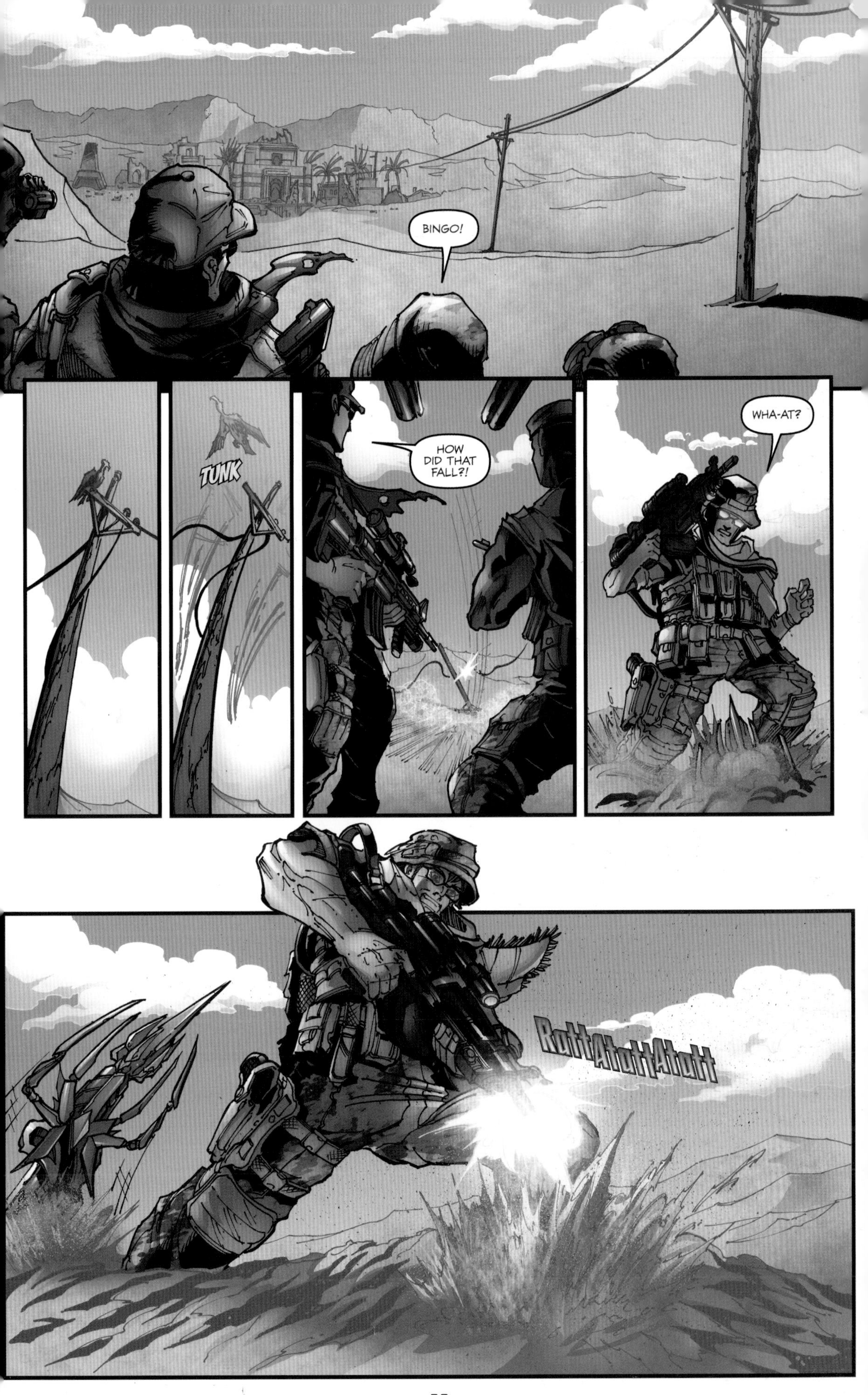
BINGO!
TUNK
HOW DID THAT FALL?!
WHA-AT?
RattAtattAtatt

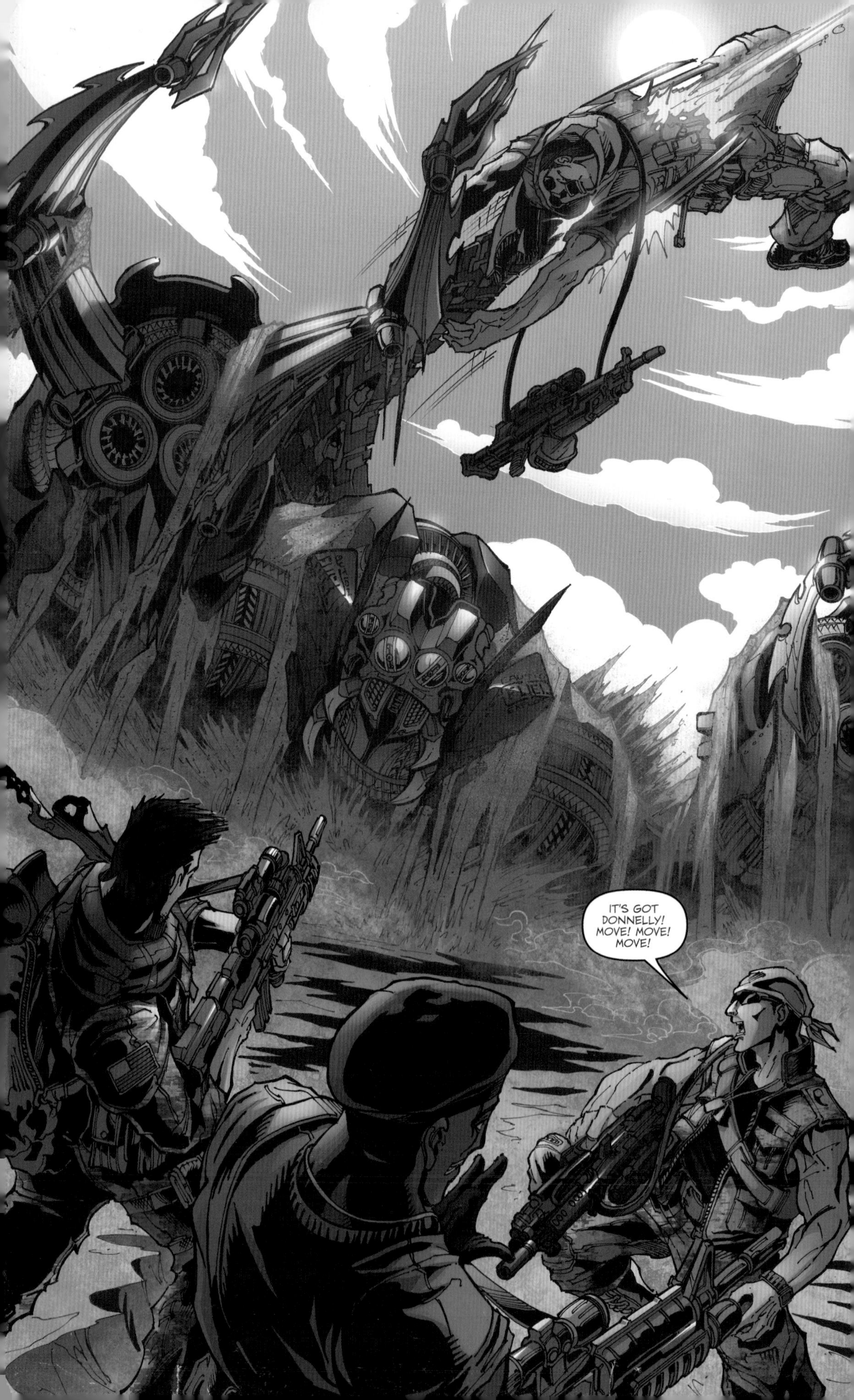
IT'S GOT DONNELLY! MOVE! MOVE! MOVE!

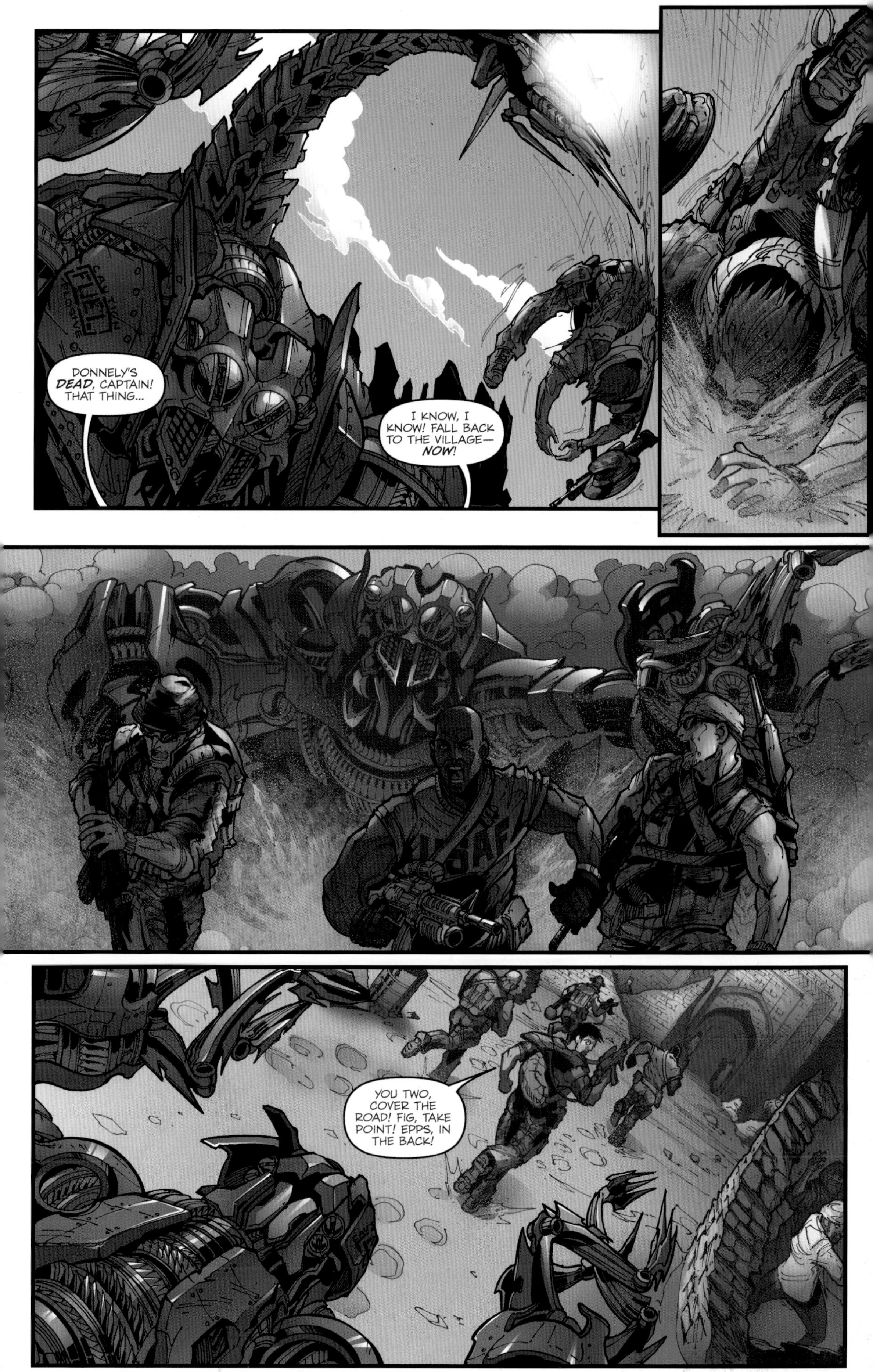
FUEL
DONNELY'S *DEAD*, CAPTAIN! THAT THING...
I KNOW, I KNOW! FALL BACK TO THE VILLAGE— *NOW*!
USAF
YOU TWO, COVER THE ROAD! FIG, TAKE POINT! EPPS, IN THE BACK!

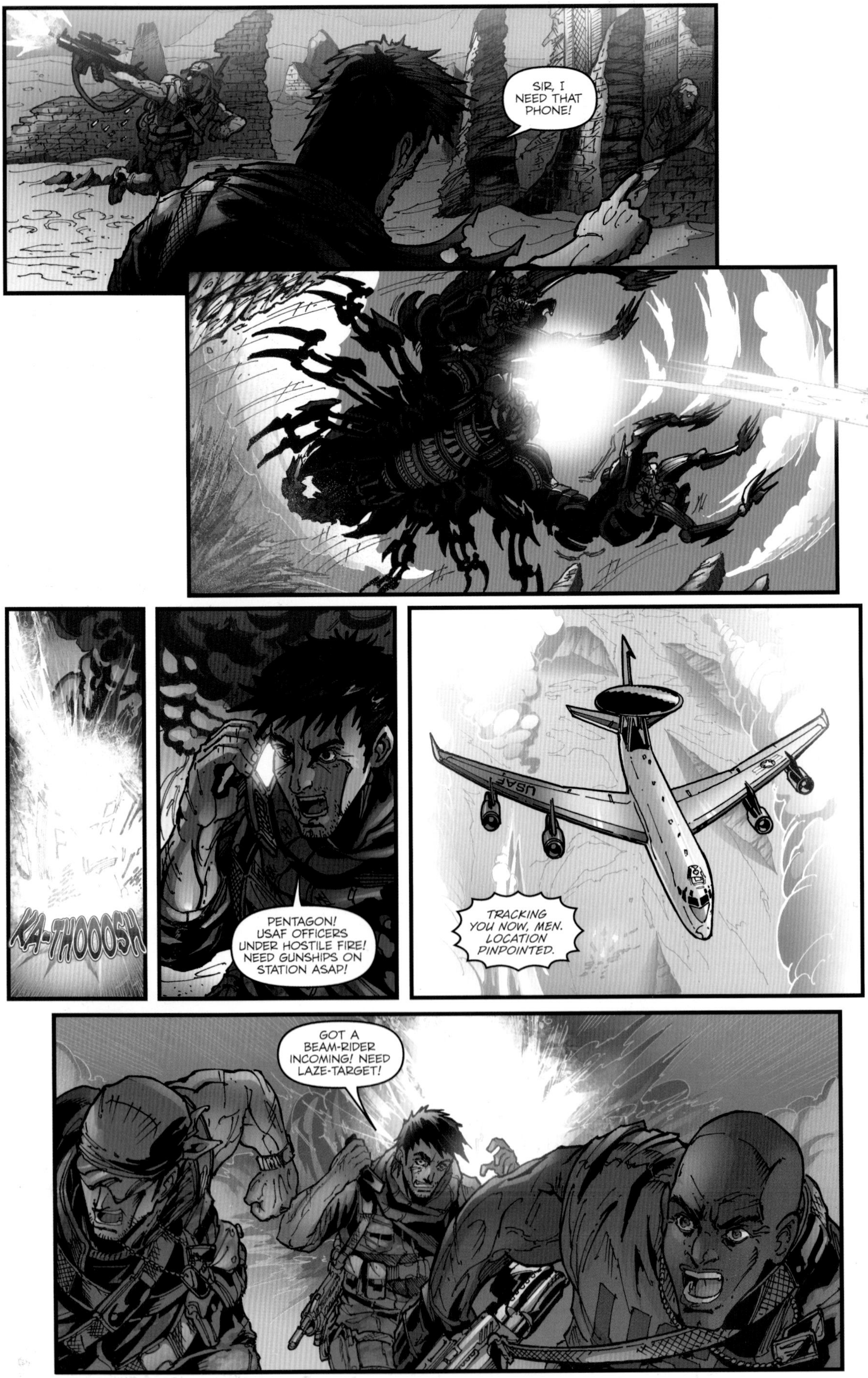
SIR, I NEED THAT PHONE!
KA-THOOOSH
PENTAGON! USAF OFFICERS UNDER HOSTILE FIRE! NEED GUNSHIPS ON STATION ASAP!
USAF
TRACKING YOU NOW, MEN. LOCATION PINPOINTED.
GOT A BEAM-RIDER INCOMING! NEED LAZE-TARGET!

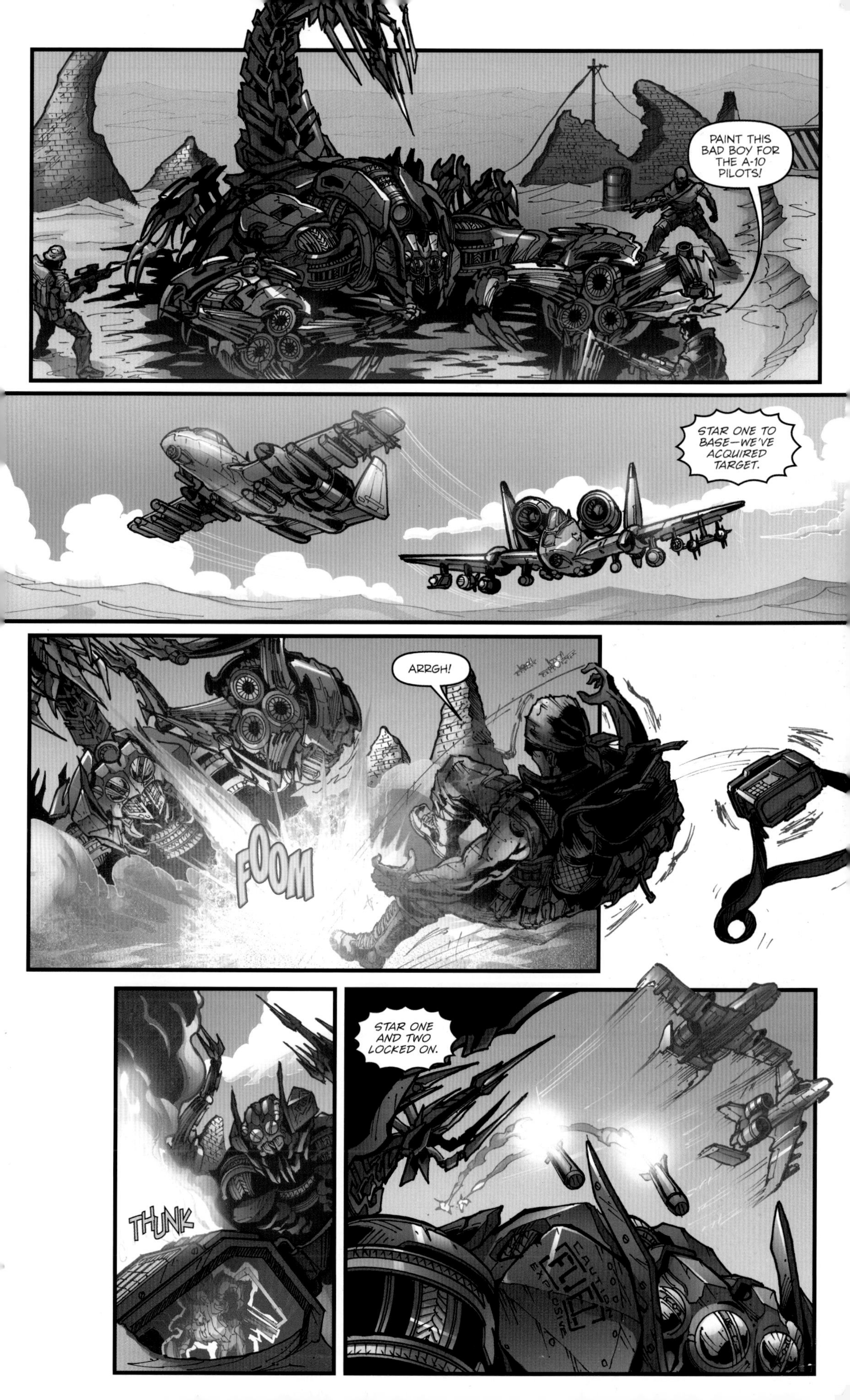
PAINT THIS BAD BOY FOR THE A-10 PILOTS!
STAR ONE TO BASE—WE'VE ACQUIRED TARGET.
ARRGH!
FOOM
THUNK
STAR ONE AND TWO LOCKED ON.

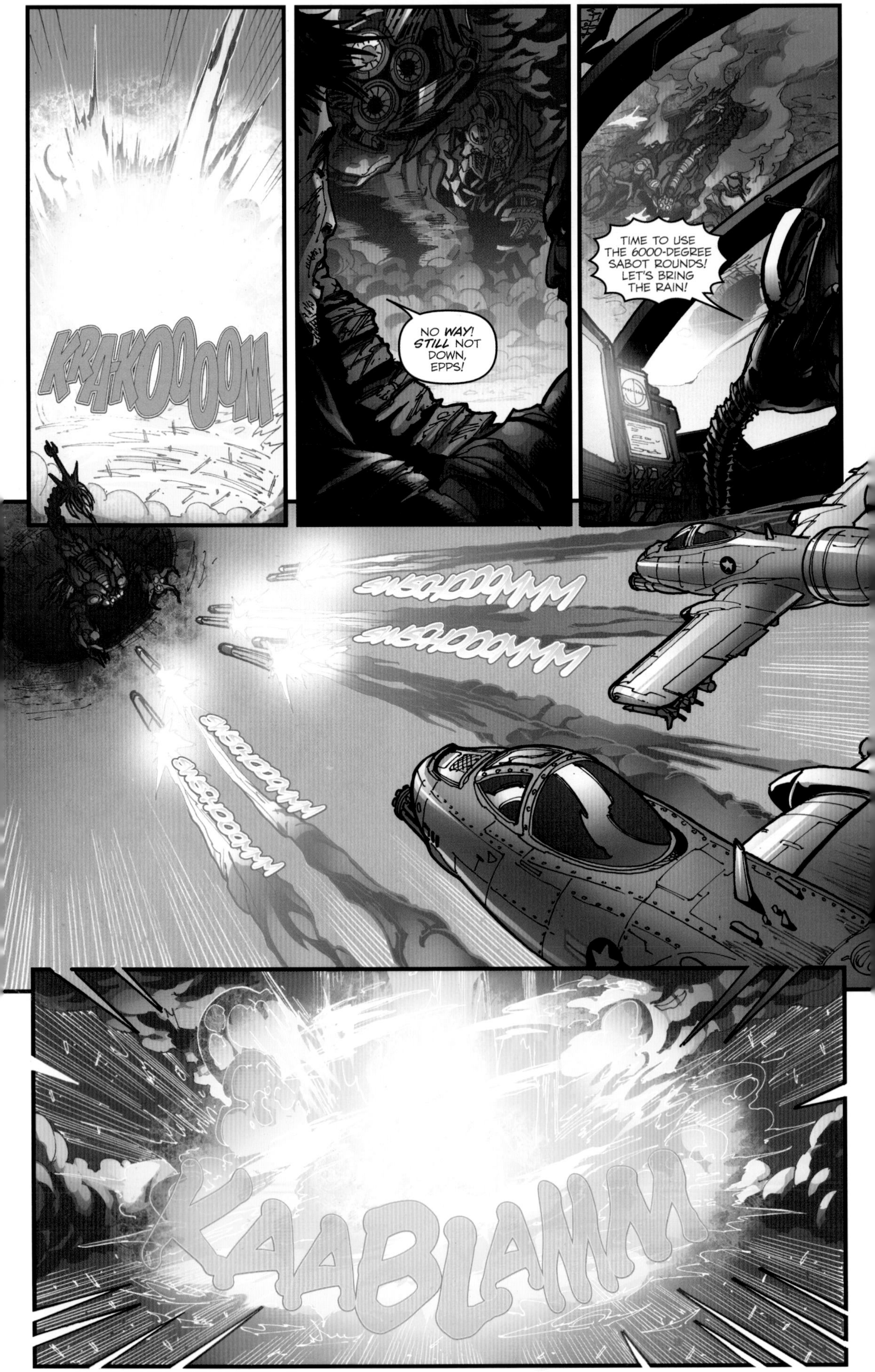
KRA-KOOOOM
NO WAY! STILL NOT DOWN, EPPS!
TIME TO USE THE 6000-DEGREE SABOT ROUNDS! LET'S BRING THE RAIN!
KAABLAMM

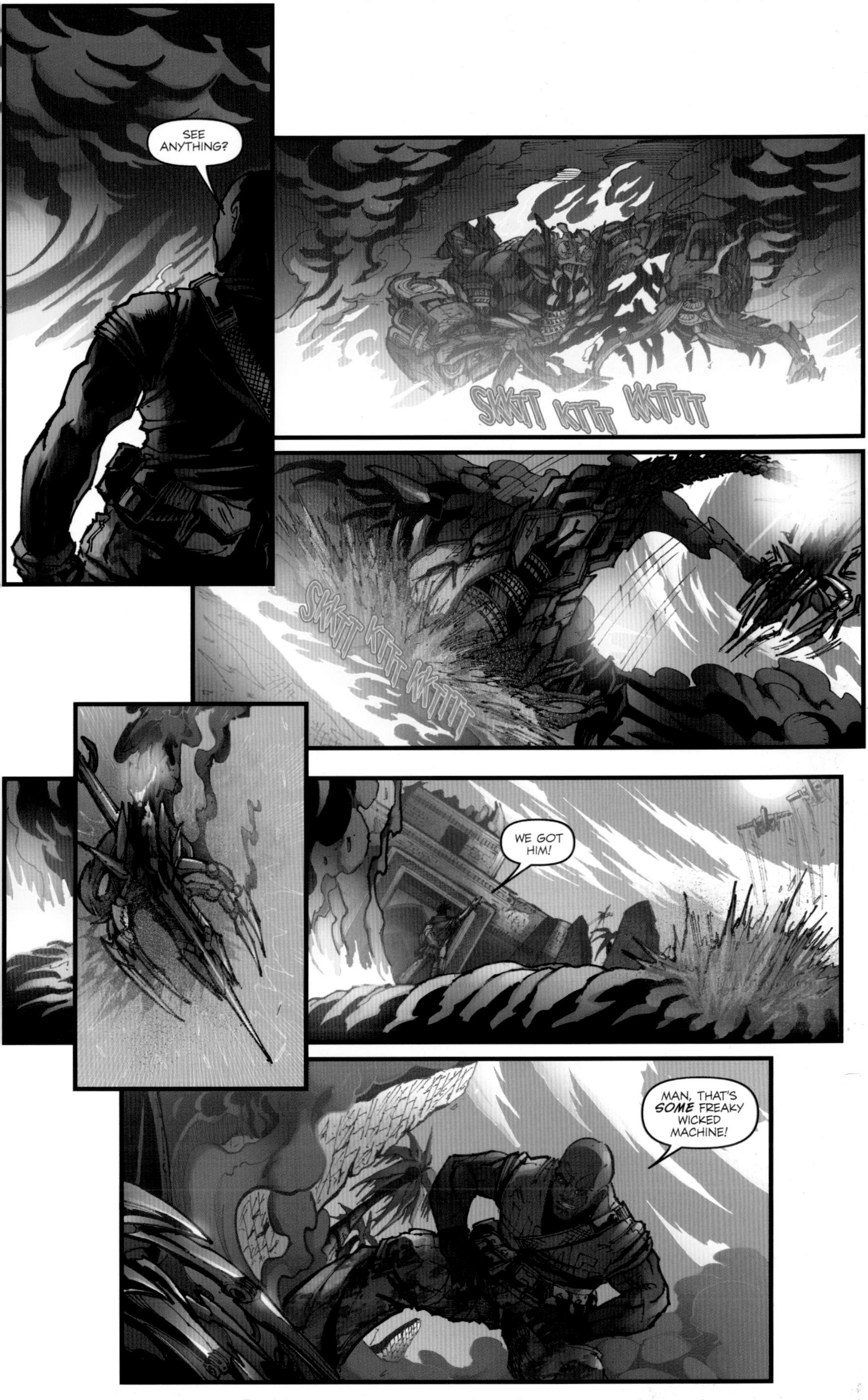
SEE ANYTHING?
SKKTT KTTT KKTTTT
SKKTT KTTT KKTTTT
WE GOT HIM!
MAN, THAT'S **SOME** FREAKY WICKED MACHINE!

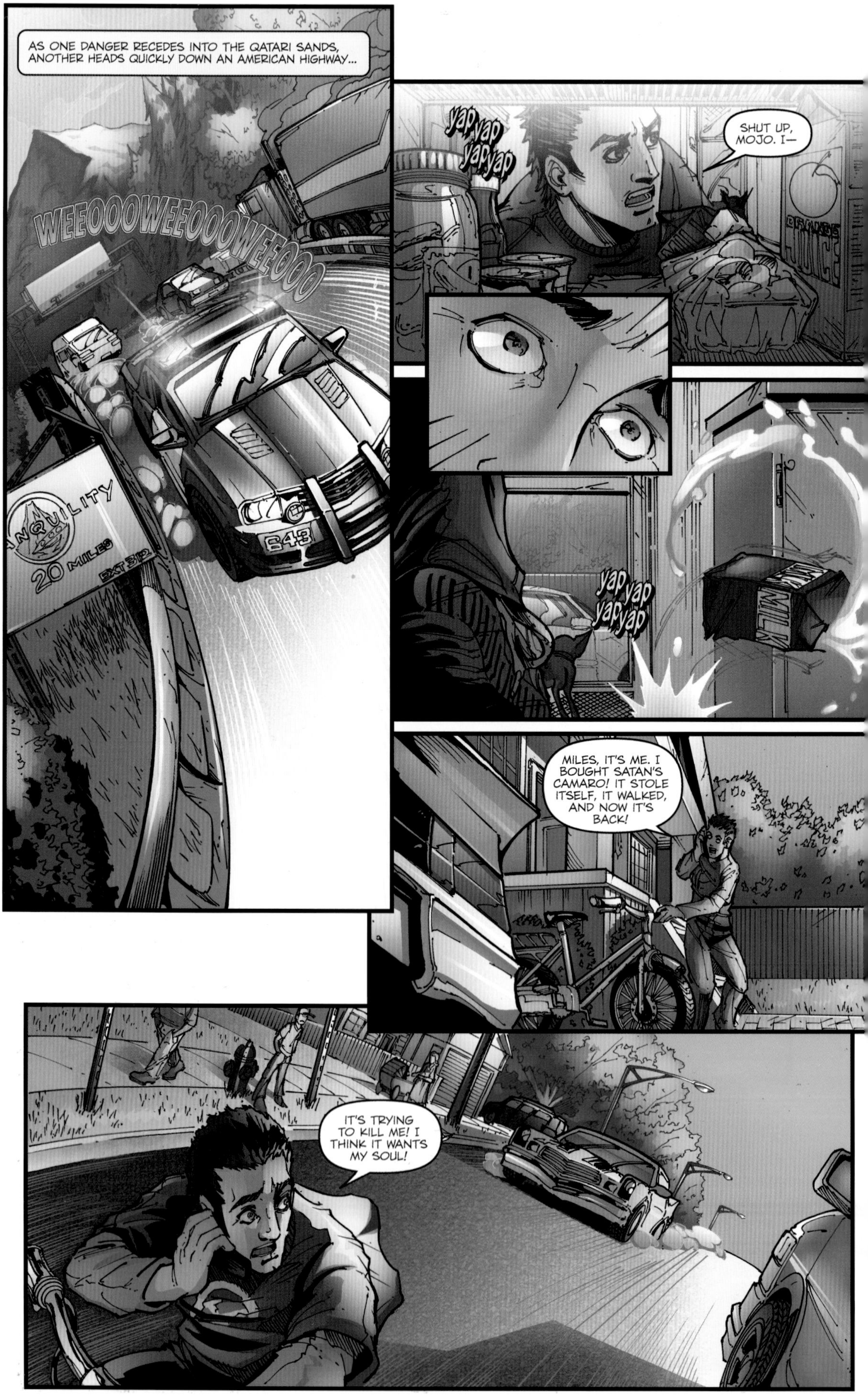
AS ONE DANGER RECEDES INTO THE QATARI SANDS, ANOTHER HEADS QUICKLY DOWN AN AMERICAN HIGHWAY...
WEEOOOWEEOOOWEEOOO
20 MILES
EXT 312
643
yap yap yap yap
SHUT UP, MOJO. I—
ORANGE JUICE
yap yap yap yap
MILK
MILES, IT'S ME. I BOUGHT SATAN'S CAMARO! IT STOLE ITSELF, IT WALKED, AND NOW IT'S BACK!
IT'S TRYING TO KILL ME! I THINK IT WANTS MY SOUL!

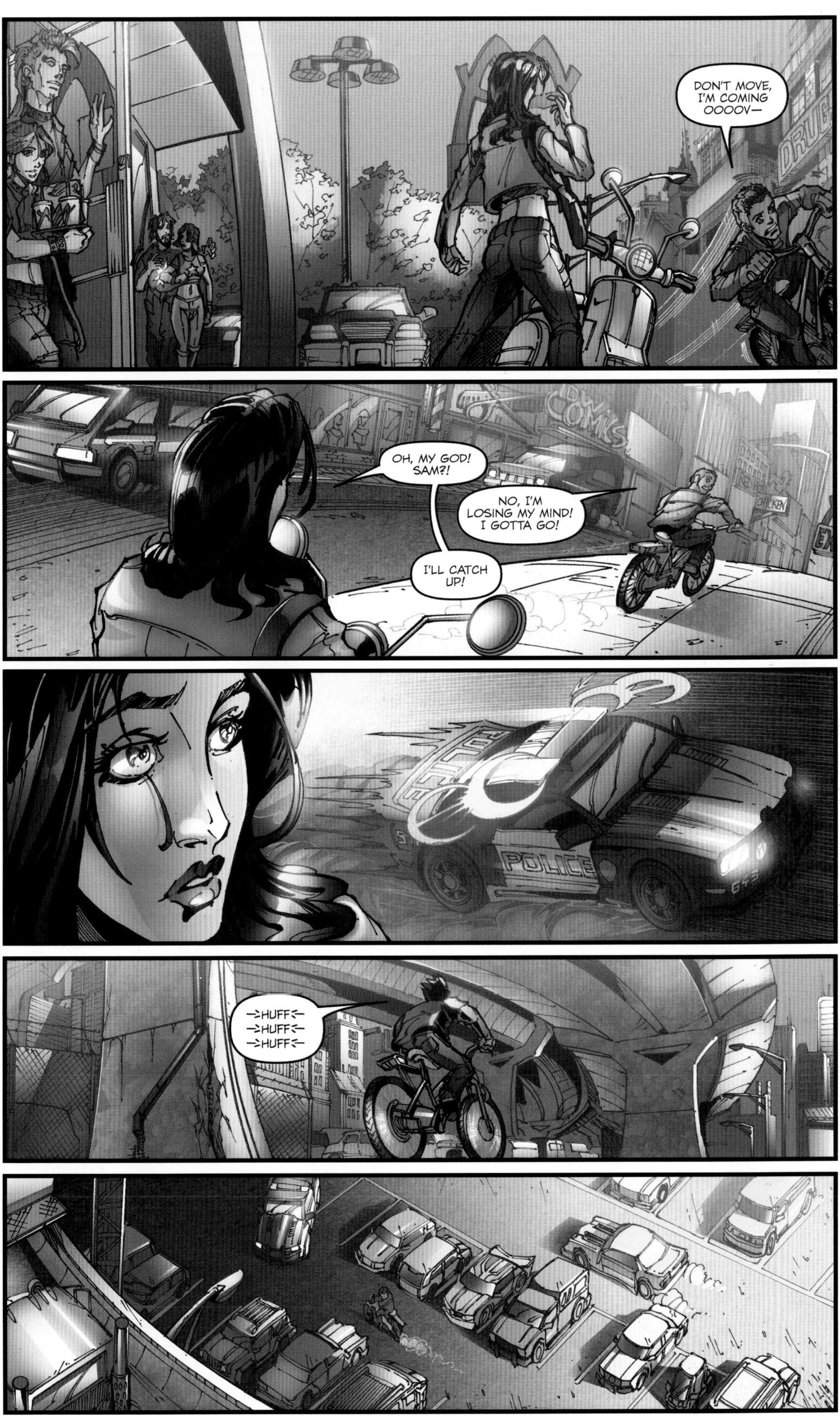
DON'T MOVE, I'M COMING OOOOV—
DRUG
OH, MY GOD! SAM?!
COMICS
NO, I'M LOSING MY MIND! I GOTTA GO!
CHICKEN
I'LL CATCH UP!
POLICE
—HUFF—
—HUFF—
—HUFF—

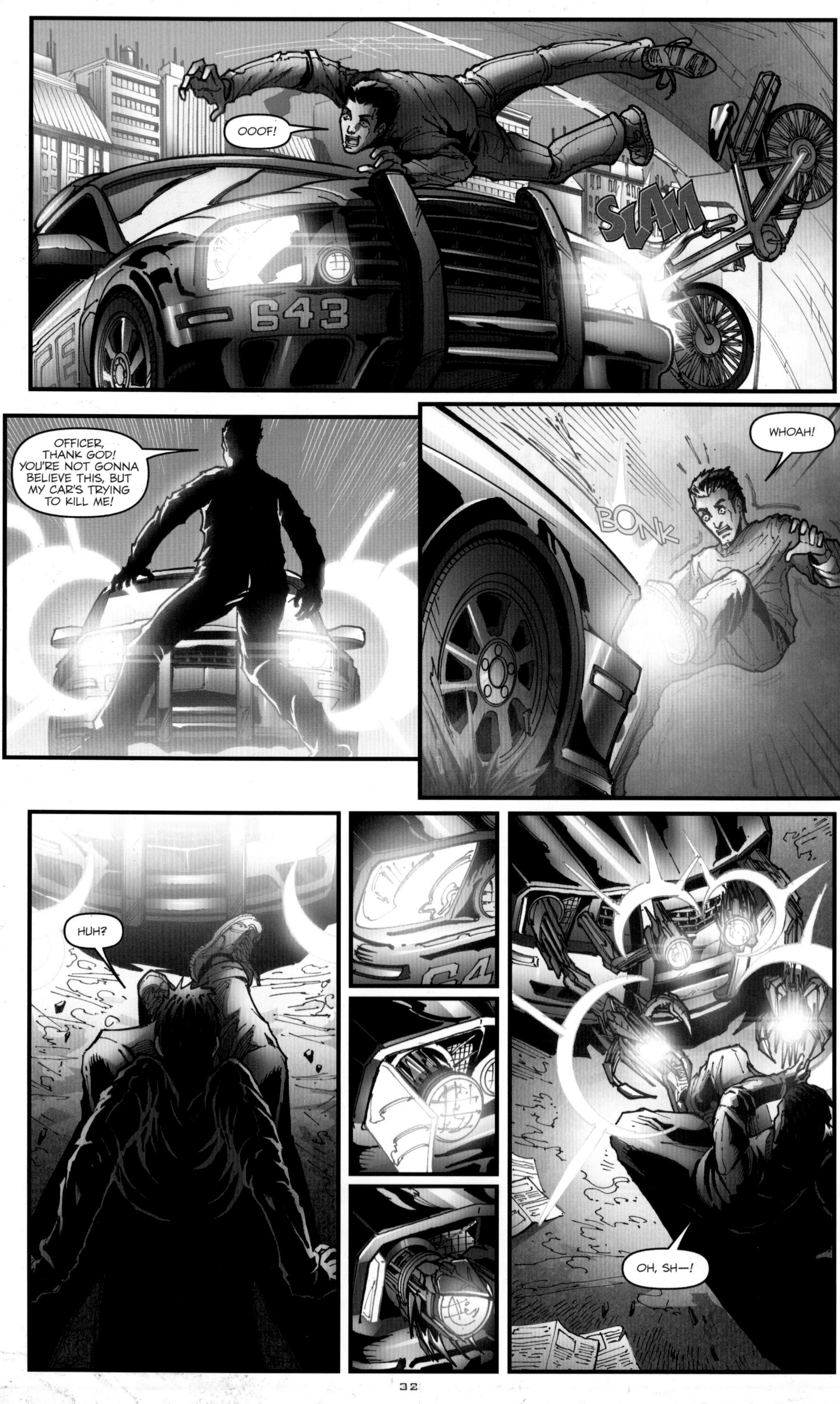
OOOF!
SLAM
643
OFFICER, THANK GOD! YOU'RE NOT GONNA BELIEVE THIS, BUT MY CAR'S TRYING TO KILL ME!
WHOAH!
BONK
HUH?
OH, SH—!

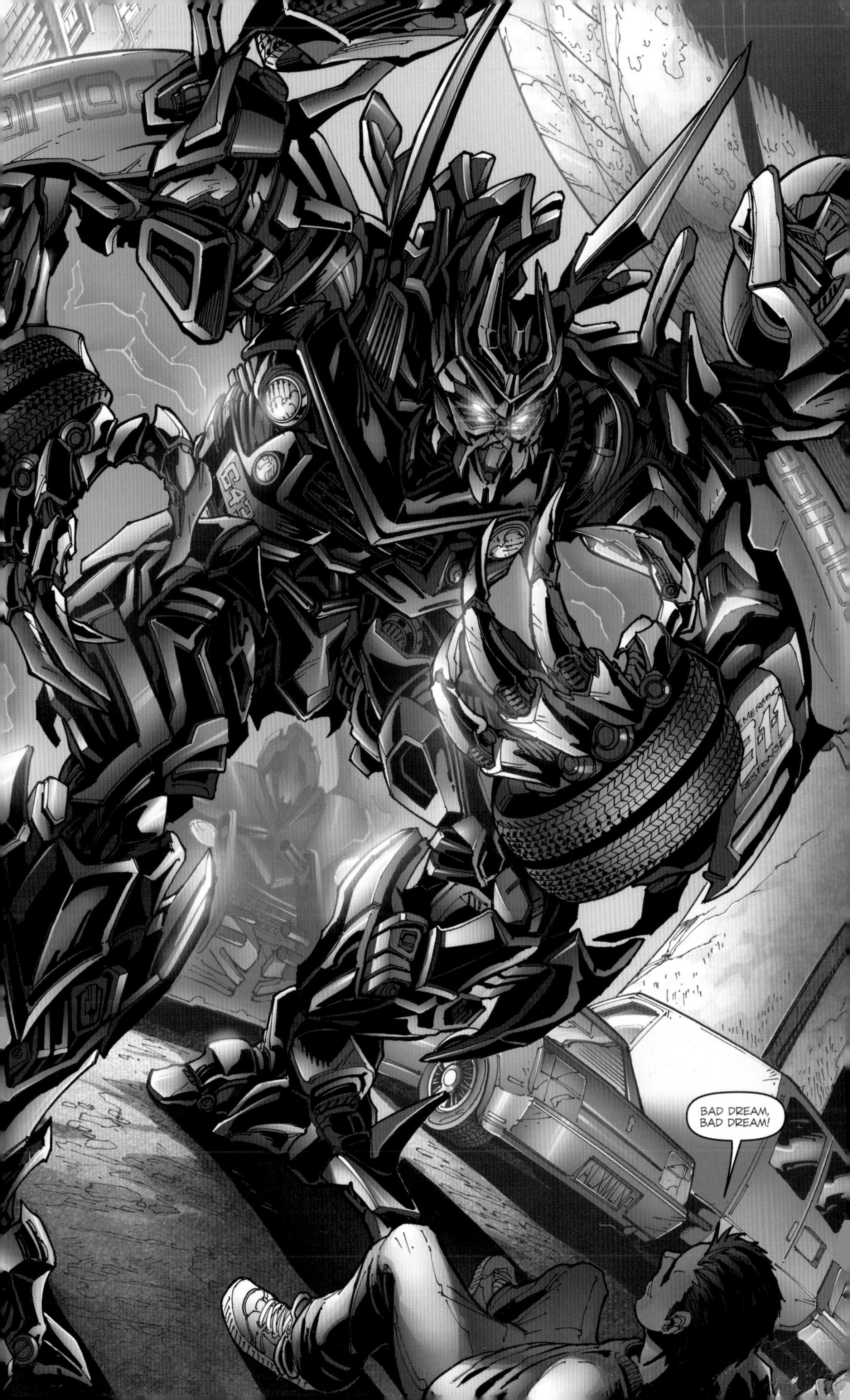
BAD DREAM, BAD DREAM!

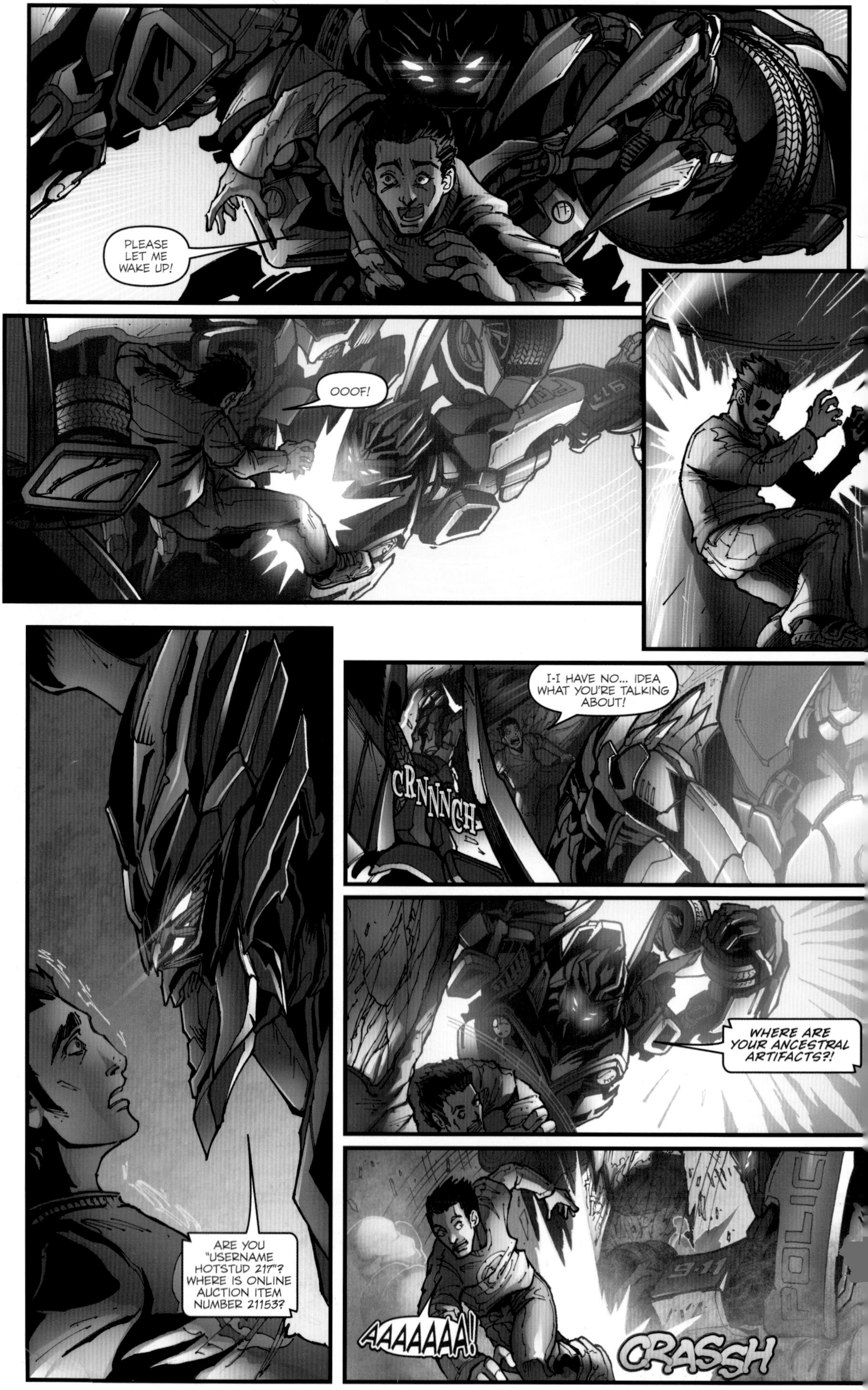
PLEASE LET ME WAKE UP!
OOOF!
CRNNNCH
I-I HAVE NO... IDEA WHAT YOU'RE TALKING ABOUT!
WHERE ARE YOUR ANCESTRAL ARTIFACTS?!
ARE YOU "USERNAME HOTSTUD 217"? WHERE IS ONLINE AUCTION ITEM NUMBER 21153?
AAAAAAA!
CRASSH

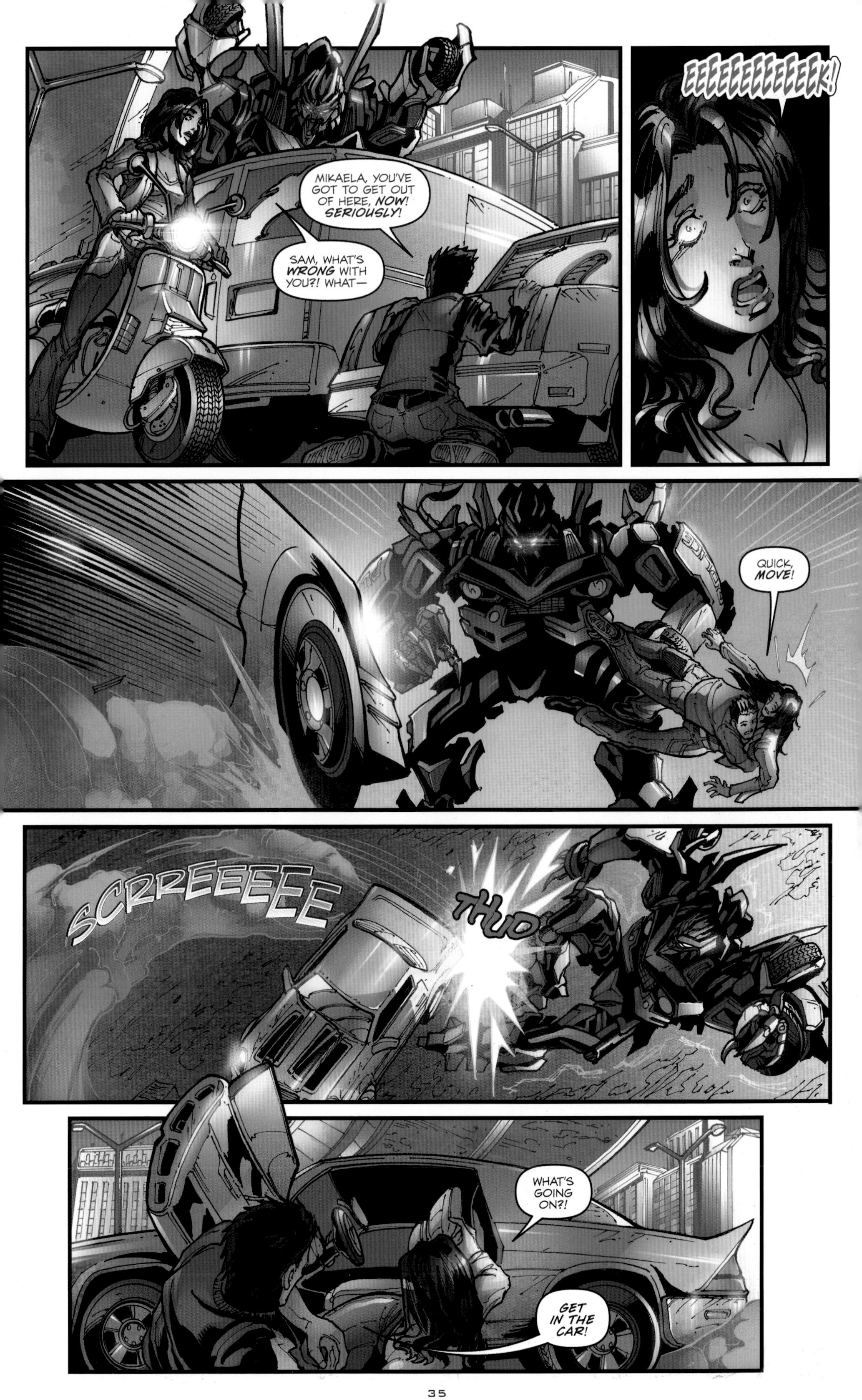
MIKAELA, YOU'VE GOT TO GET OUT OF HERE, NOW! SERIOUSLY!
SAM, WHAT'S WRONG WITH YOU?! WHAT—
EEEEEEEEEEEEEK!
QUICK, MOVE!
SCRREEEEEE
THUD
WHAT'S GOING ON?!
GET IN THE CAR!

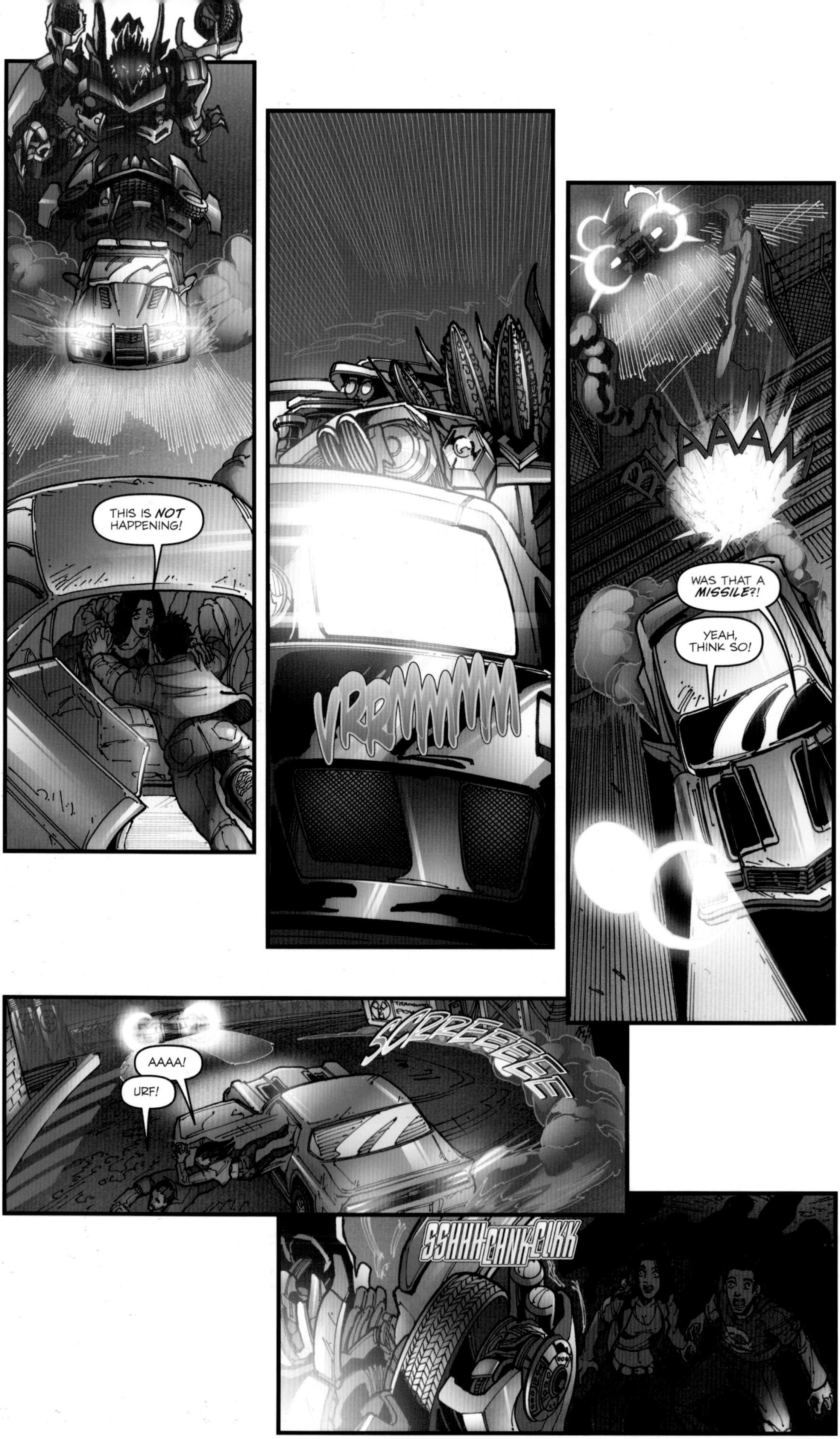
THIS IS NOT HAPPENING!
VRRMMMMM
BLAAAM
WAS THAT A MISSILE?!
YEAH, THINK SO!
SCREEEEE
AAAA!
URF!
SSHHKCHNKCLIKK

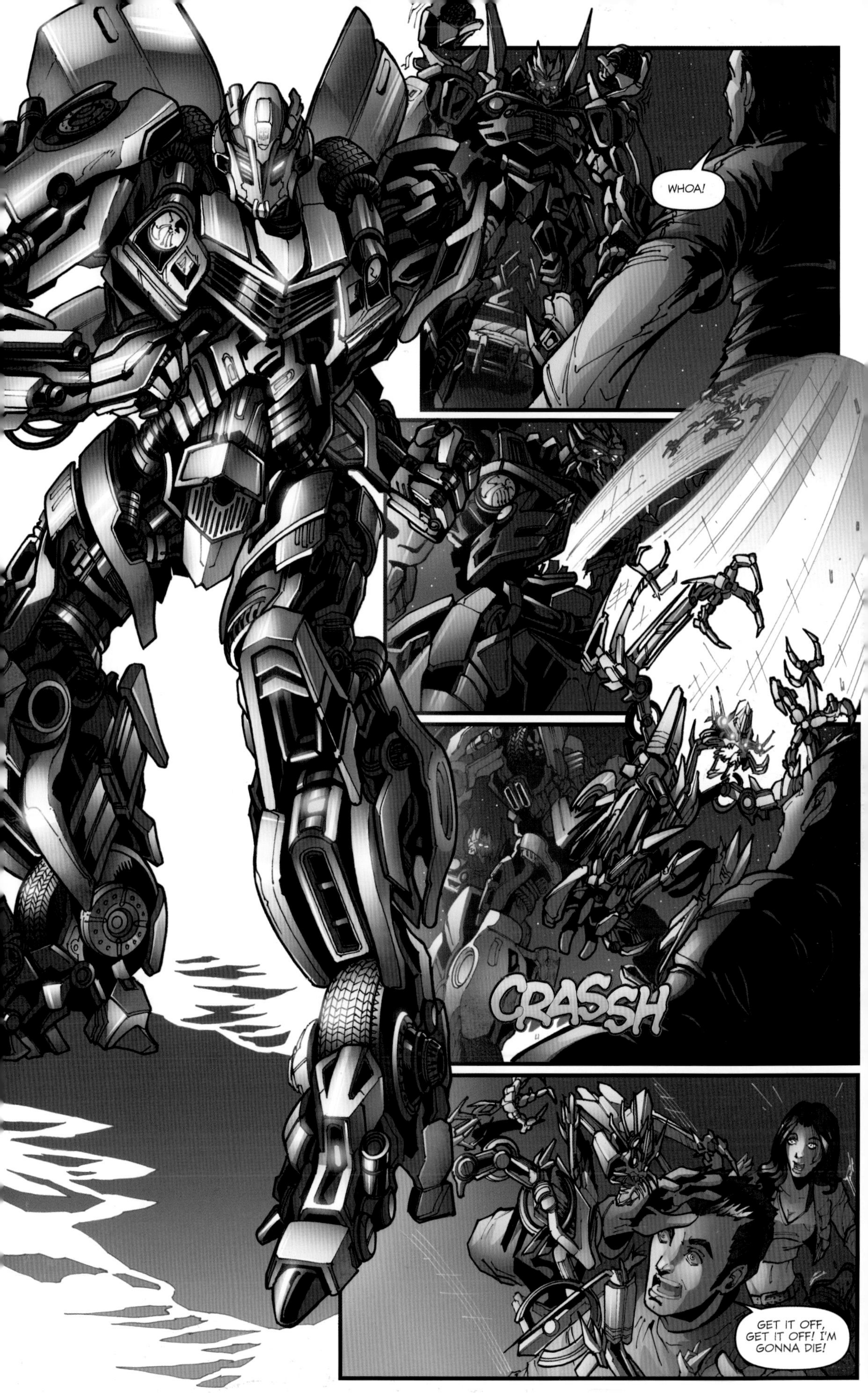
WHOA!
CRASSH
GET IT OFF, GET IT OFF! I'M GONNA DIE!

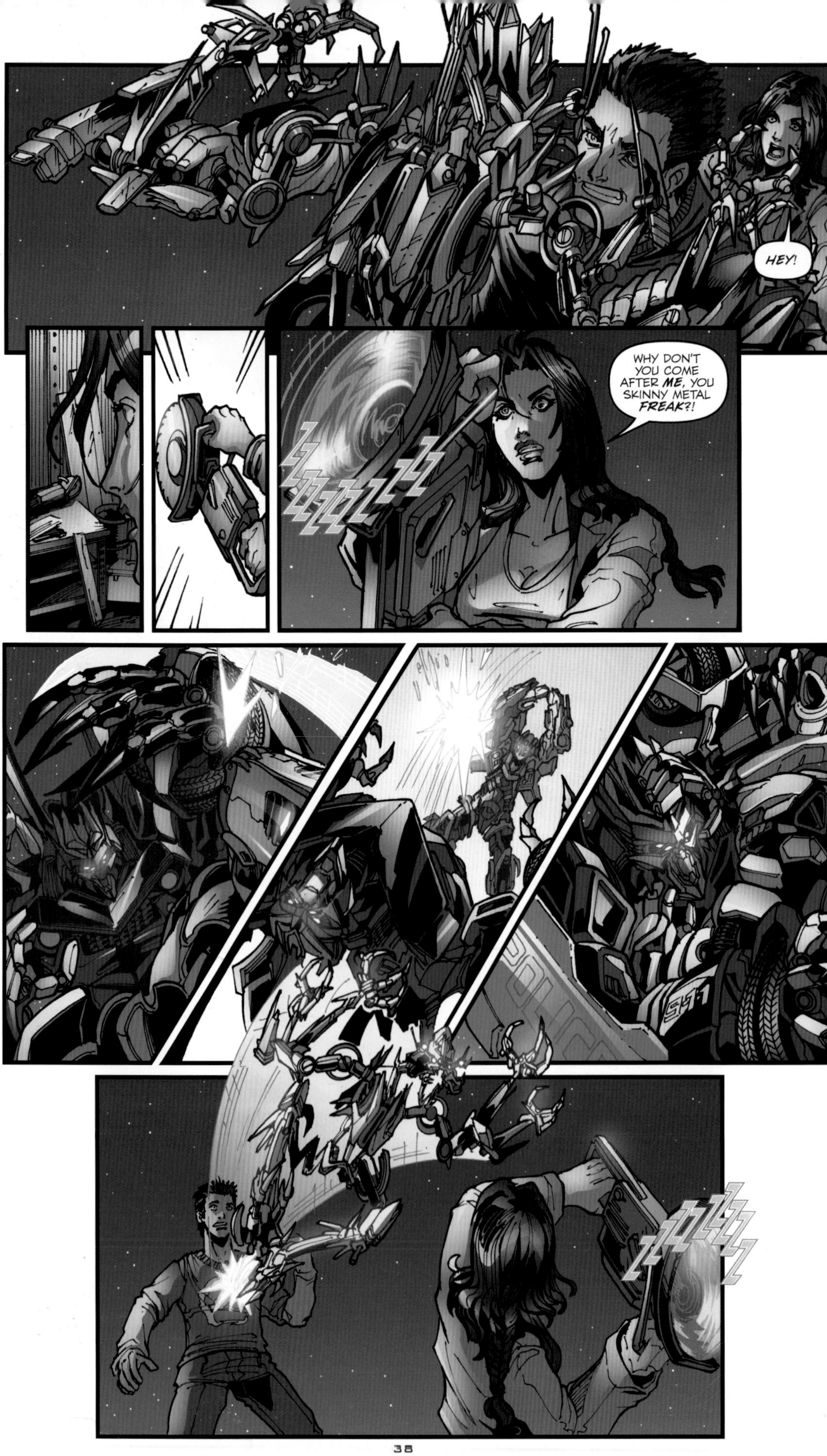
HEY!
WHY DON'T YOU COME AFTER *ME*, YOU SKINNY METAL *FREAK*?!

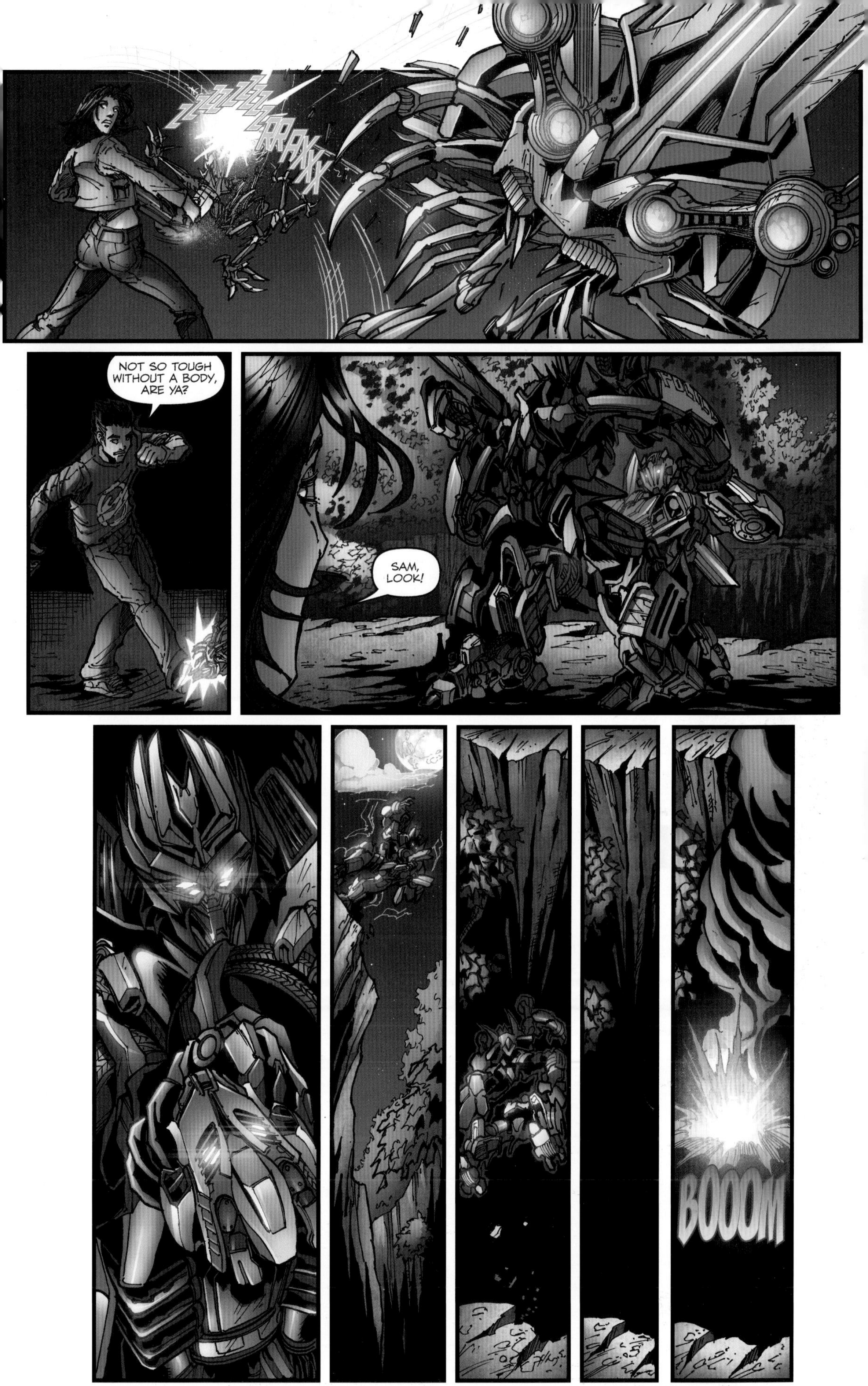
ZZZZZZZZZRRAXXX
NOT SO TOUGH WITHOUT A BODY, ARE YA?
SAM, LOOK!
BOOOM

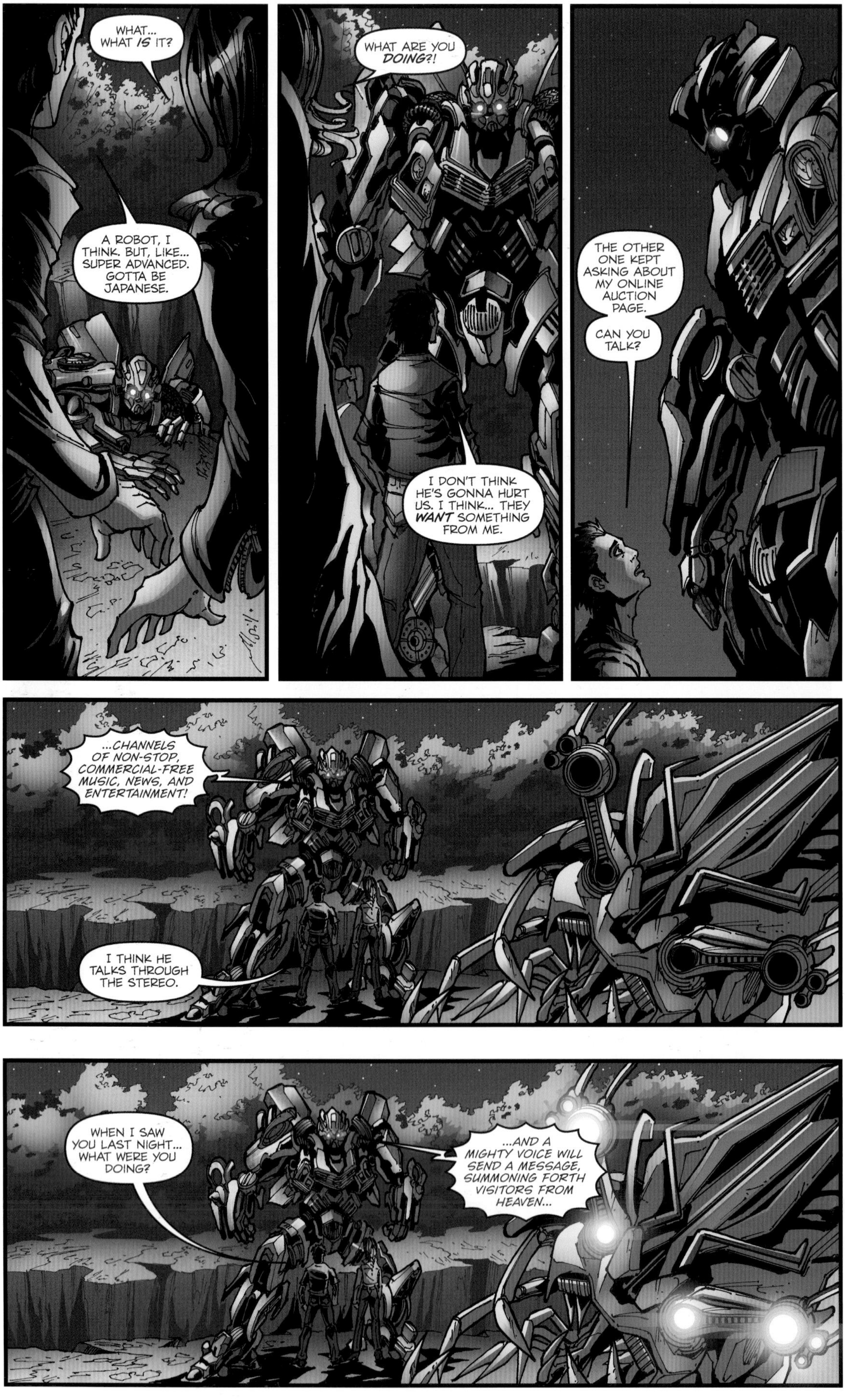
WHAT... WHAT IS IT?
A ROBOT, I THINK. BUT, LIKE... SUPER ADVANCED. GOTTA BE JAPANESE.
WHAT ARE YOU DOING?!
I DON'T THINK HE'S GONNA HURT US. I THINK... THEY WANT SOMETHING FROM ME.
THE OTHER ONE KEPT ASKING ABOUT MY ONLINE AUCTION PAGE.
CAN YOU TALK?
...CHANNELS OF NON-STOP, COMMERCIAL-FREE MUSIC, NEWS, AND ENTERTAINMENT!
I THINK HE TALKS THROUGH THE STEREO.
WHEN I SAW YOU LAST NIGHT... WHAT WERE YOU DOING?
...AND A MIGHTY VOICE WILL SEND A MESSAGE, SUMMONING FORTH VISITORS FROM HEAVEN...

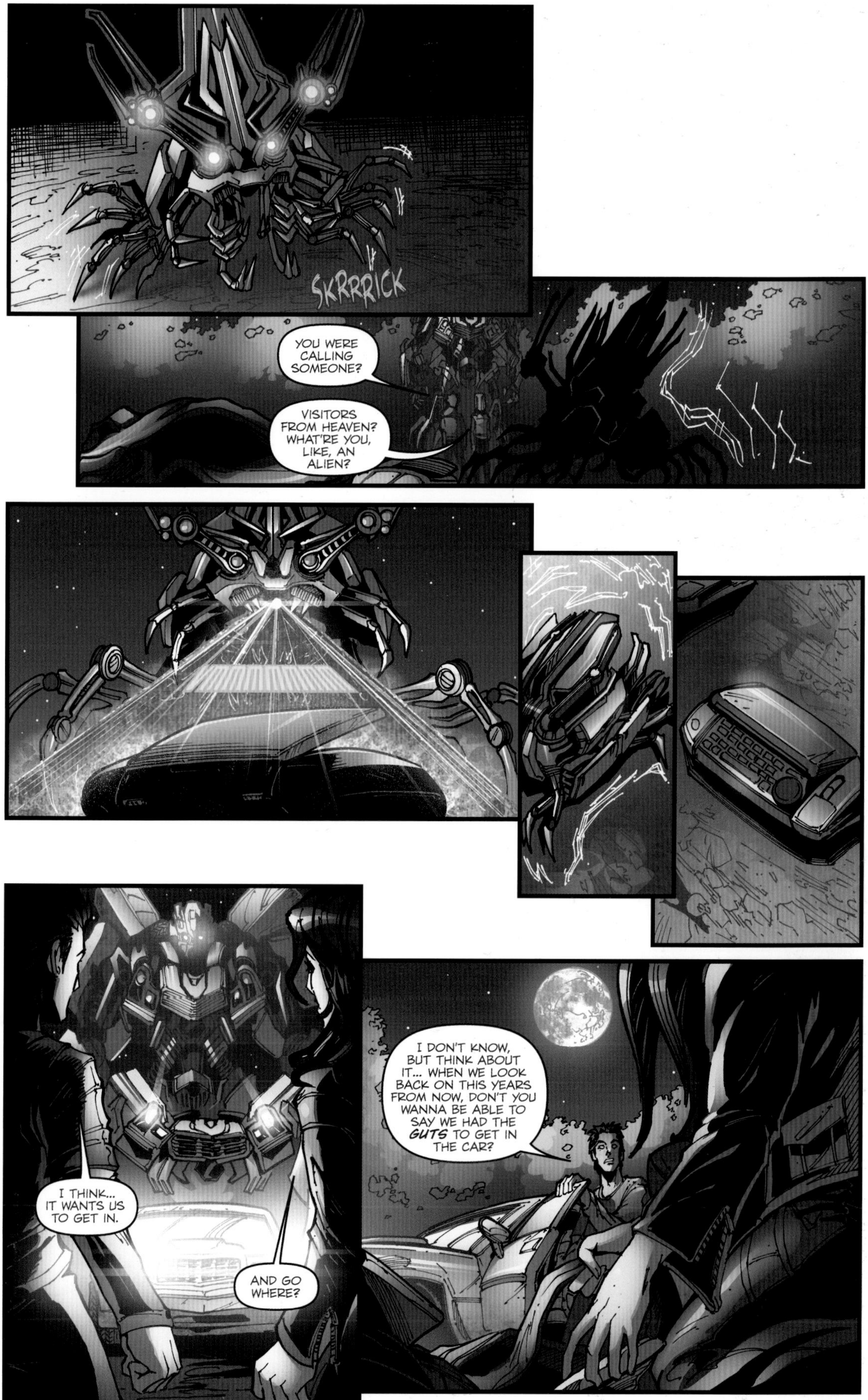
SKRRRICK
YOU WERE CALLING SOMEONE?
VISITORS FROM HEAVEN? WHAT'RE YOU, LIKE, AN ALIEN?
I THINK... IT WANTS US TO GET IN.
AND GO WHERE?
I DON'T KNOW, BUT THINK ABOUT IT... WHEN WE LOOK BACK ON THIS YEARS FROM NOW, DON'T YOU WANNA BE ABLE TO SAY WE HAD THE GUTS TO GET IN THE CAR?

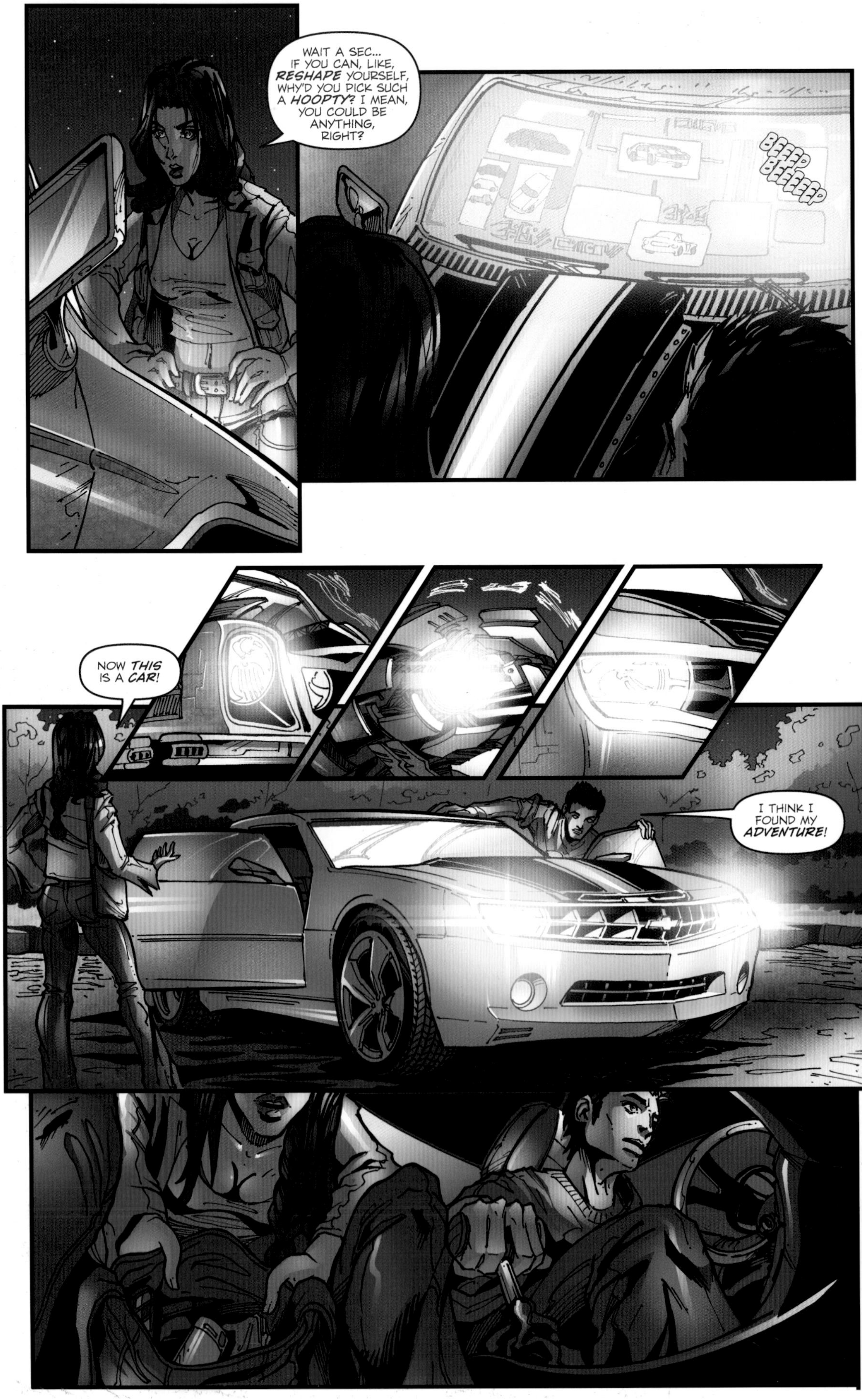
WAIT A SEC... IF YOU CAN, LIKE, RESHAPE YOURSELF, WHY'D YOU PICK SUCH A HOOPTY? I MEAN, YOU COULD BE ANYTHING, RIGHT?
BEEEP BEEEEEP
NOW THIS IS A CAR!
I THINK I FOUND MY ADVENTURE!

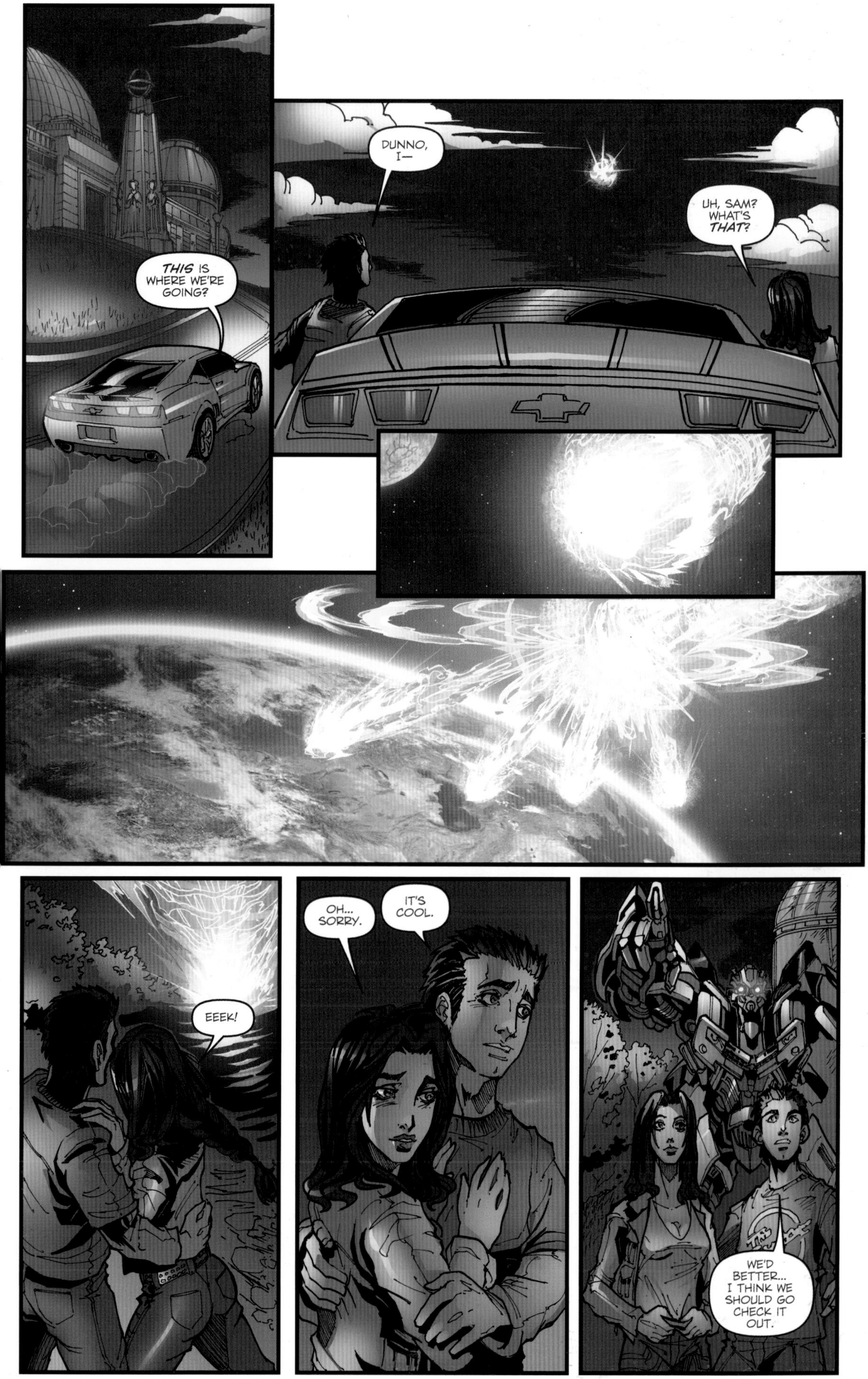
THIS IS WHERE WE'RE GOING?
DUNNO, I—
UH, SAM? WHAT'S THAT?
EEEK!
OH... SORRY.
IT'S COOL.
WE'D BETTER... I THINK WE SHOULD GO CHECK IT OUT.

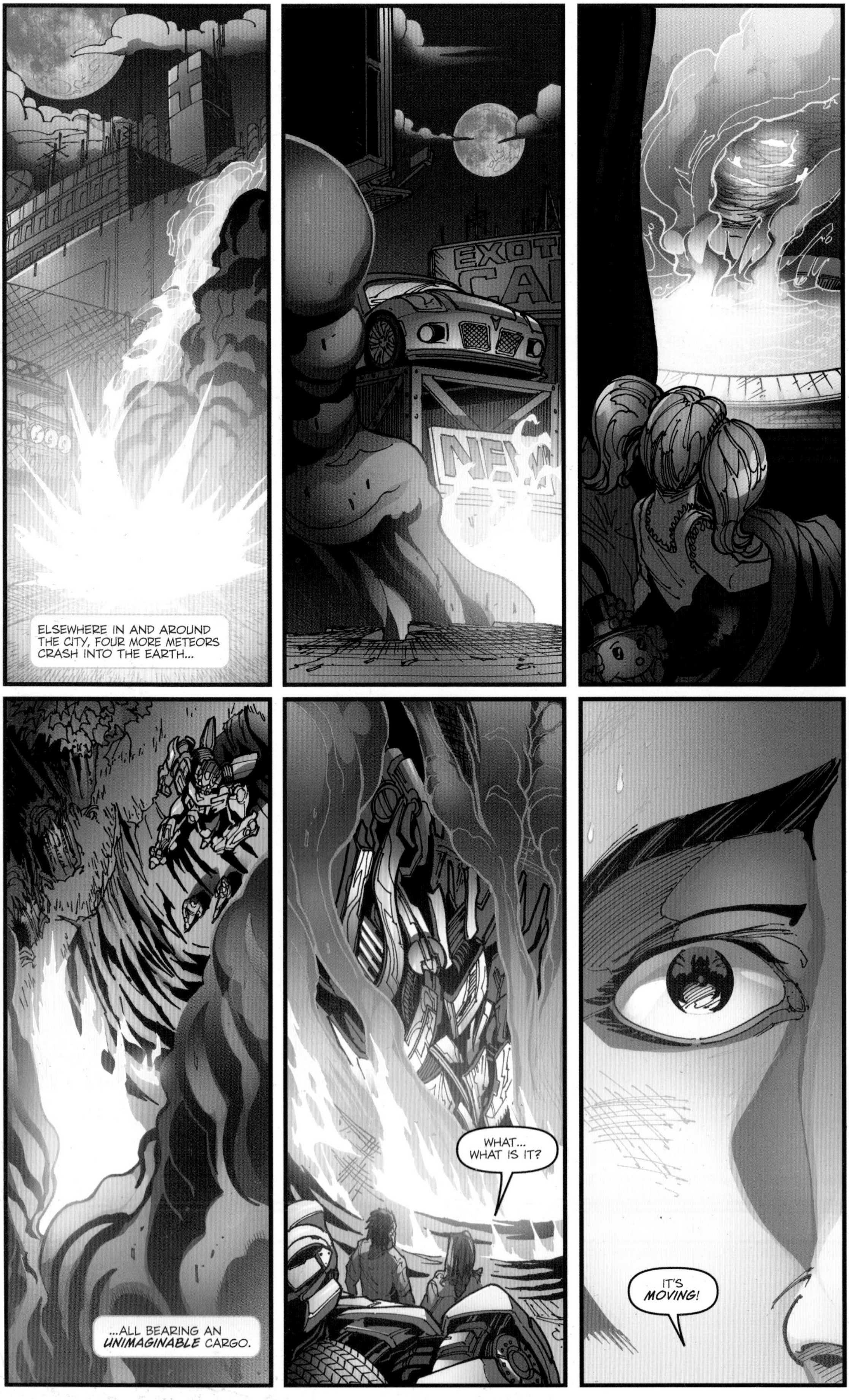
ELSEWHERE IN AND AROUND THE CITY, FOUR MORE METEORS CRASH INTO THE EARTH...
...ALL BEARING AN *UNIMAGINABLE* CARGO.
WHAT... WHAT IS IT?
IT'S *MOVING!*

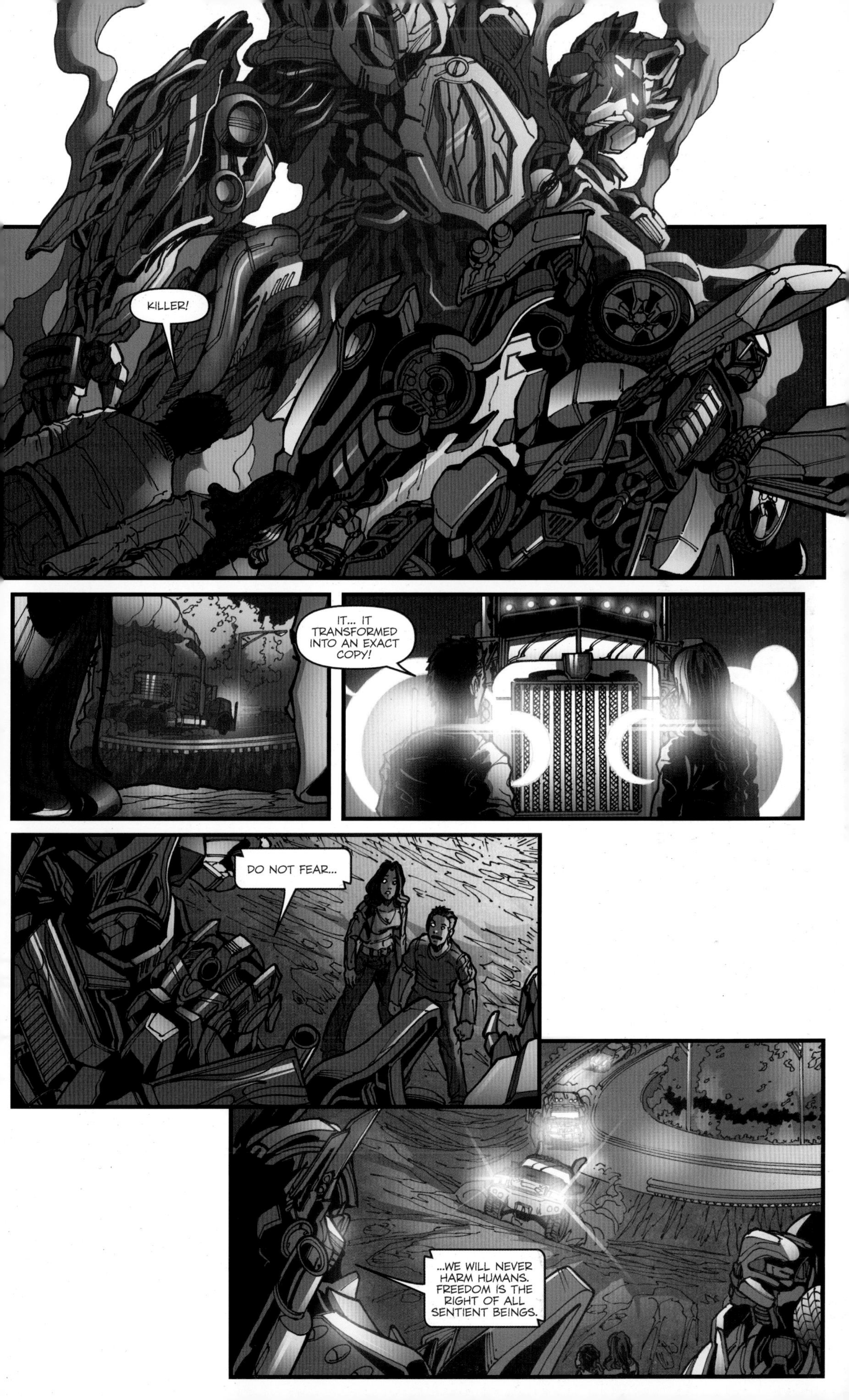
KILLER!
IT... IT TRANSFORMED INTO AN EXACT COPY!
DO NOT FEAR...
...WE WILL NEVER HARM HUMANS. FREEDOM IS THE RIGHT OF ALL SENTIENT BEINGS.

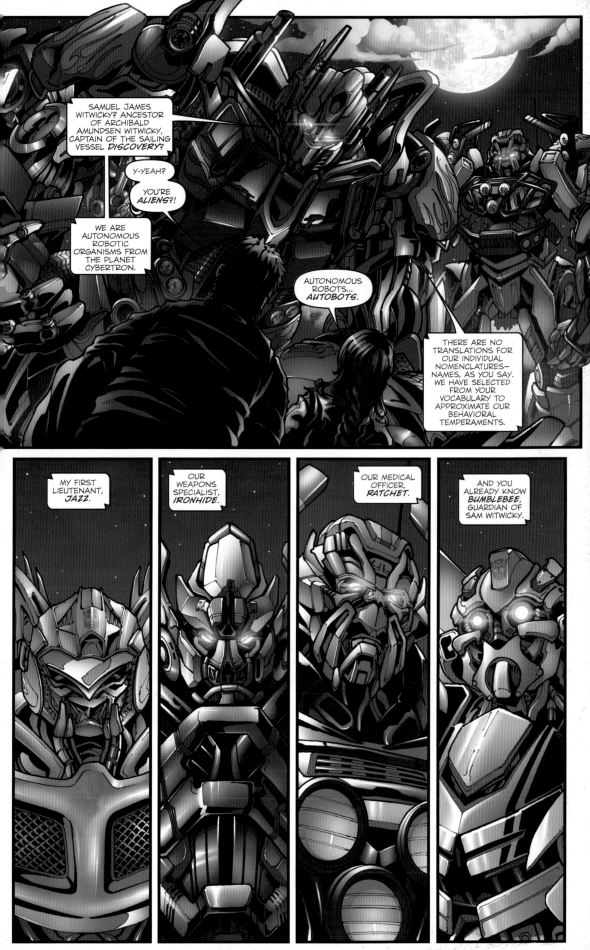

SAMUEL JAMES WITWICKY? ANCESTOR OF ARCHIBALD AMUNDSEN WITWICKY, CAPTAIN OF THE SAILING VESSEL *DISCOVERY*?

Y-YEAH?

YOU'RE *ALIENS*?!

WE ARE AUTONOMOUS ROBOTIC ORGANISMS FROM THE PLANET CYBERTRON.

AUTONOMOUS ROBOTS... *AUTOBOTS.*

THERE ARE NO TRANSLATIONS FOR OUR INDIVIDUAL NOMENCLATURES— NAMES, AS YOU SAY. WE HAVE SELECTED FROM YOUR VOCABULARY TO APPROXIMATE OUR BEHAVIORAL TEMPERAMENTS.

MY FIRST LIEUTENANT, *JAZZ.*

OUR WEAPONS SPECIALIST, *IRONHIDE.*

OUR MEDICAL OFFICER... *RATCHET.*

AND YOU ALREADY KNOW *BUMBLEBEE,* GUARDIAN OF SAM WITWICKY.

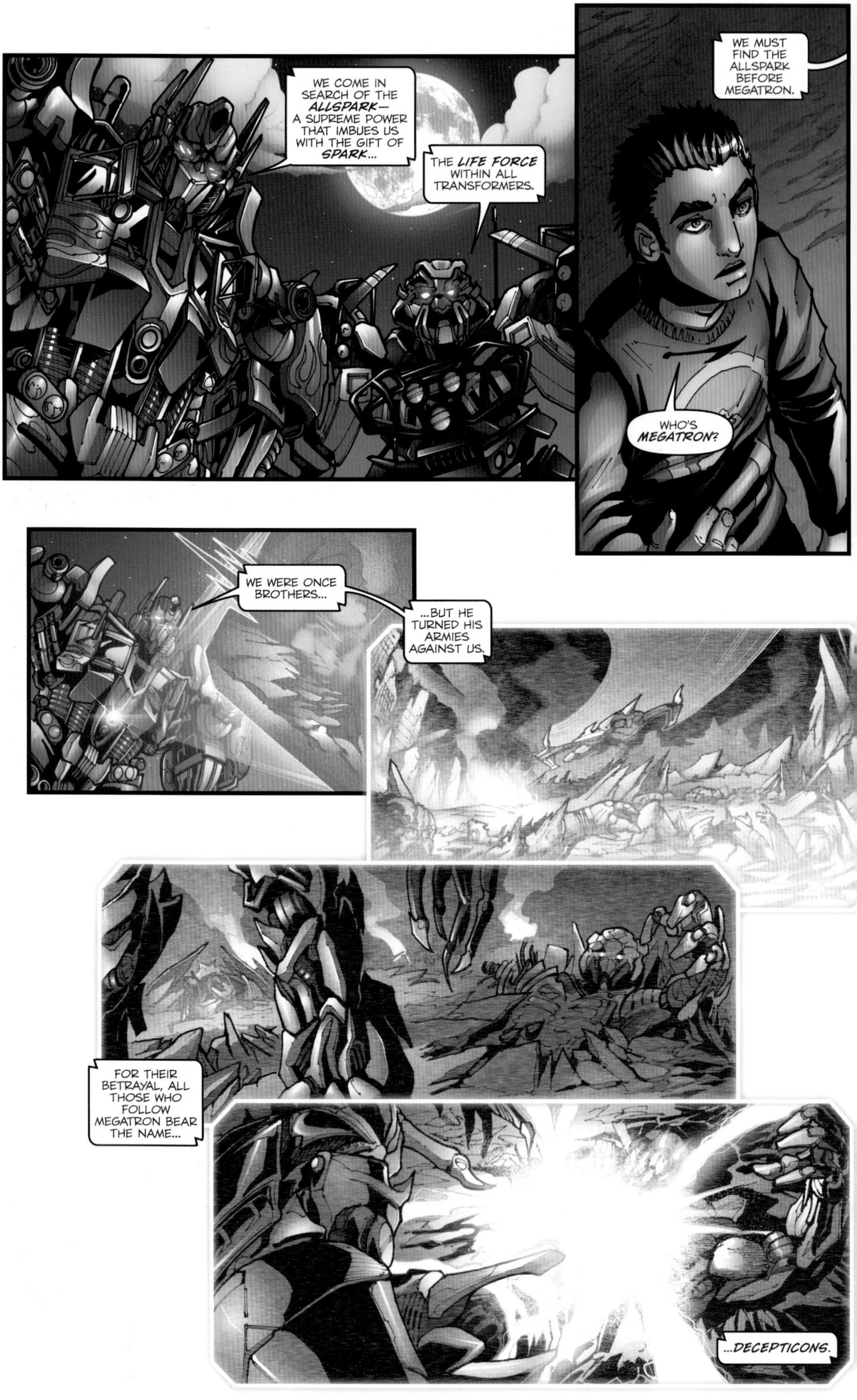
WE COME IN SEARCH OF THE ALLSPARK— A SUPREME POWER THAT IMBUES US WITH THE GIFT OF SPARK...
THE LIFE FORCE WITHIN ALL TRANSFORMERS.
WE MUST FIND THE ALLSPARK BEFORE MEGATRON.
WHO'S MEGATRON?
WE WERE ONCE BROTHERS...
...BUT HE TURNED HIS ARMIES AGAINST US.
FOR THEIR BETRAYAL, ALL THOSE WHO FOLLOW MEGATRON BEAR THE NAME...
...DECEPTICONS.

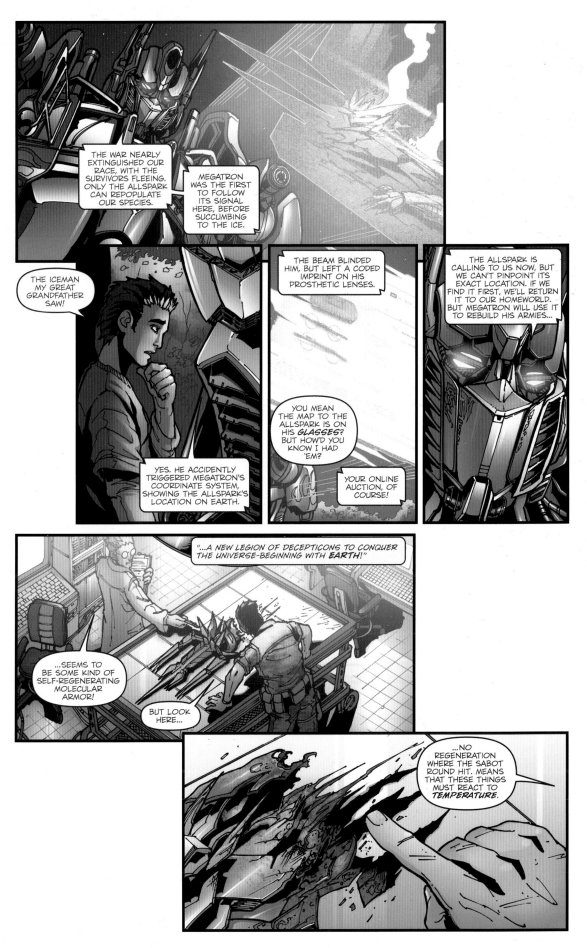

THE WAR NEARLY EXTINGUISHED OUR RACE, WITH THE SURVIVORS FLEEING. ONLY THE ALLSPARK CAN REPOPULATE OUR SPECIES.

MEGATRON WAS THE FIRST TO FOLLOW ITS SIGNAL HERE, BEFORE SUCCUMBING TO THE ICE.

THE ICEMAN MY GREAT GRANDFATHER SAW!

THE BEAM BLINDED HIM, BUT LEFT A CODED IMPRINT ON HIS PROSTHETIC LENSES.

THE ALLSPARK IS CALLING TO US NOW, BUT WE CAN'T PINPOINT ITS EXACT LOCATION. IF WE FIND IT FIRST, WE'LL RETURN IT TO OUR HOMEWORLD. BUT MEGATRON WILL USE IT TO REBUILD HIS ARMIES...

YES. HE ACCIDENTLY TRIGGERED MEGATRON'S COORDINATE SYSTEM, SHOWING THE ALLSPARK'S LOCATION ON EARTH.

YOU MEAN THE MAP TO THE ALLSPARK IS ON HIS *GLASSES?* BUT HOW'D YOU KNOW I HAD 'EM?

YOUR ONLINE AUCTION, OF COURSE!

"...A NEW LEGION OF DECEPTICONS TO CONQUER THE UNIVERSE—BEGINNING WITH *EARTH!*"

...SEEMS TO BE SOME KIND OF SELF-REGENERATING MOLECULAR ARMOR!

BUT LOOK HERE...

...NO REGENERATION WHERE THE SABOT ROUND HIT. MEANS THAT THESE THINGS MUST REACT TO *TEMPERATURE*.

49

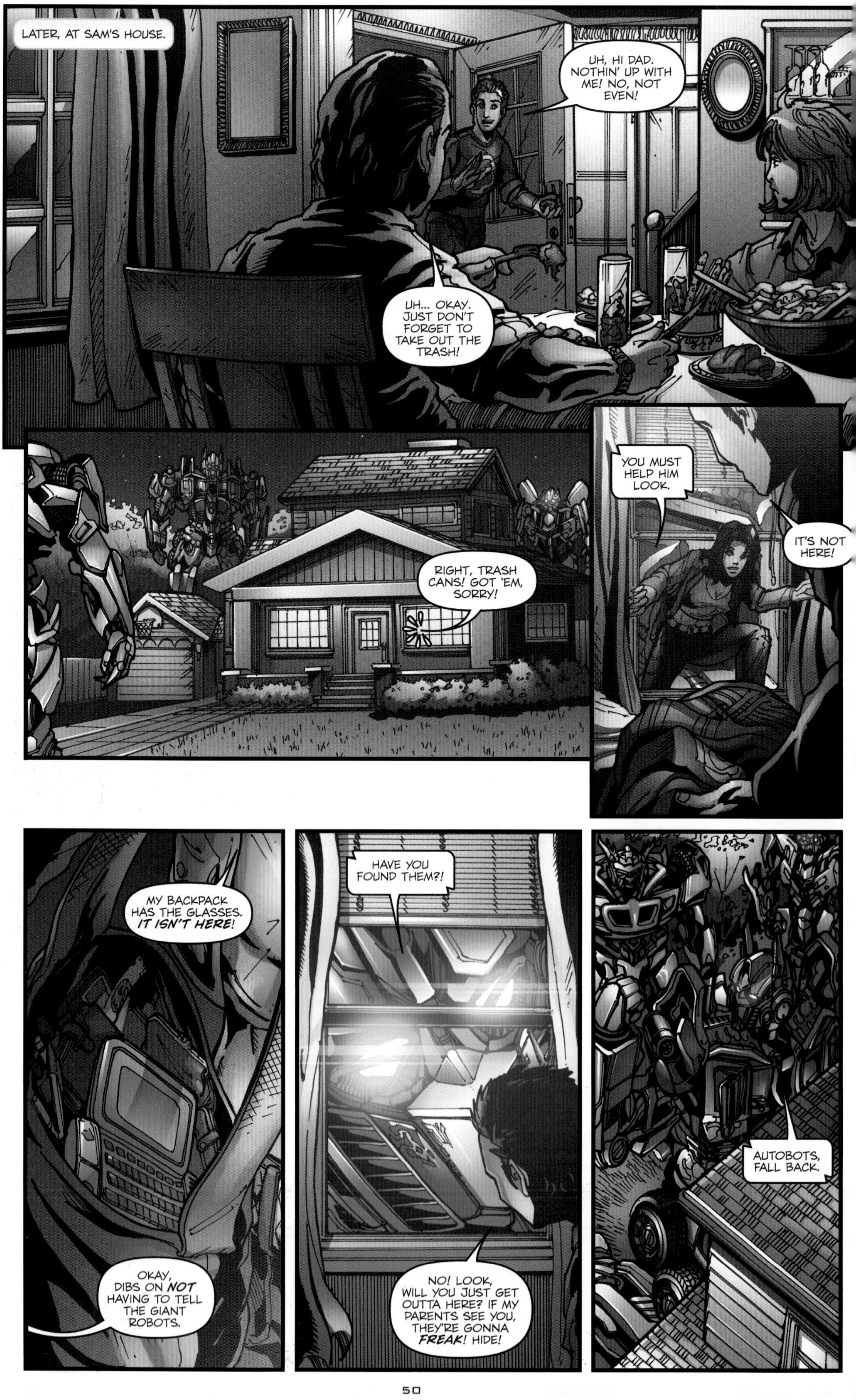
LATER, AT SAM'S HOUSE.
UH, HI DAD. NOTHIN' UP WITH ME! NO, NOT EVEN!
UH... OKAY. JUST DON'T FORGET TO TAKE OUT THE TRASH!
RIGHT, TRASH CANS! GOT 'EM, SORRY!
YOU MUST HELP HIM LOOK.
IT'S NOT HERE!
MY BACKPACK HAS THE GLASSES. *IT ISN'T HERE!*
OKAY, DIBS ON **NOT** HAVING TO TELL THE GIANT ROBOTS.
HAVE YOU FOUND THEM?!
NO! LOOK, WILL YOU JUST GET OUTTA HERE? IF MY PARENTS SEE YOU, THEY'RE GONNA **FREAK**! HIDE!
AUTOBOTS, FALL BACK.

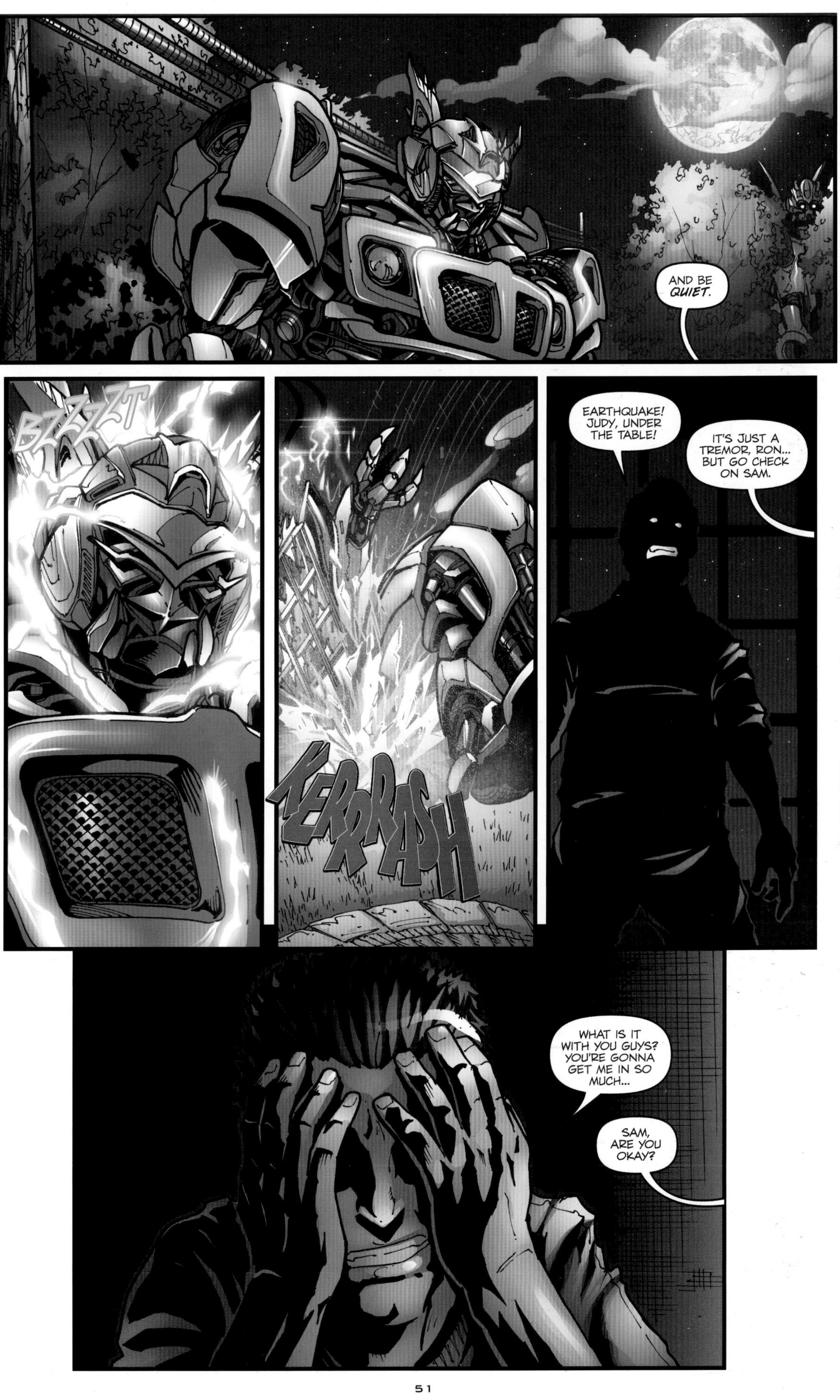
AND BE QUIET.
BZZZZT
KERRASH
EARTHQUAKE! JUDY, UNDER THE TABLE!
IT'S JUST A TREMOR, RON... BUT GO CHECK ON SAM.
WHAT IS IT WITH YOU GUYS? YOU'RE GONNA GET ME IN SO MUCH...
SAM, ARE YOU OKAY?

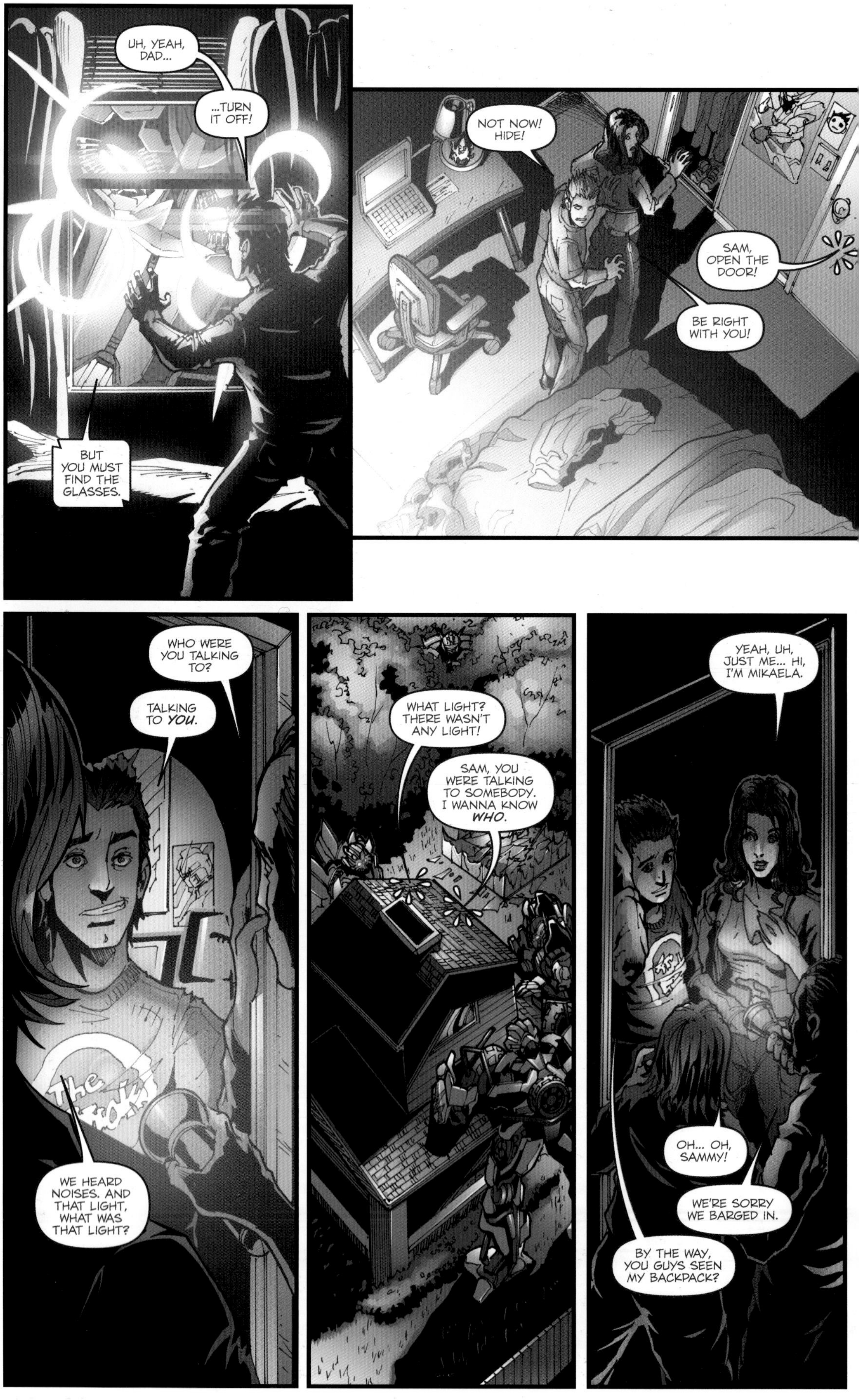
UH, YEAH, DAD...
...TURN IT OFF!
BUT YOU MUST FIND THE GLASSES.
NOT NOW! HIDE!
SAM, OPEN THE DOOR!
BE RIGHT WITH YOU!
WHO WERE YOU TALKING TO?
TALKING TO *YOU*.
WE HEARD NOISES. AND THAT LIGHT, WHAT WAS THAT LIGHT?
WHAT LIGHT? THERE WASN'T ANY LIGHT!
SAM, YOU WERE TALKING TO SOMEBODY. I WANNA KNOW *WHO*.
YEAH, UH, JUST ME... HI, I'M MIKAELA.
OH... OH, SAMMY!
WE'RE SORRY WE BARGED IN.
BY THE WAY, YOU GUYS SEEN MY BACKPACK?

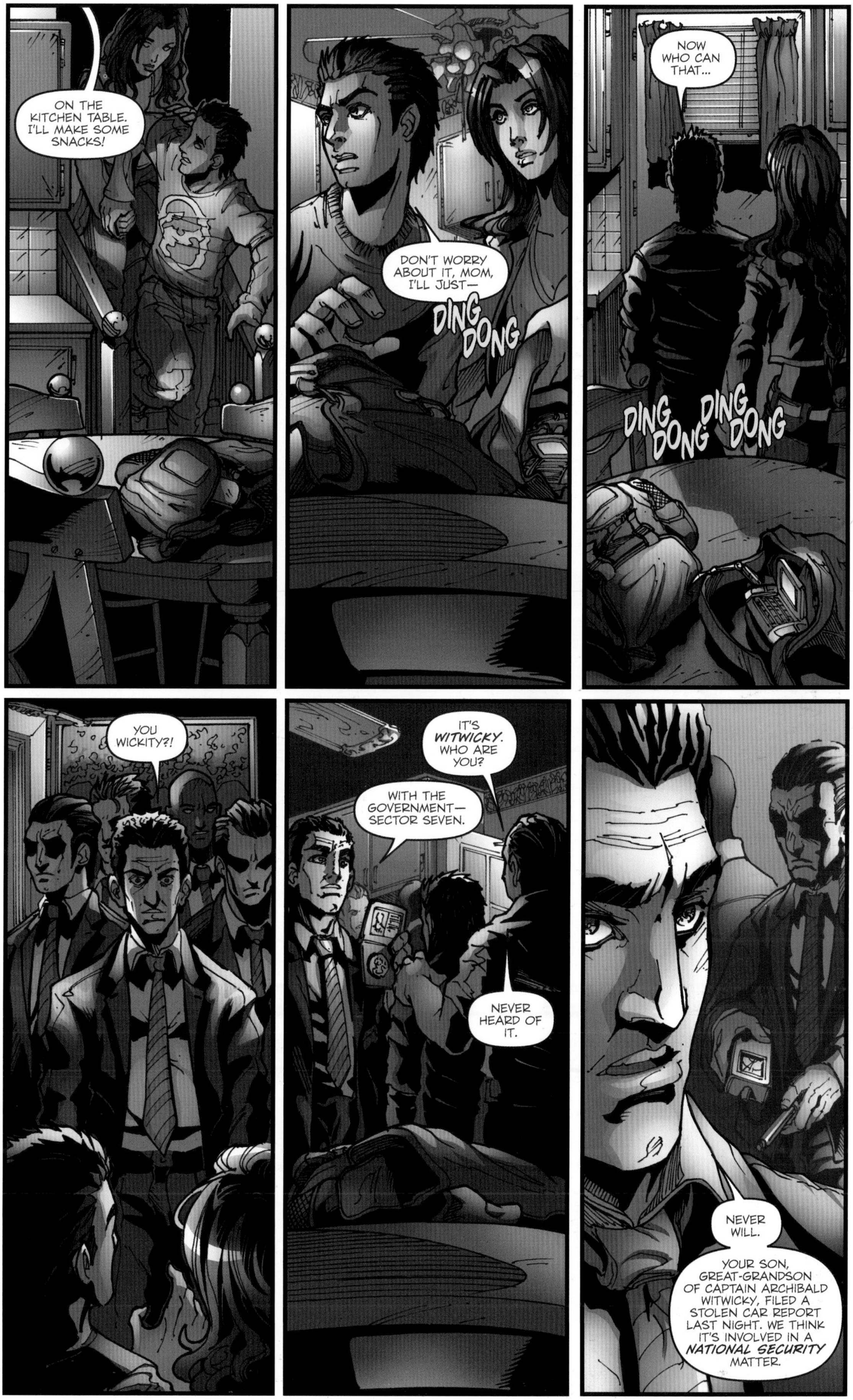
ON THE KITCHEN TABLE. I'LL MAKE SOME SNACKS!
DON'T WORRY ABOUT IT, MOM, I'LL JUST—
DING DONG
NOW WHO CAN THAT...
DING DONG DING DONG
YOU WICKITY?!
IT'S WITWICKY. WHO ARE YOU?
WITH THE GOVERNMENT— SECTOR SEVEN.
NEVER HEARD OF IT.
NEVER WILL.
YOUR SON, GREAT-GRANDSON OF CAPTAIN ARCHIBALD WITWICKY, FILED A STOLEN CAR REPORT LAST NIGHT. WE THINK IT'S INVOLVED IN A NATIONAL SECURITY MATTER.

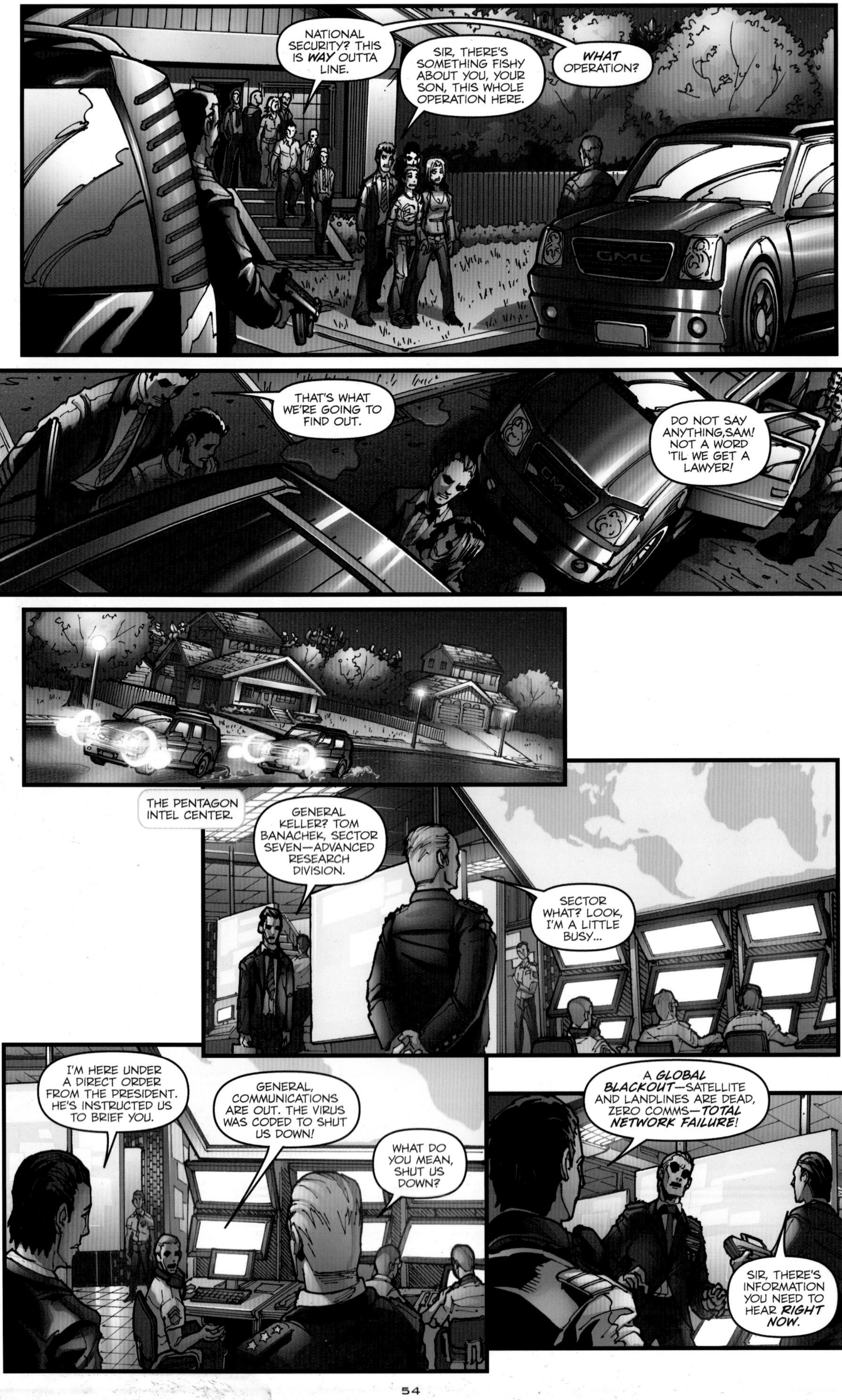
NATIONAL SECURITY? THIS IS WAY OUTTA LINE.
SIR, THERE'S SOMETHING FISHY ABOUT YOU, YOUR SON, THIS WHOLE OPERATION HERE.
WHAT OPERATION?
THAT'S WHAT WE'RE GOING TO FIND OUT.
DO NOT SAY ANYTHING,SAM! NOT A WORD 'TIL WE GET A LAWYER!
THE PENTAGON INTEL CENTER.
GENERAL KELLER? TOM BANACHEK, SECTOR SEVEN—ADVANCED RESEARCH DIVISION.
SECTOR WHAT? LOOK, I'M A LITTLE BUSY...
I'M HERE UNDER A DIRECT ORDER FROM THE PRESIDENT. HE'S INSTRUCTED US TO BRIEF YOU.
GENERAL, COMMUNICATIONS ARE OUT. THE VIRUS WAS CODED TO SHUT US DOWN!
WHAT DO YOU MEAN, SHUT US DOWN?
A GLOBAL BLACKOUT—SATELLITE AND LANDLINES ARE DEAD, ZERO COMMS—TOTAL NETWORK FAILURE!
SIR, THERE'S INFORMATION YOU NEED TO HEAR RIGHT NOW.

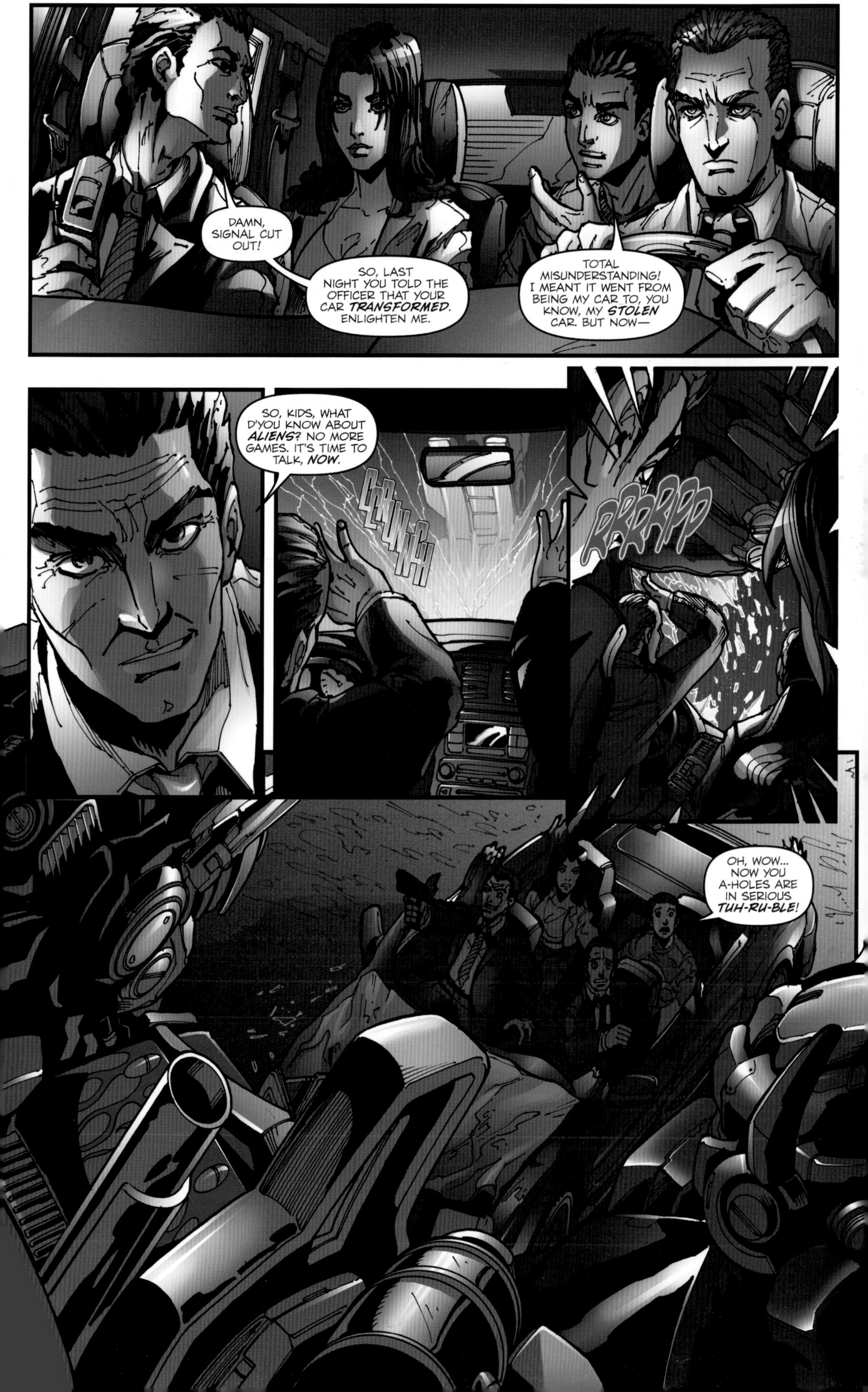
DAMN, SIGNAL CUT OUT!
SO, LAST NIGHT YOU TOLD THE OFFICER THAT YOUR CAR TRANSFORMED. ENLIGHTEN ME.
TOTAL MISUNDERSTANDING! I MEANT IT WENT FROM BEING MY CAR TO, YOU KNOW, MY STOLEN CAR. BUT NOW—
SO, KIDS, WHAT D'YOU KNOW ABOUT ALIENS? NO MORE GAMES. IT'S TIME TO TALK, NOW.
CCRUNCH
RRRRIPP
OH, WOW... NOW YOU A-HOLES ARE IN SERIOUS TUH-RU-BLE!

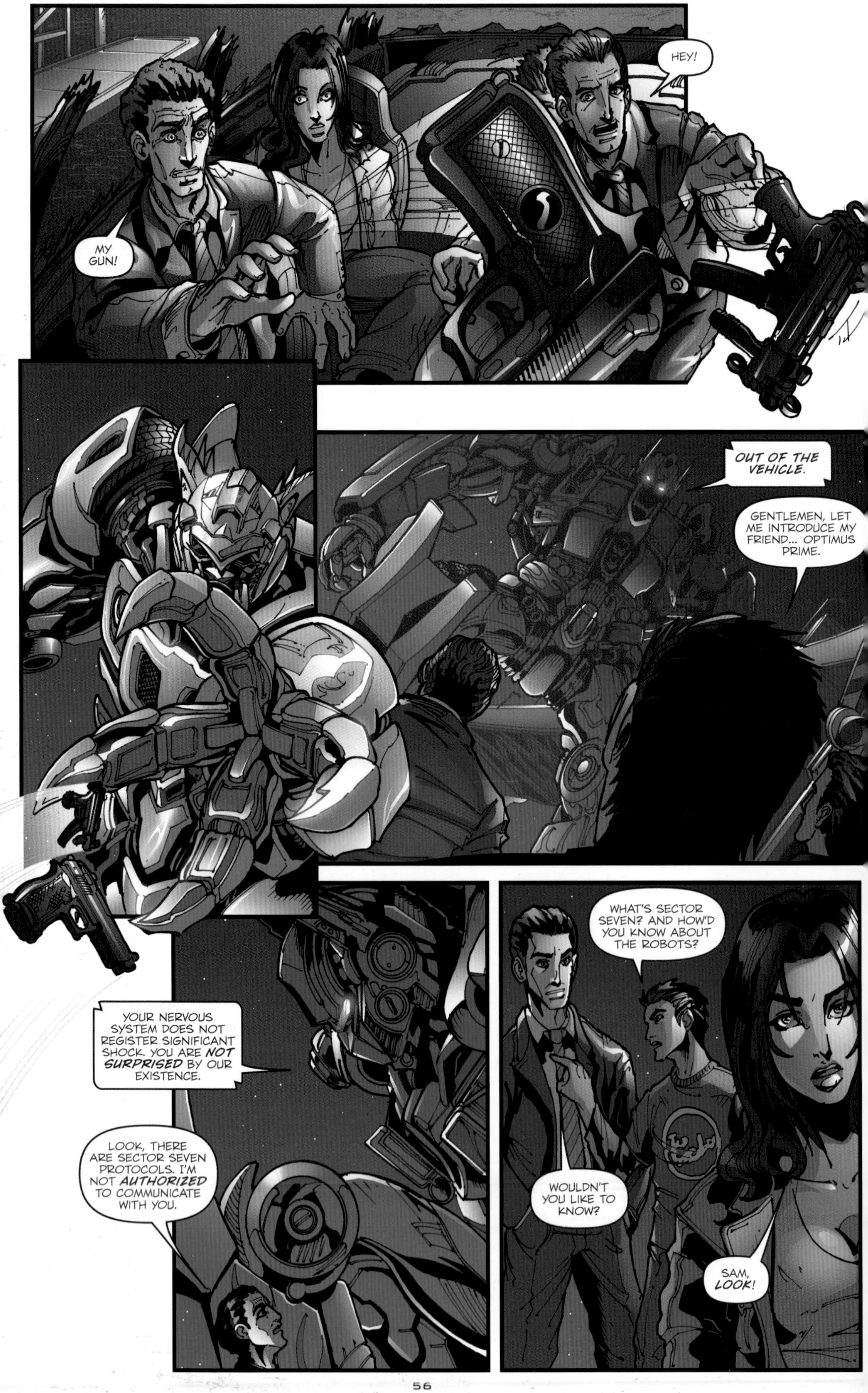
HEY!
MY GUN!
OUT OF THE VEHICLE.
GENTLEMEN, LET ME INTRODUCE MY FRIEND... OPTIMUS PRIME.
YOUR NERVOUS SYSTEM DOES NOT REGISTER SIGNIFICANT SHOCK. YOU ARE NOT SURPRISED BY OUR EXISTENCE.
LOOK, THERE ARE SECTOR SEVEN PROTOCOLS. I'M NOT AUTHORIZED TO COMMUNICATE WITH YOU.
WHAT'S SECTOR SEVEN? AND HOW'D YOU KNOW ABOUT THE ROBOTS?
WOULDN'T YOU LIKE TO KNOW?
SAM, LOOK!

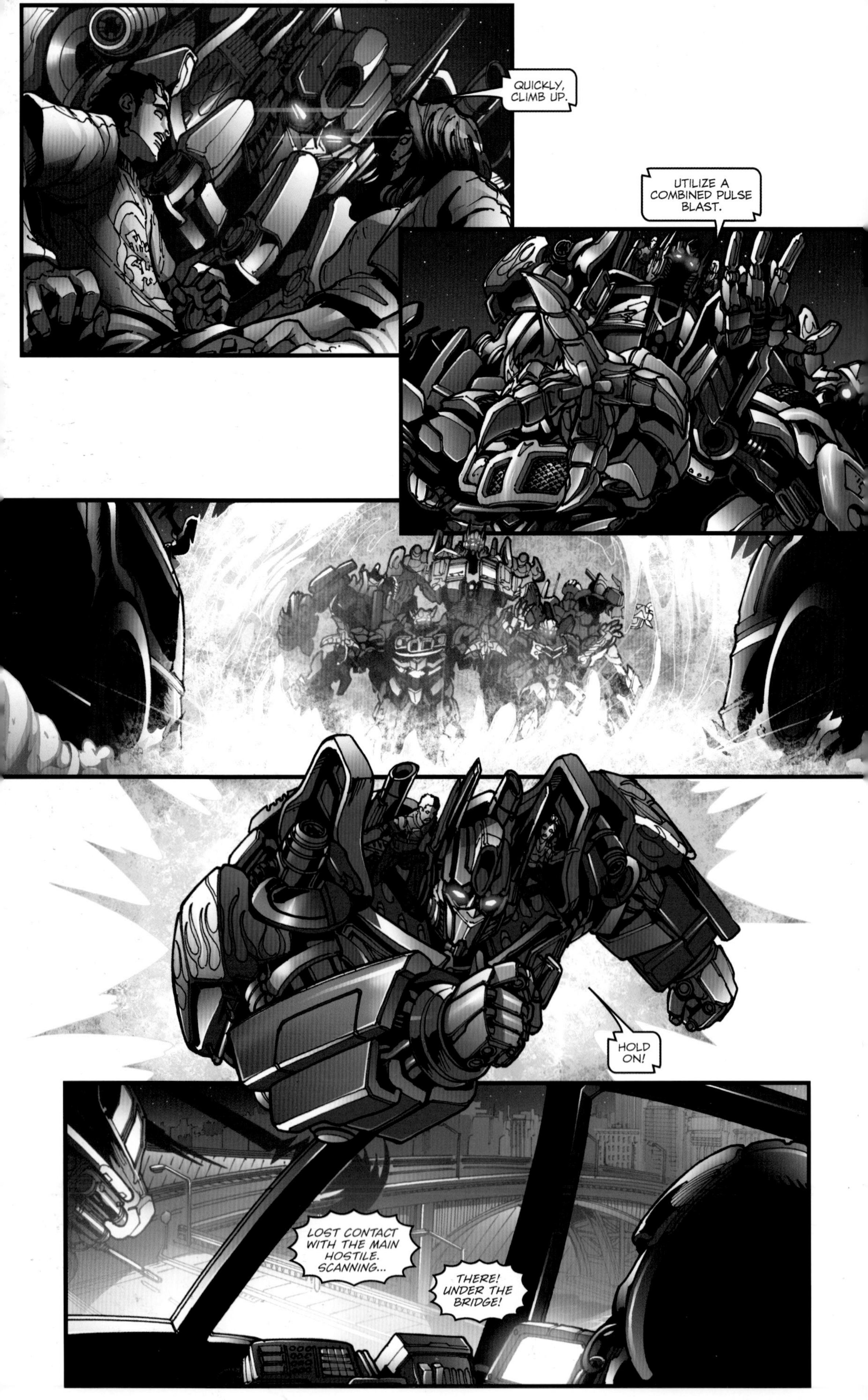
QUICKLY, CLIMB UP.
UTILIZE A COMBINED PULSE BLAST.
HOLD ON!
LOST CONTACT WITH THE MAIN HOSTILE. SCANNING...
THERE! UNDER THE BRIDGE!

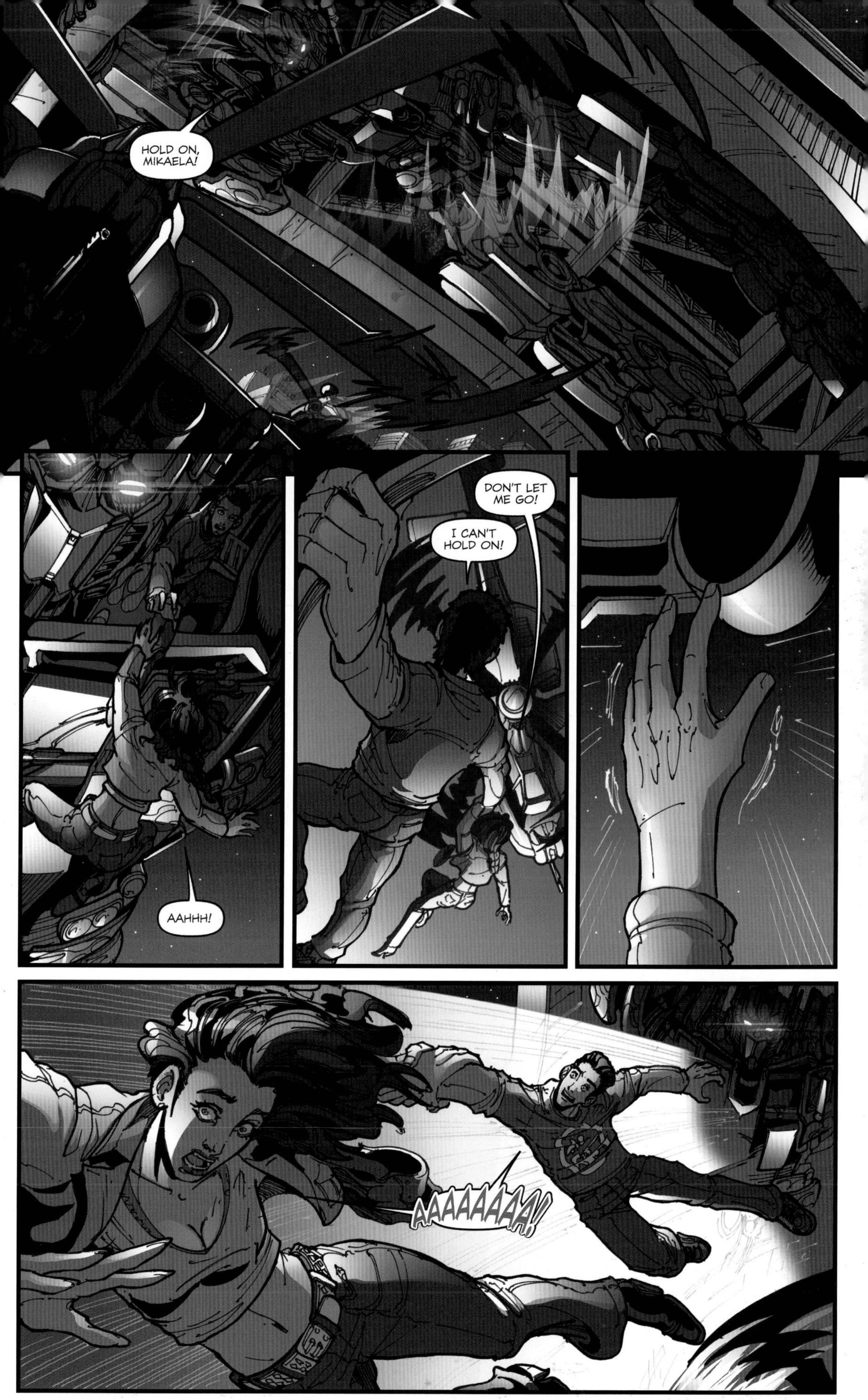
HOLD ON, MIKAELA!
AAHHH!
DON'T LET ME GO!
I CAN'T HOLD ON!
AAAAAAAA!

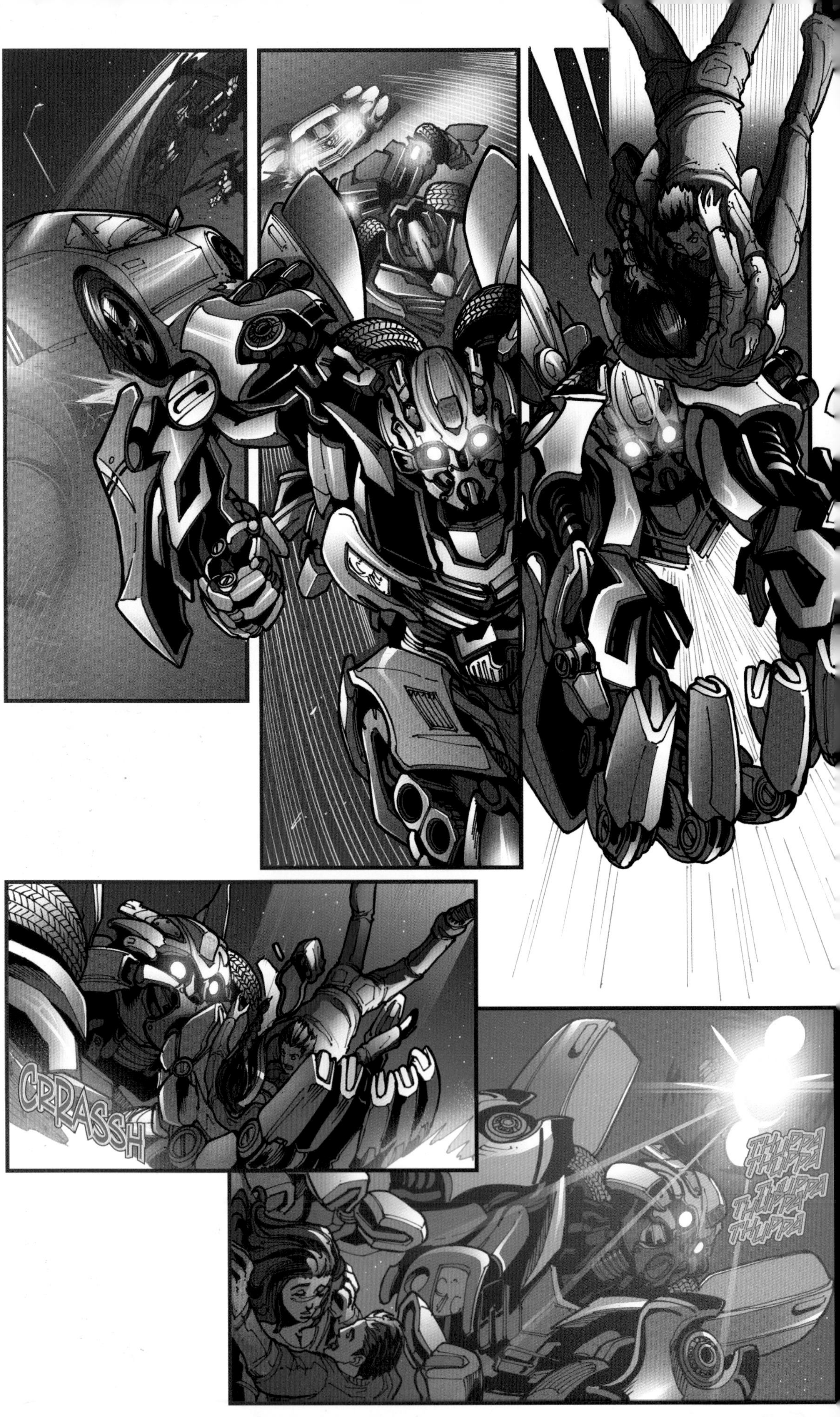
CRRASSH
THUPPA
THUPPA
THUPPA
THUPPA
THUPPA

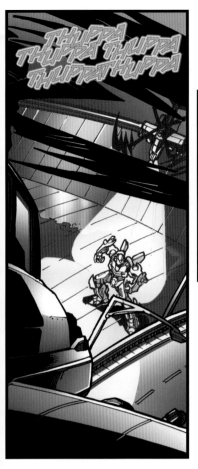

THUPPA THUPPA THUPPA THUPPA THUPPA

FOOSH

FOOSH

STOP IT! YOU'RE HURTING HIM!

HSSSS

GET THE HELL AWAY FROM HIM! HE'S NOT GONNA HURT ANYONE!

GET IN THERE, NOW!

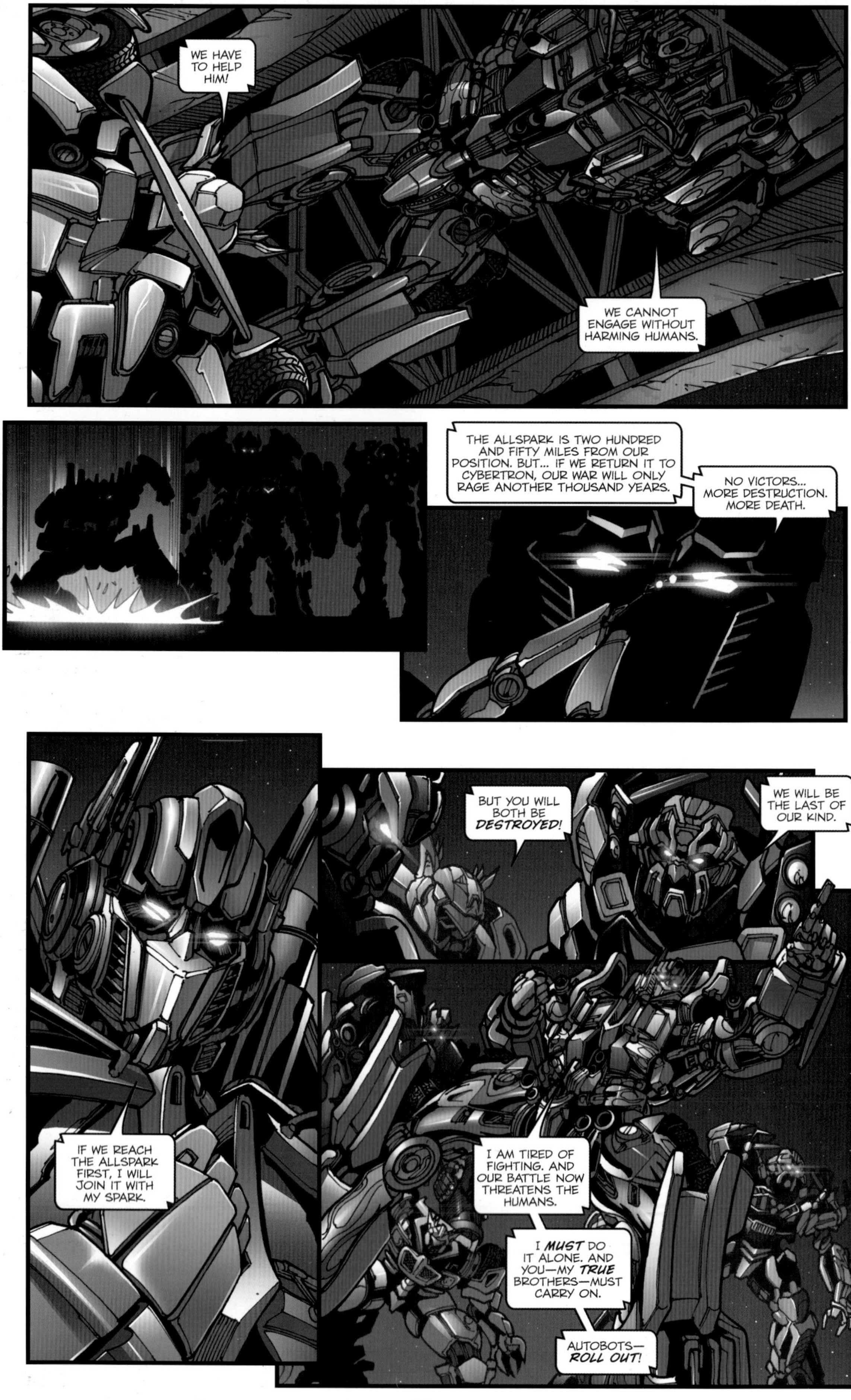
WE HAVE TO HELP HIM!
WE CANNOT ENGAGE WITHOUT HARMING HUMANS.
THE ALLSPARK IS TWO HUNDRED AND FIFTY MILES FROM OUR POSITION. BUT... IF WE RETURN IT TO CYBERTRON, OUR WAR WILL ONLY RAGE ANOTHER THOUSAND YEARS.
NO VICTORS... MORE DESTRUCTION. MORE DEATH.
IF WE REACH THE ALLSPARK FIRST, I WILL JOIN IT WITH MY SPARK.
BUT YOU WILL BOTH BE DESTROYED!
WE WILL BE THE LAST OF OUR KIND.
I AM TIRED OF FIGHTING. AND OUR BATTLE NOW THREATENS THE HUMANS.
I MUST DO IT ALONE. AND YOU—MY TRUE BROTHERS—MUST CARRY ON.
AUTOBOTS— ROLL OUT!

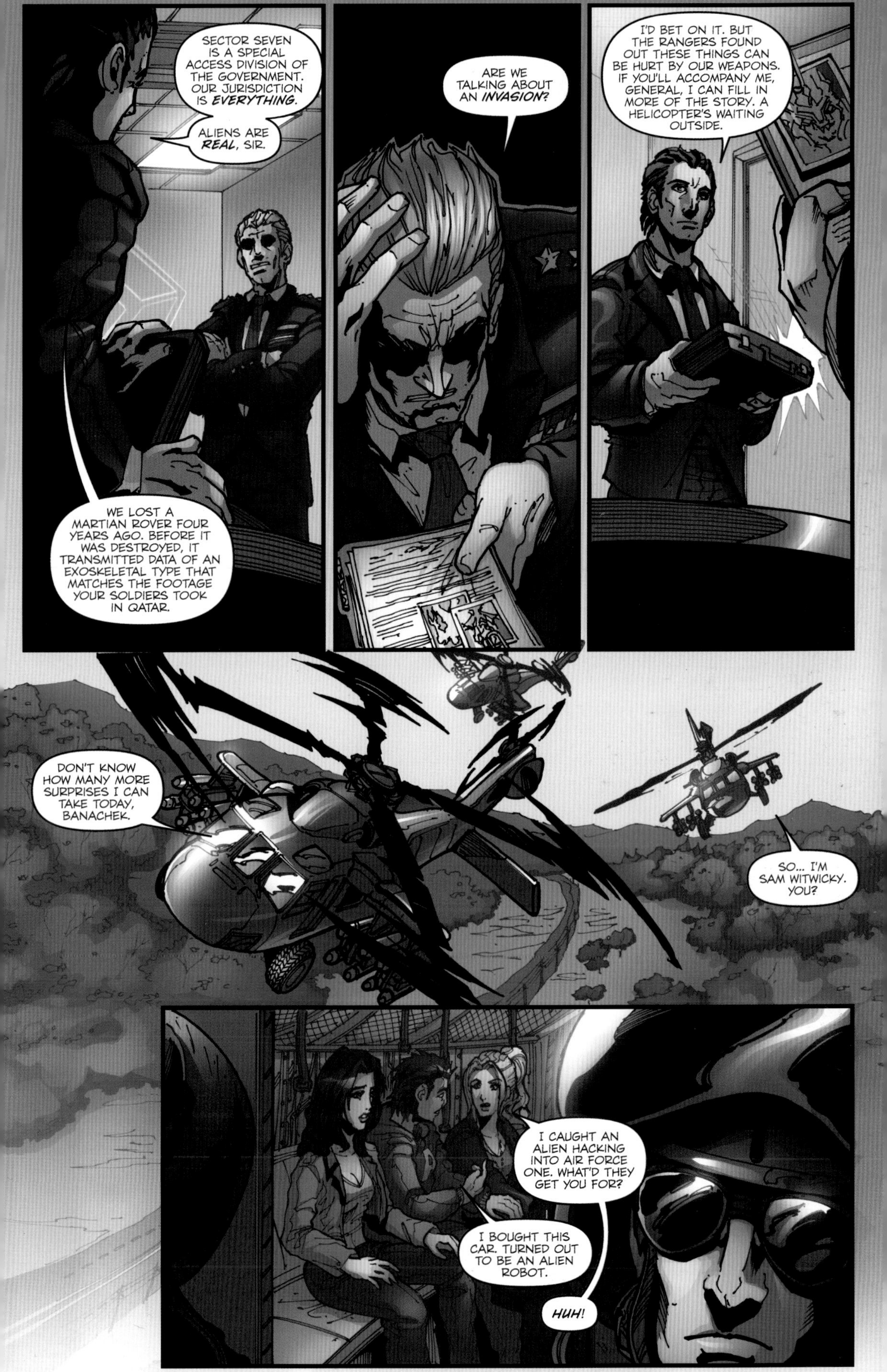
SECTOR SEVEN IS A SPECIAL ACCESS DIVISION OF THE GOVERNMENT. OUR JURISDICTION IS EVERYTHING.
ALIENS ARE REAL, SIR.
WE LOST A MARTIAN ROVER FOUR YEARS AGO. BEFORE IT WAS DESTROYED, IT TRANSMITTED DATA OF AN EXOSKELETAL TYPE THAT MATCHES THE FOOTAGE YOUR SOLDIERS TOOK IN QATAR.
ARE WE TALKING ABOUT AN INVASION?
I'D BET ON IT. BUT THE RANGERS FOUND OUT THESE THINGS CAN BE HURT BY OUR WEAPONS. IF YOU'LL ACCOMPANY ME, GENERAL, I CAN FILL IN MORE OF THE STORY. A HELICOPTER'S WAITING OUTSIDE.
DON'T KNOW HOW MANY MORE SURPRISES I CAN TAKE TODAY, BANACHEK.
SO... I'M SAM WITWICKY. YOU?
I CAUGHT AN ALIEN HACKING INTO AIR FORCE ONE. WHAT'D THEY GET YOU FOR?
I BOUGHT THIS CAR. TURNED OUT TO BE AN ALIEN ROBOT.
HUH!

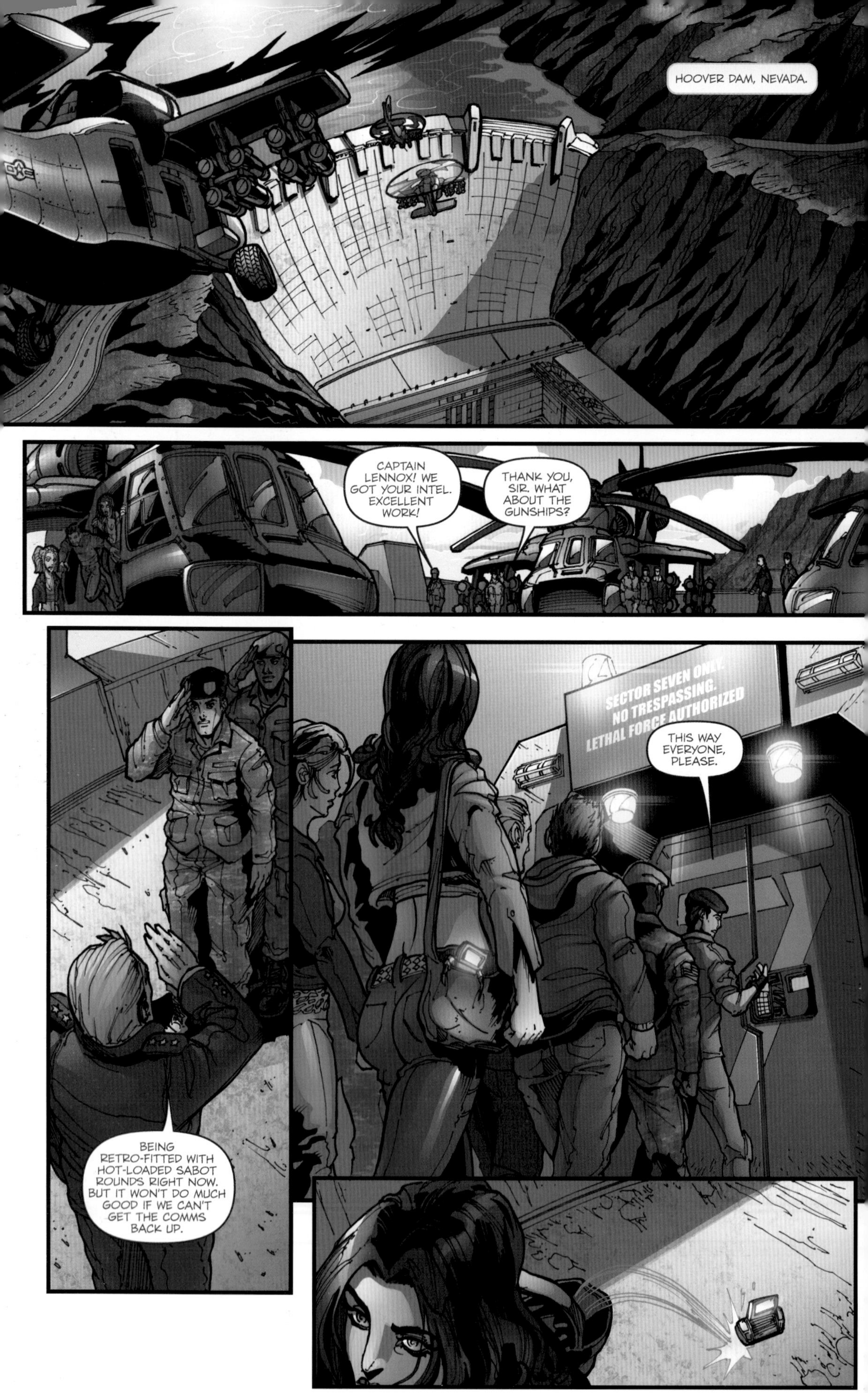
HOOVER DAM, NEVADA.
CAPTAIN LENNOX! WE GOT YOUR INTEL. EXCELLENT WORK!
THANK YOU, SIR. WHAT ABOUT THE GUNSHIPS?
BEING RETRO-FITTED WITH HOT-LOADED SABOT ROUNDS RIGHT NOW. BUT IT WON'T DO MUCH GOOD IF WE CAN'T GET THE COMMS BACK UP.
SECTOR SEVEN ONLY. NO TRESPASSING. LETHAL FORCE AUTHORIZED
THIS WAY EVERYONE, PLEASE.

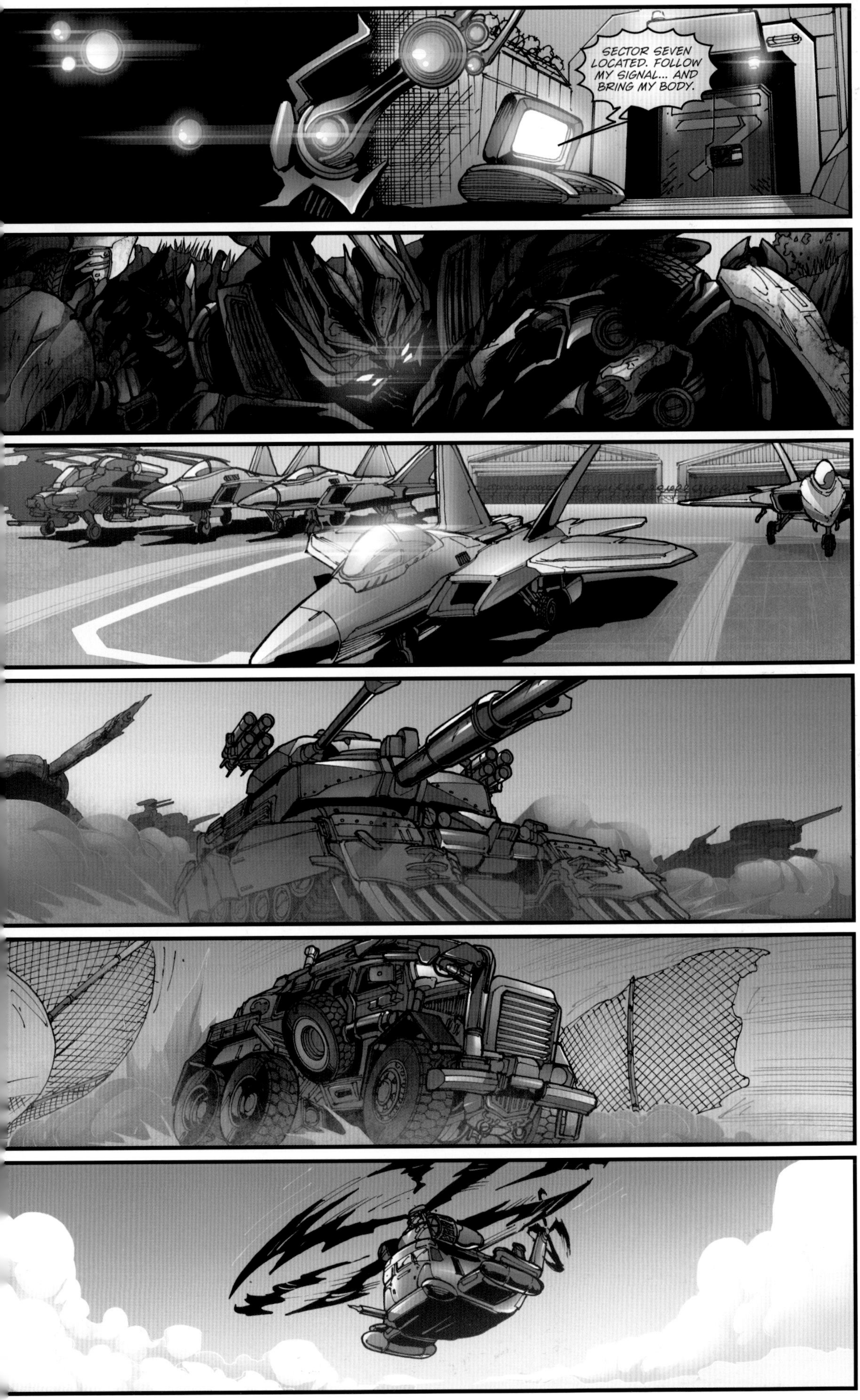
SECTOR SEVEN LOCATED. FOLLOW MY SIGNAL... AND BRING MY BODY.

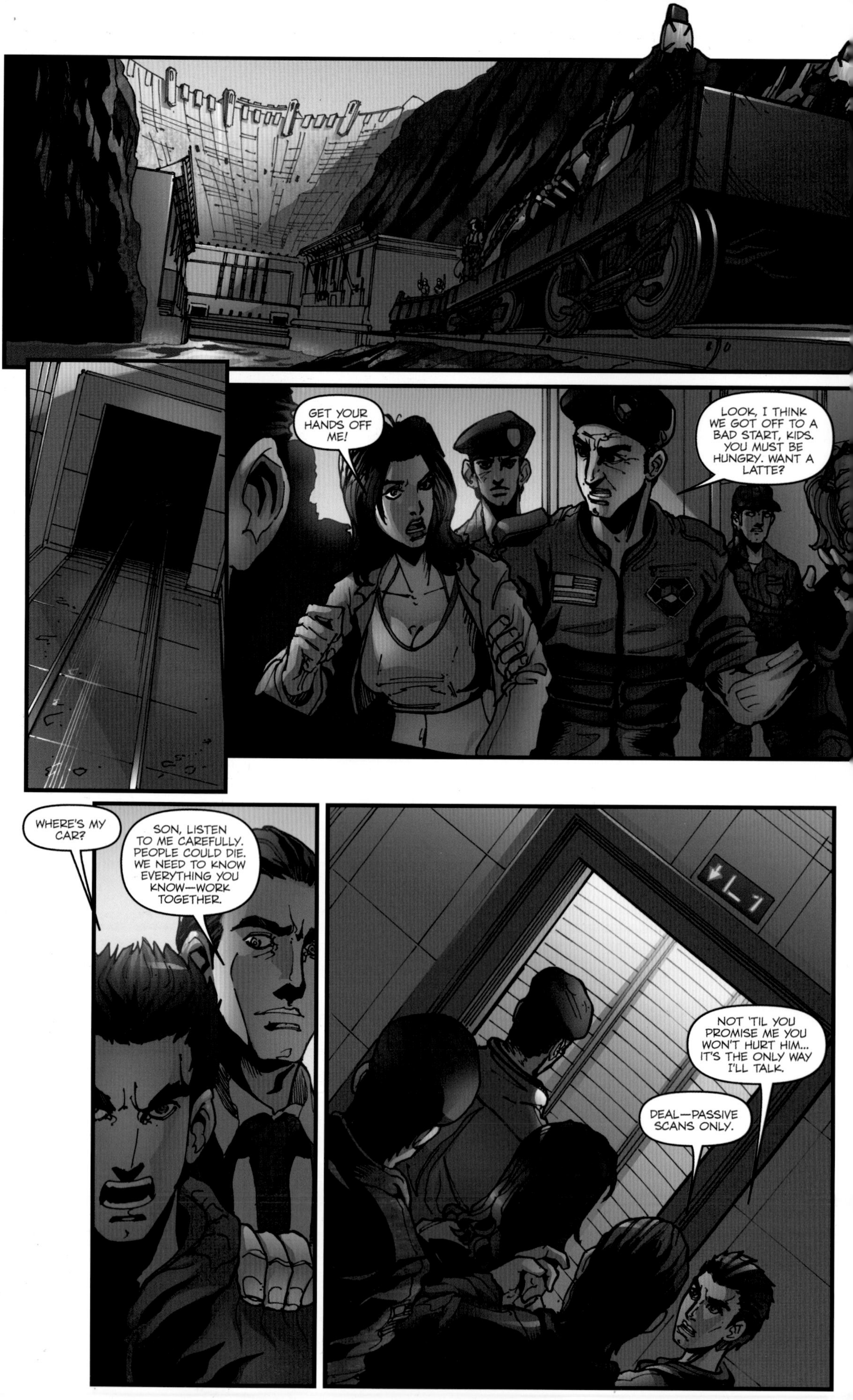
GET YOUR HANDS OFF ME!
LOOK, I THINK WE GOT OFF TO A BAD START, KIDS. YOU MUST BE HUNGRY. WANT A LATTE?
WHERE'S MY CAR?
SON, LISTEN TO ME CAREFULLY. PEOPLE COULD DIE. WE NEED TO KNOW EVERYTHING YOU KNOW—WORK TOGETHER.
NOT 'TIL YOU PROMISE ME YOU WON'T HURT HIM... IT'S THE ONLY WAY I'LL TALK.
DEAL—PASSIVE SCANS ONLY.

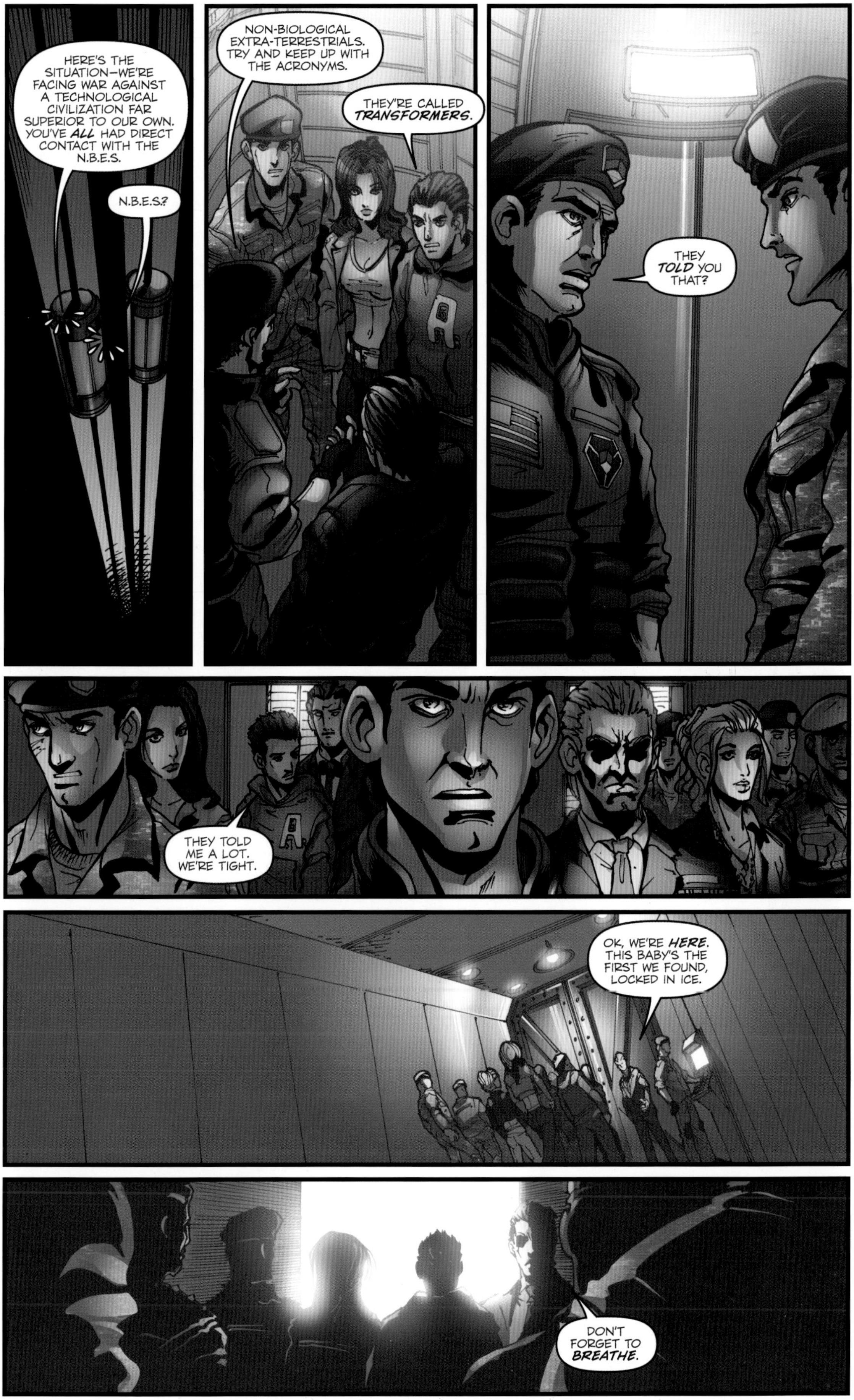
HERE'S THE SITUATION—WE'RE FACING WAR AGAINST A TECHNOLOGICAL CIVILIZATION FAR SUPERIOR TO OUR OWN. YOU'VE ALL HAD DIRECT CONTACT WITH THE N.B.E.S.
N.B.E.S?
NON-BIOLOGICAL EXTRA-TERRESTRIALS. TRY AND KEEP UP WITH THE ACRONYMS.
THEY'RE CALLED TRANSFORMERS.
THEY TOLD YOU THAT?
THEY TOLD ME A LOT. WE'RE TIGHT.
OK, WE'RE HERE. THIS BABY'S THE FIRST WE FOUND, LOCKED IN ICE.
DON'T FORGET TO BREATHE.

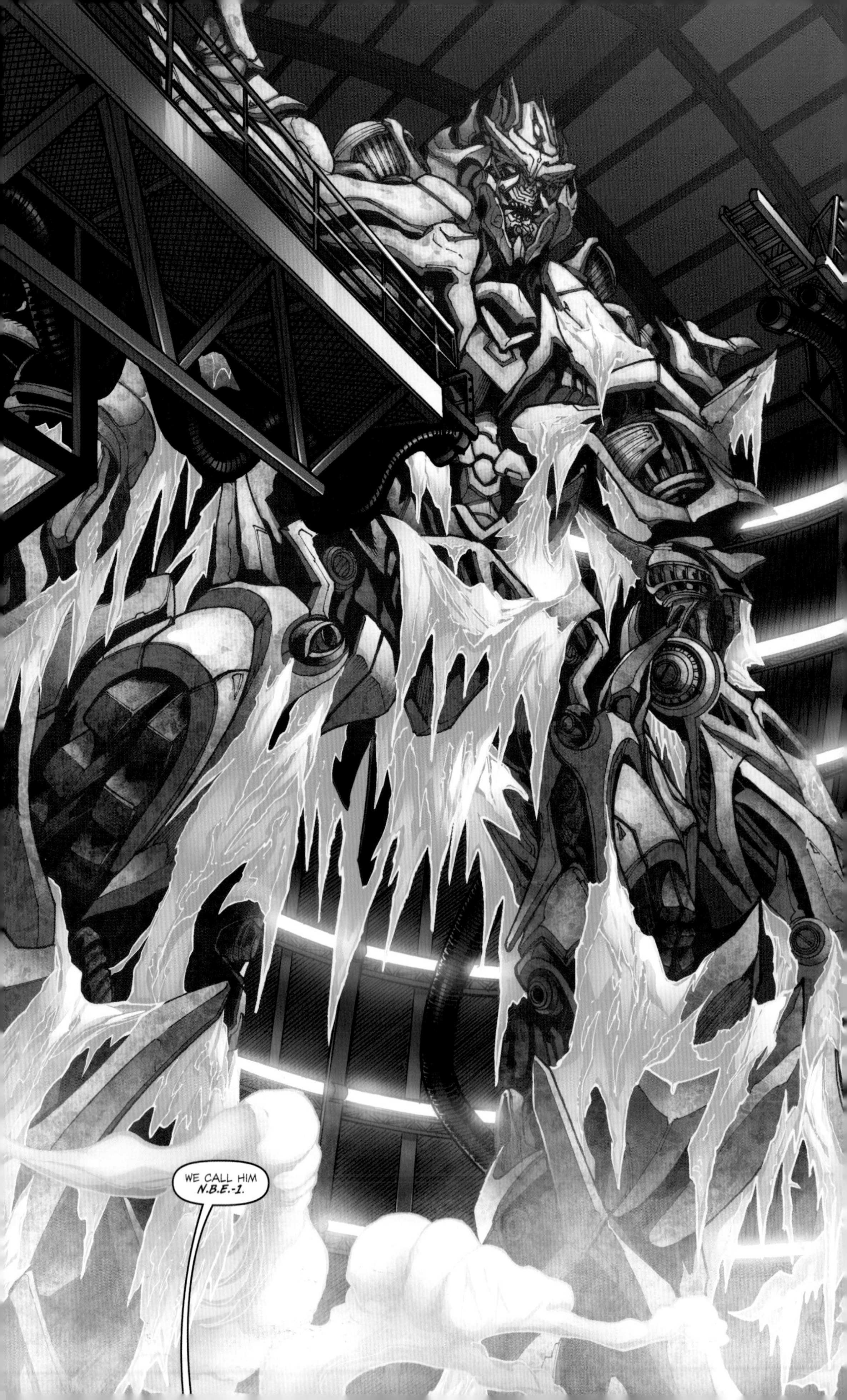
WE CALL HIM N.B.E.-1.

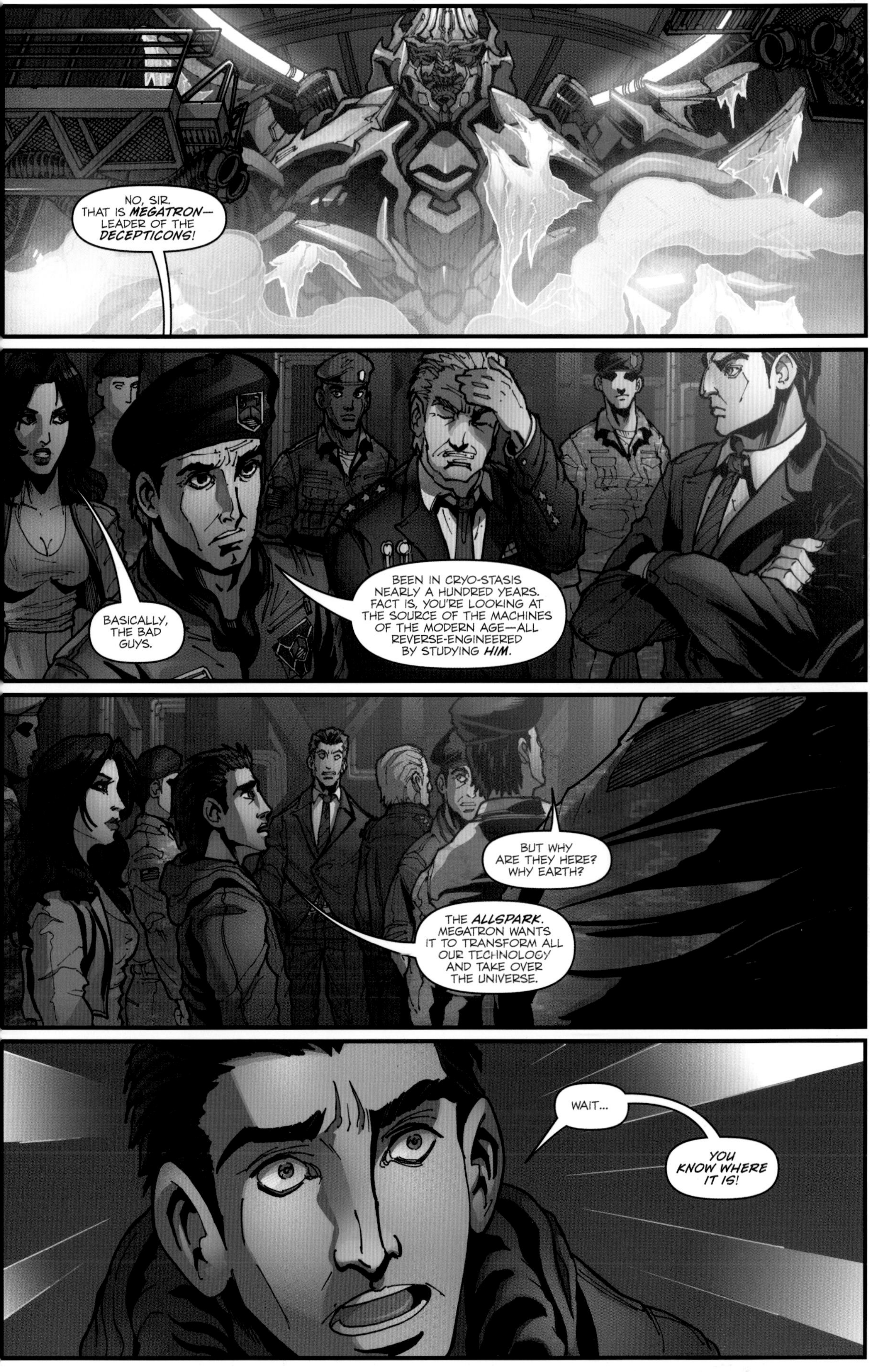
NO, SIR. THAT IS *MEGATRON*— LEADER OF THE *DECEPTICONS*!
BASICALLY, THE BAD GUYS.
BEEN IN CRYO-STASIS NEARLY A HUNDRED YEARS. FACT IS, YOU'RE LOOKING AT THE SOURCE OF THE MACHINES OF THE MODERN AGE—ALL REVERSE-ENGINEERED BY STUDYING *HIM*.
BUT WHY ARE THEY HERE? WHY EARTH?
THE *ALLSPARK*. MEGATRON WANTS IT TO TRANSFORM ALL OUR TECHNOLOGY AND TAKE OVER THE UNIVERSE.
WAIT...
YOU KNOW WHERE IT IS!

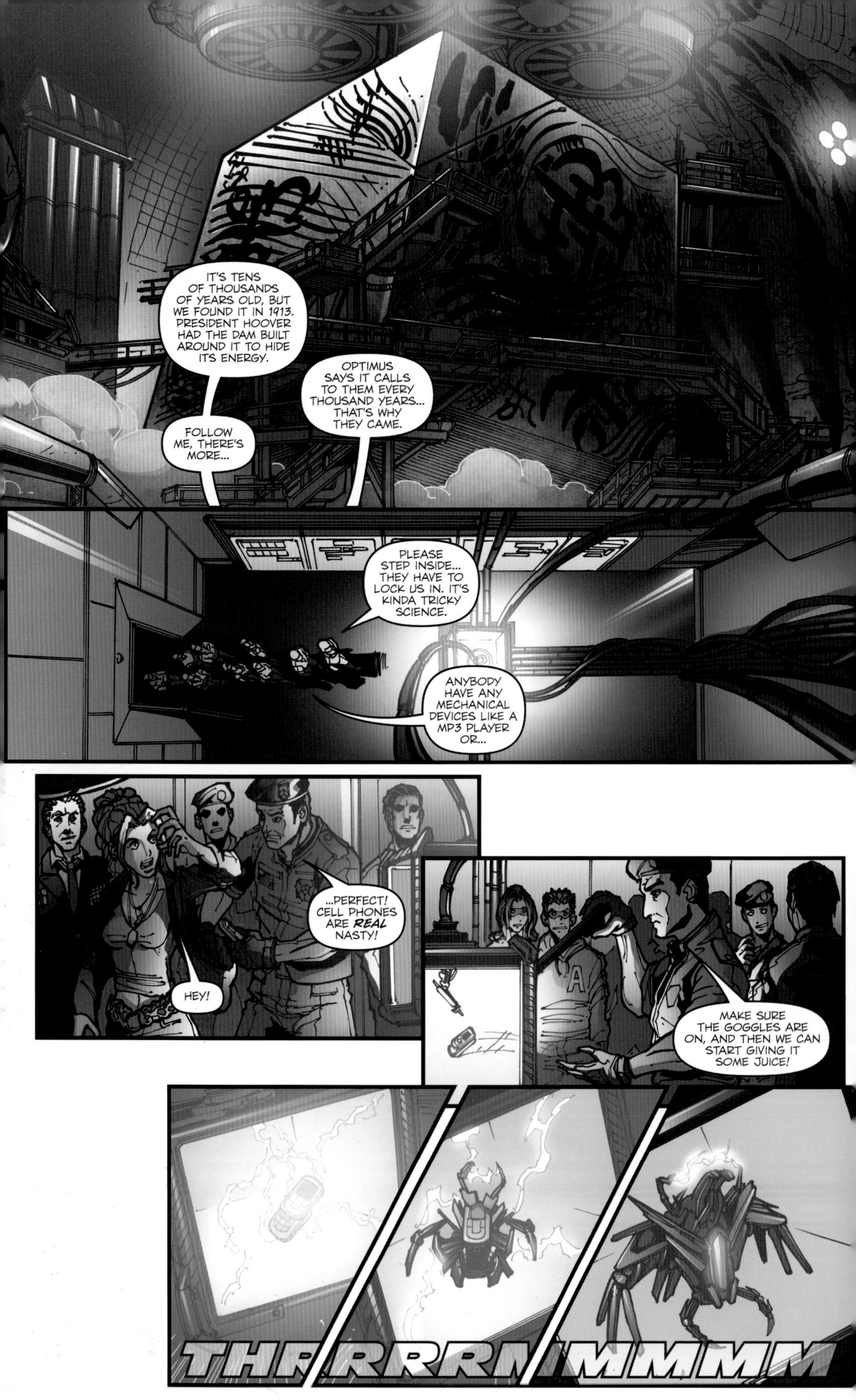
IT'S TENS OF THOUSANDS OF YEARS OLD, BUT WE FOUND IT IN 1913. PRESIDENT HOOVER HAD THE DAM BUILT AROUND IT TO HIDE ITS ENERGY.
FOLLOW ME, THERE'S MORE...
OPTIMUS SAYS IT CALLS TO THEM EVERY THOUSAND YEARS... THAT'S WHY THEY CAME.
PLEASE STEP INSIDE... THEY HAVE TO LOCK US IN. IT'S KINDA TRICKY SCIENCE.
ANYBODY HAVE ANY MECHANICAL DEVICES LIKE A MP3 PLAYER OR...
...PERFECT! CELL PHONES ARE *REAL* NASTY!
HEY!
MAKE SURE THE GOGGLES ARE ON, AND THEN WE CAN START GIVING IT SOME JUICE!
THRRRRMMMMMM

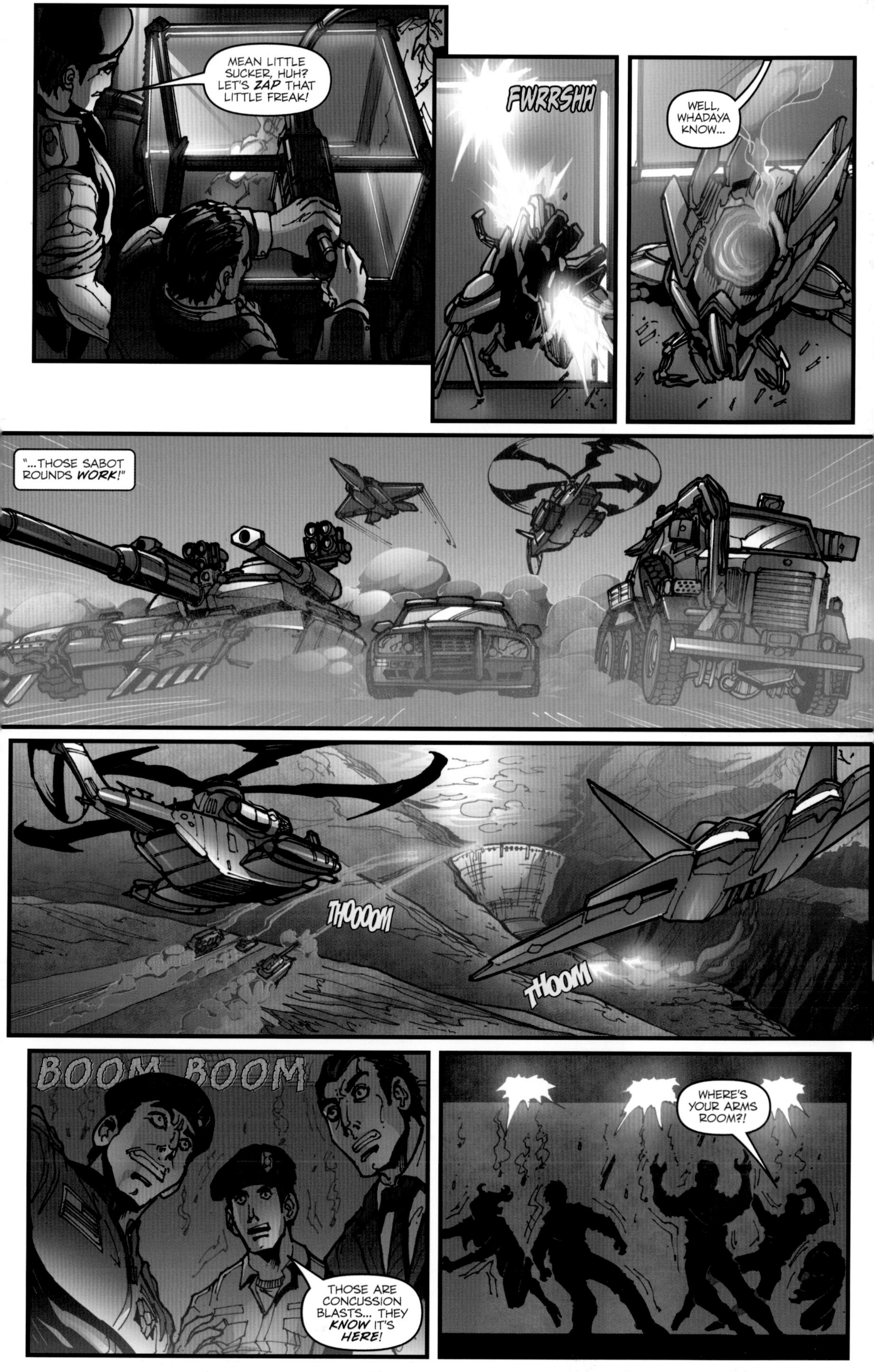
MEAN LITTLE SUCKER, HUH? LET'S ZAP THAT LITTLE FREAK!
FWRRSHH
WELL, WHADAYA KNOW...
"...THOSE SABOT ROUNDS WORK!"
THOOOOM
THOOM
BOOM BOOM
THOSE ARE CONCUSSION BLASTS... THEY KNOW IT'S HERE!
WHERE'S YOUR ARMS ROOM?!

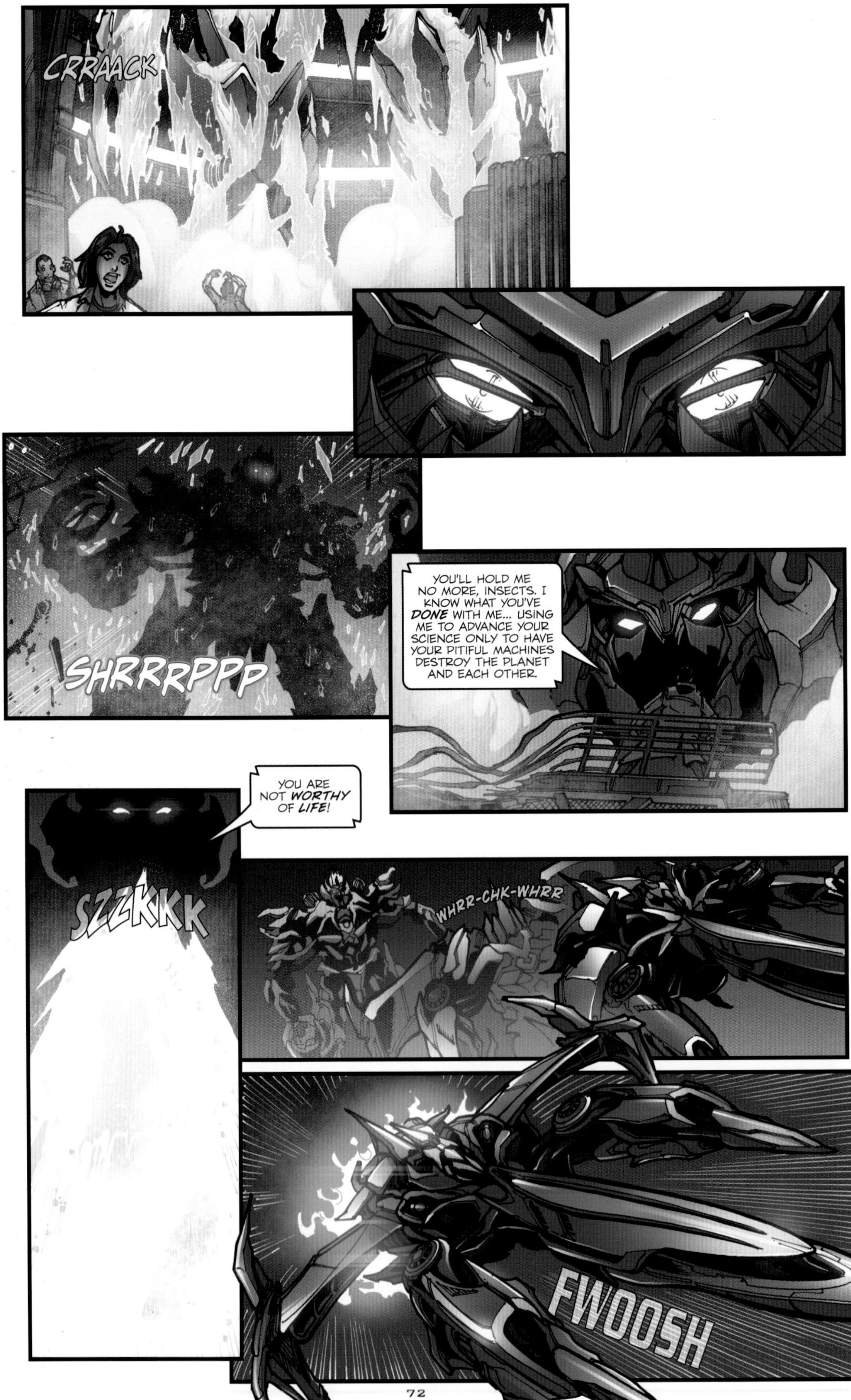
CRRAACK
SHRRRPPP
YOU'LL HOLD ME NO MORE, INSECTS. I KNOW WHAT YOU'VE DONE WITH ME... USING ME TO ADVANCE YOUR SCIENCE ONLY TO HAVE YOUR PITIFUL MACHINES DESTROY THE PLANET AND EACH OTHER.
YOU ARE NOT WORTHY OF LIFE!
SZZKKK
WHRR-CHK-WHRR
FWOOSH

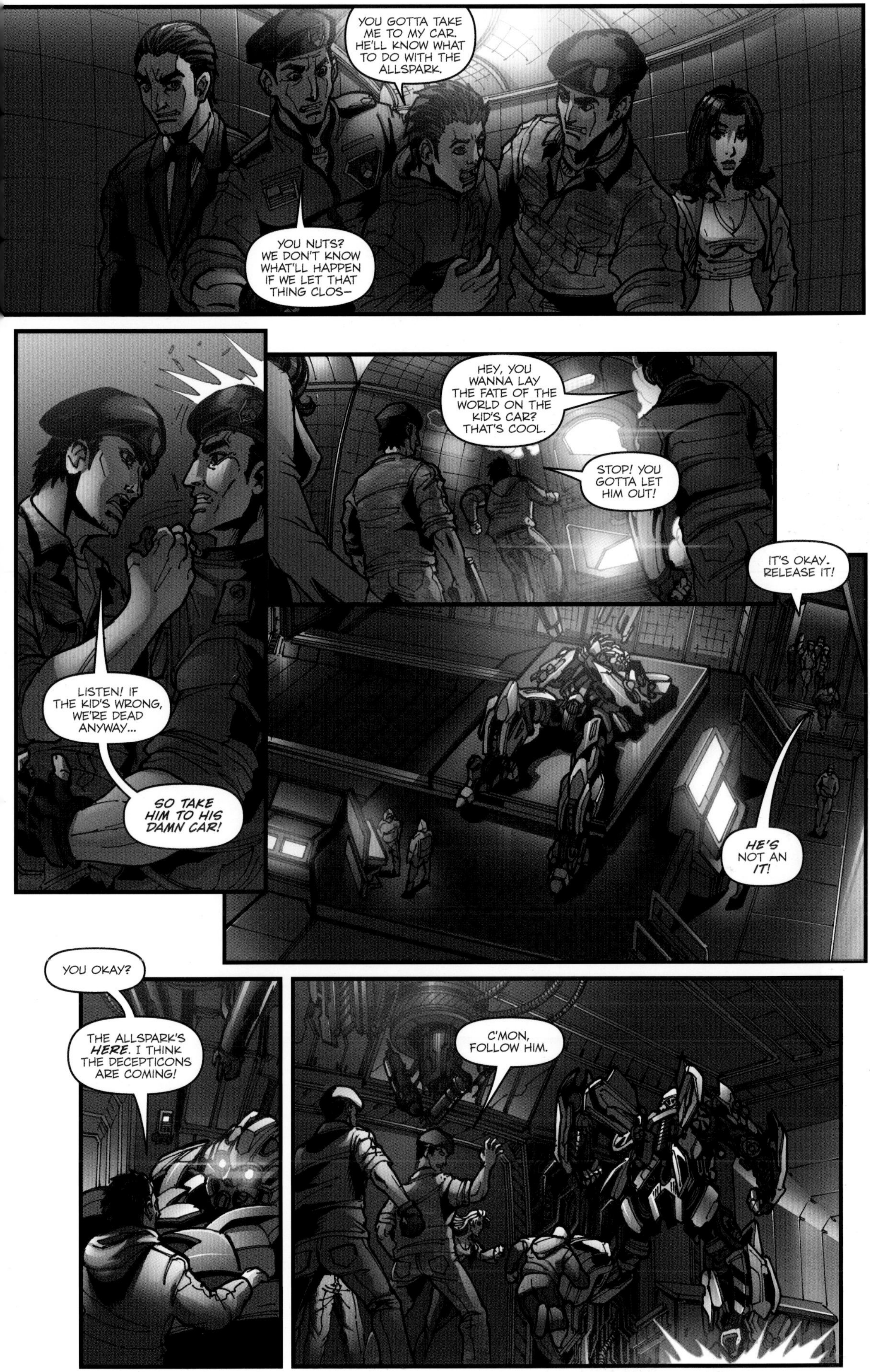
YOU GOTTA TAKE ME TO MY CAR. HE'LL KNOW WHAT TO DO WITH THE ALLSPARK.
YOU NUTS? WE DON'T KNOW WHAT'LL HAPPEN IF WE LET THAT THING CLOS—
LISTEN! IF THE KID'S WRONG, WE'RE DEAD ANYWAY...
SO TAKE HIM TO HIS DAMN CAR!
HEY, YOU WANNA LAY THE FATE OF THE WORLD ON THE KID'S CAR? THAT'S COOL.
STOP! YOU GOTTA LET HIM OUT!
IT'S OKAY. RELEASE IT!
HE'S NOT AN IT!
YOU OKAY?
THE ALLSPARK'S HERE. I THINK THE DECEPTICONS ARE COMING!
C'MON, FOLLOW HIM.

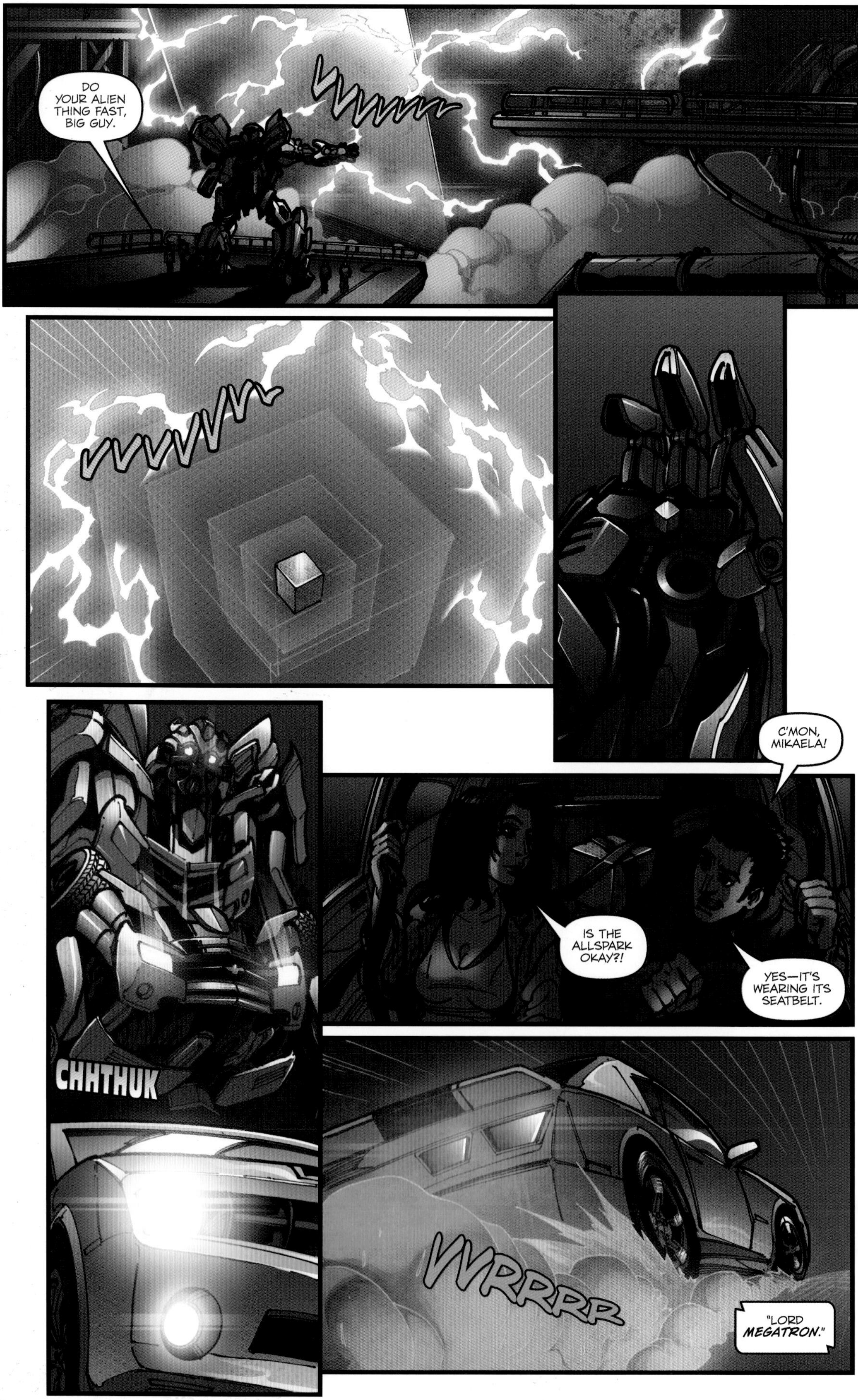
DO YOUR ALIEN THING FAST, BIG GUY.
VVVVVVVV
VVVVVVVV
C'MON, MIKAELA!
IS THE ALLSPARK OKAY?!
YES—IT'S WEARING ITS SEATBELT.
CHHTHUK
VVRRRR
"LORD MEGATRON."

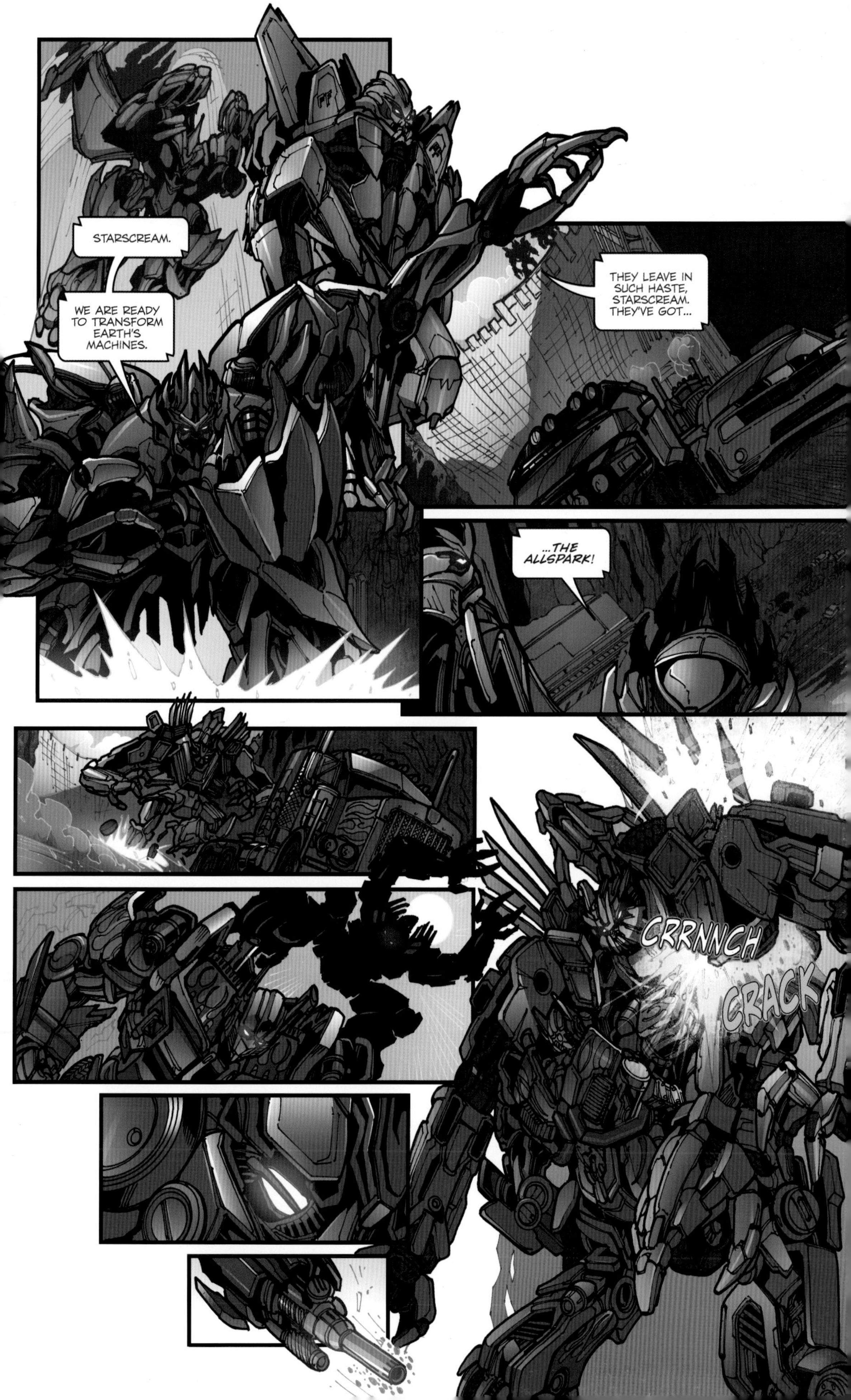
STARSCREAM.
WE ARE READY TO TRANSFORM EARTH'S MACHINES.
THEY LEAVE IN SUCH HASTE, STARSCREAM. THEY'VE GOT...
...THE ALLSPARK!
CRRNNCH
CRACK

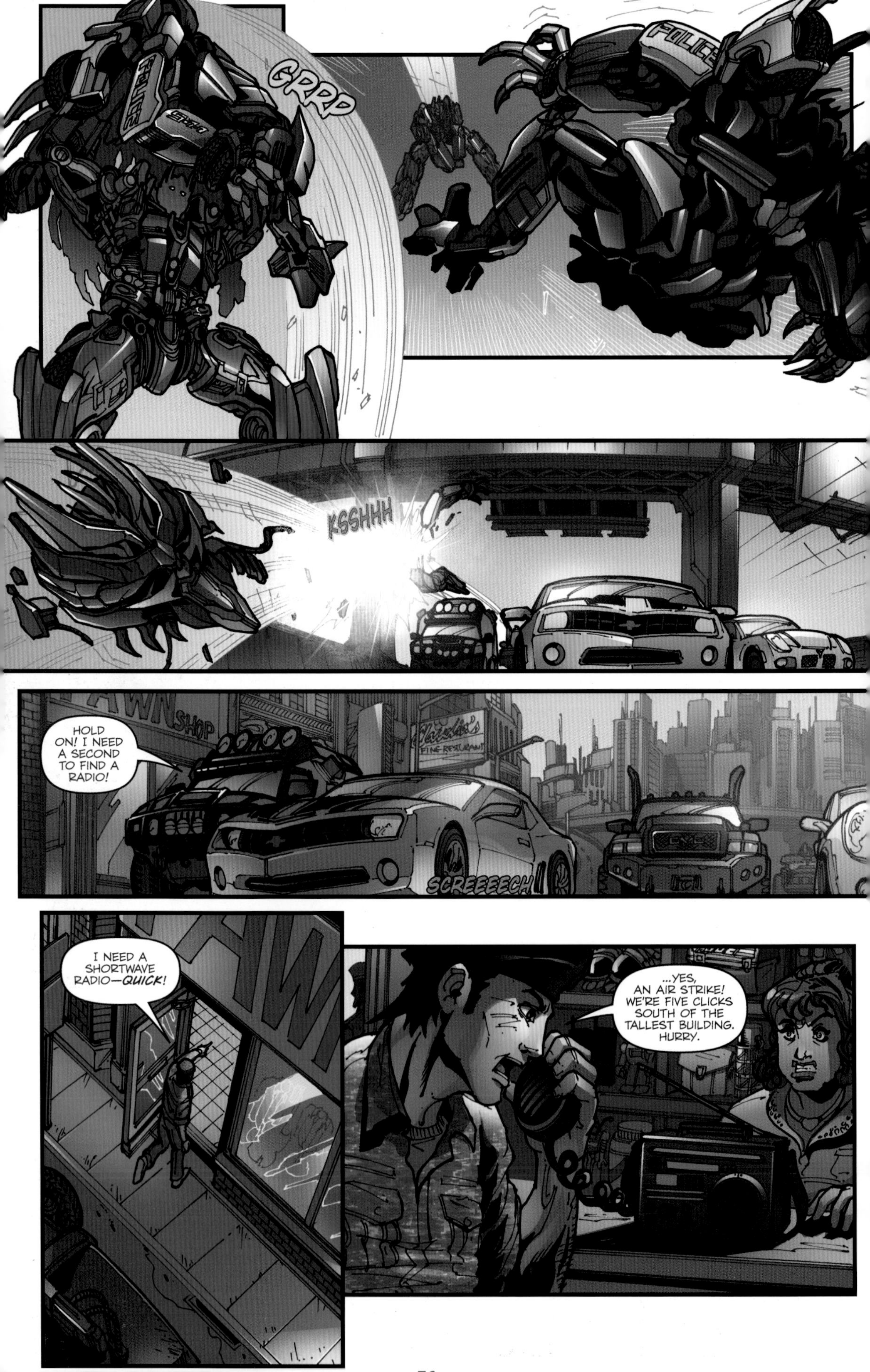
GRRP
KSSHHH
HOLD ON! I NEED A SECOND TO FIND A RADIO!
SCREEEECH
I NEED A SHORTWAVE RADIO—**QUICK**!
...YES, AN AIR STRIKE! WE'RE FIVE CLICKS SOUTH OF THE TALLEST BUILDING. HURRY.

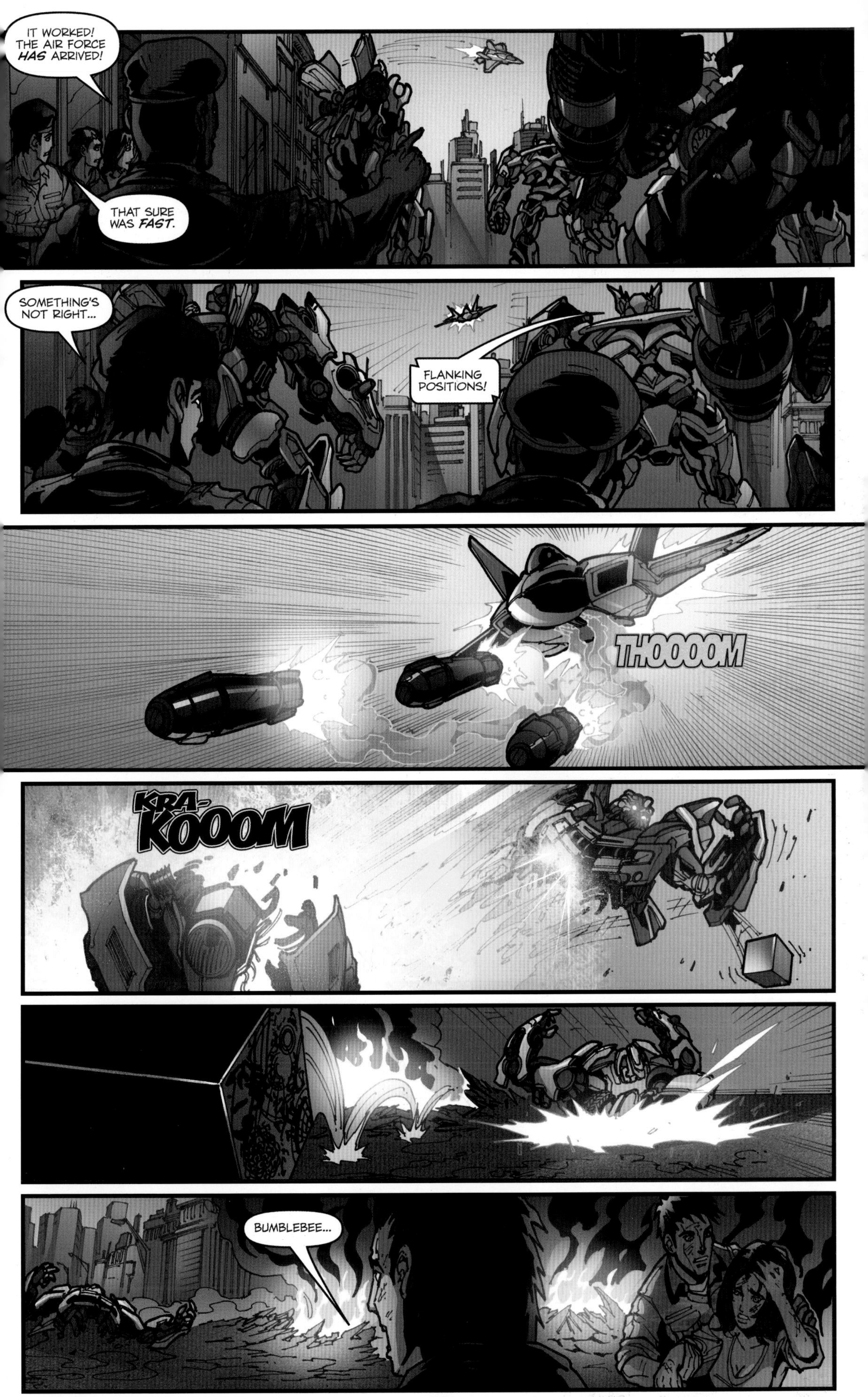
IT WORKED! THE AIR FORCE HAS ARRIVED!
THAT SURE WAS FAST.
SOMETHING'S NOT RIGHT...
FLANKING POSITIONS!
THOOOOM
KRA-KOOOM
BUMBLEBEE...

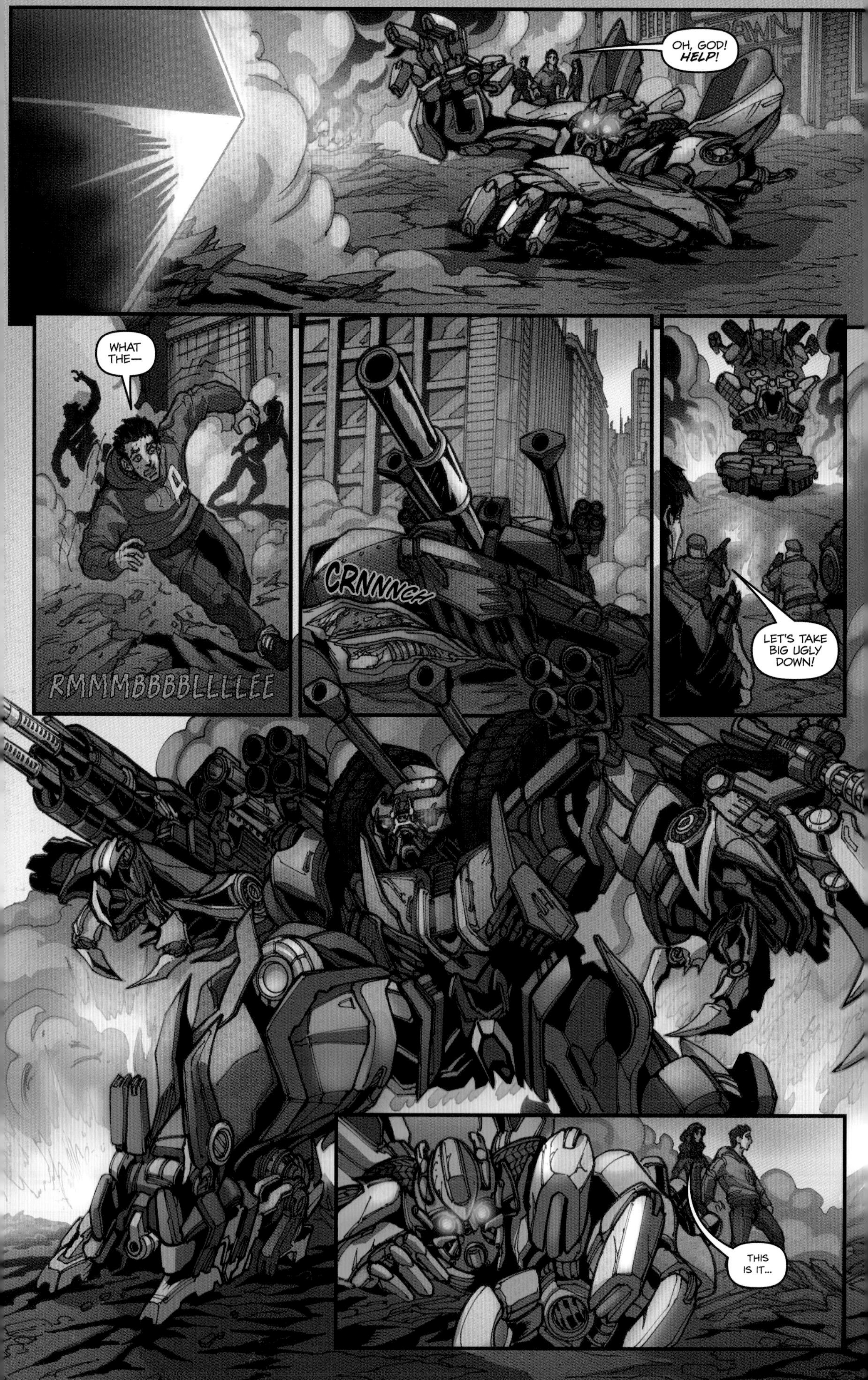
OH, GOD! **HELP!**
WHAT THE—
RMMMBBBBLLLLEE
CRNNNCH
LET'S TAKE BIG UGLY DOWN!
THIS IS IT...

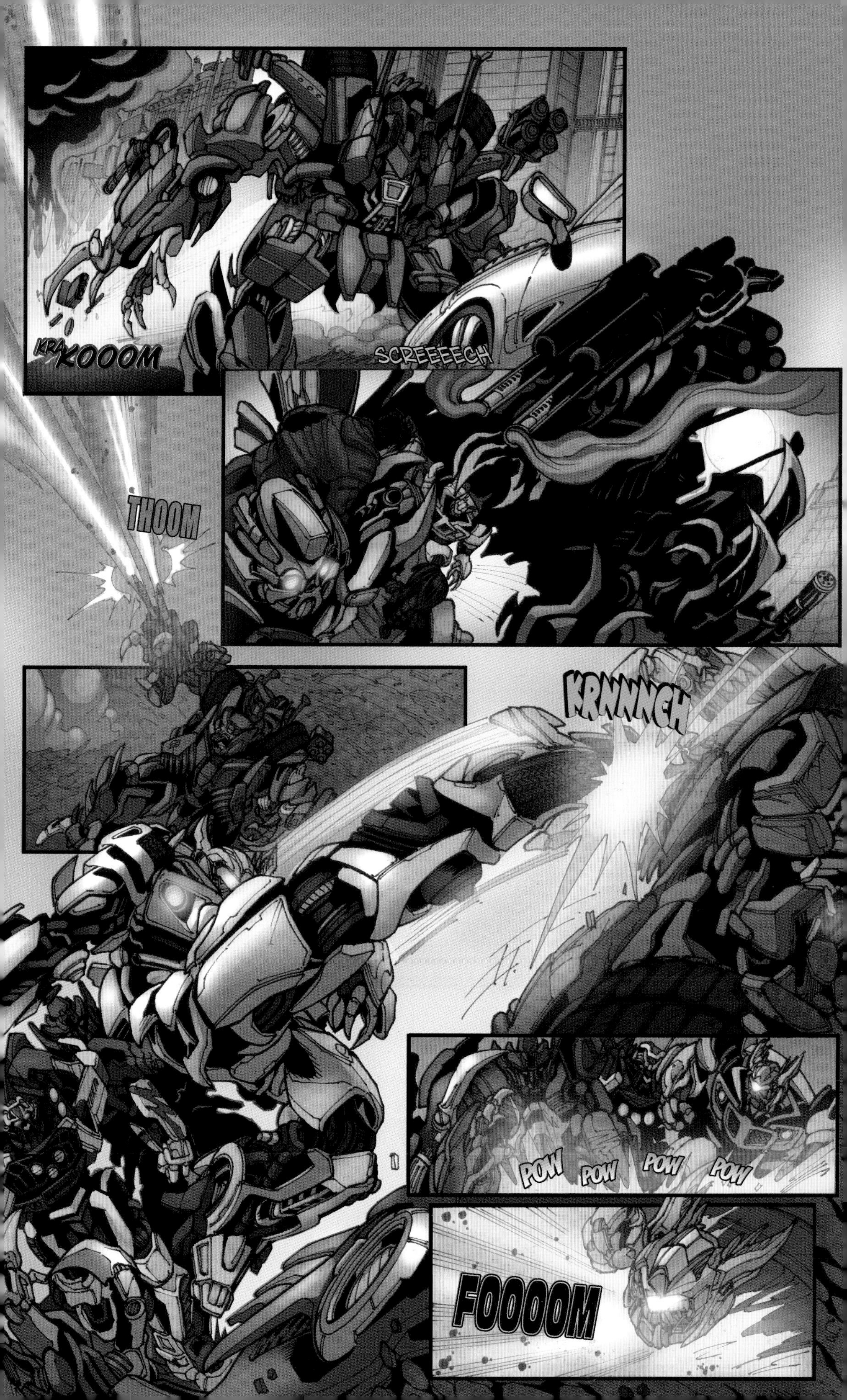
KRA KOOOM
SCREEEEECH
THOOM
KRNNNCH
POW
POW
POW
POW
FOOOOM

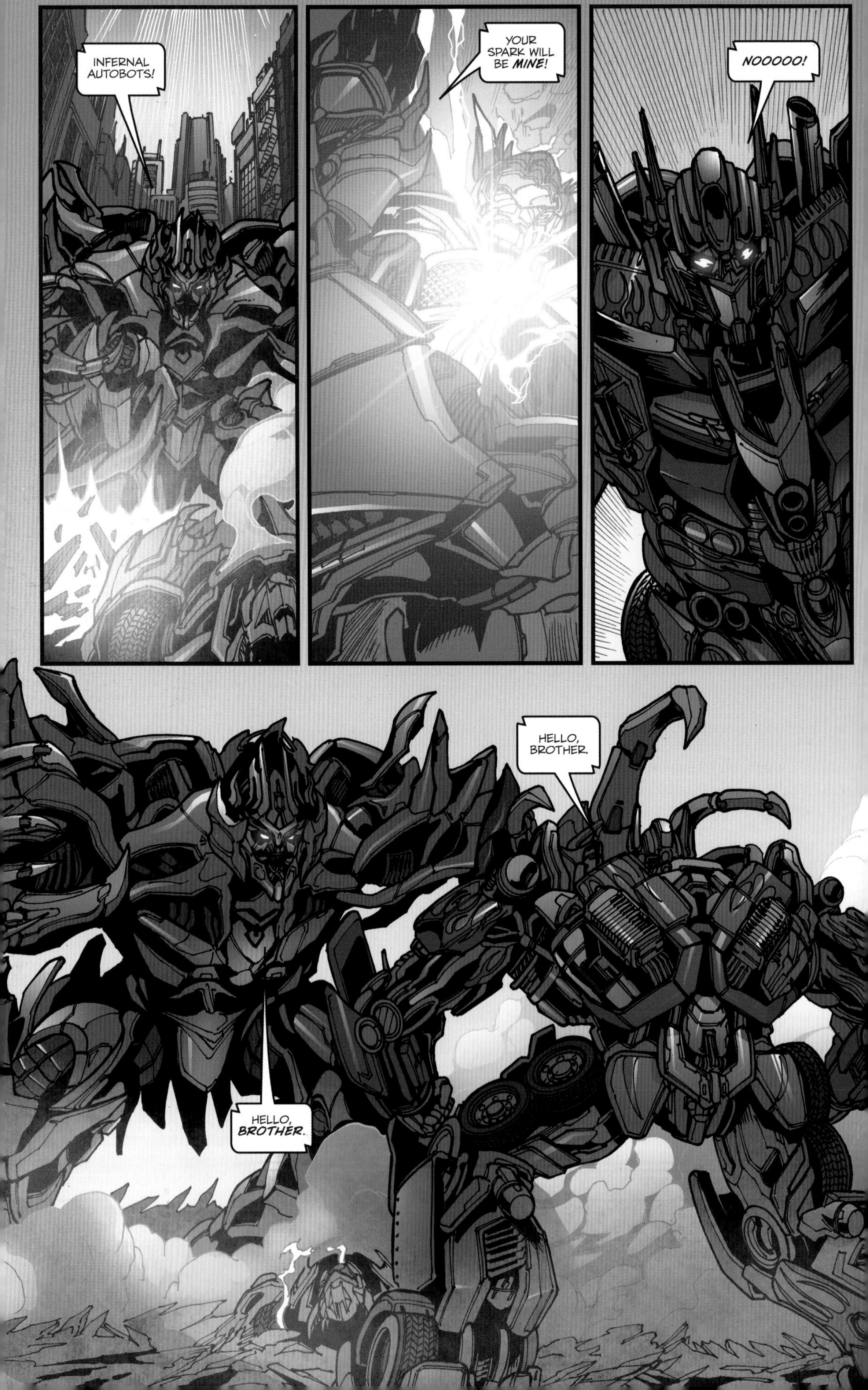
INFERNAL AUTOBOTS!
YOUR SPARK WILL BE *MINE*!
NOOOOO!
HELLO, BROTHER.
HELLO, *BROTHER*.

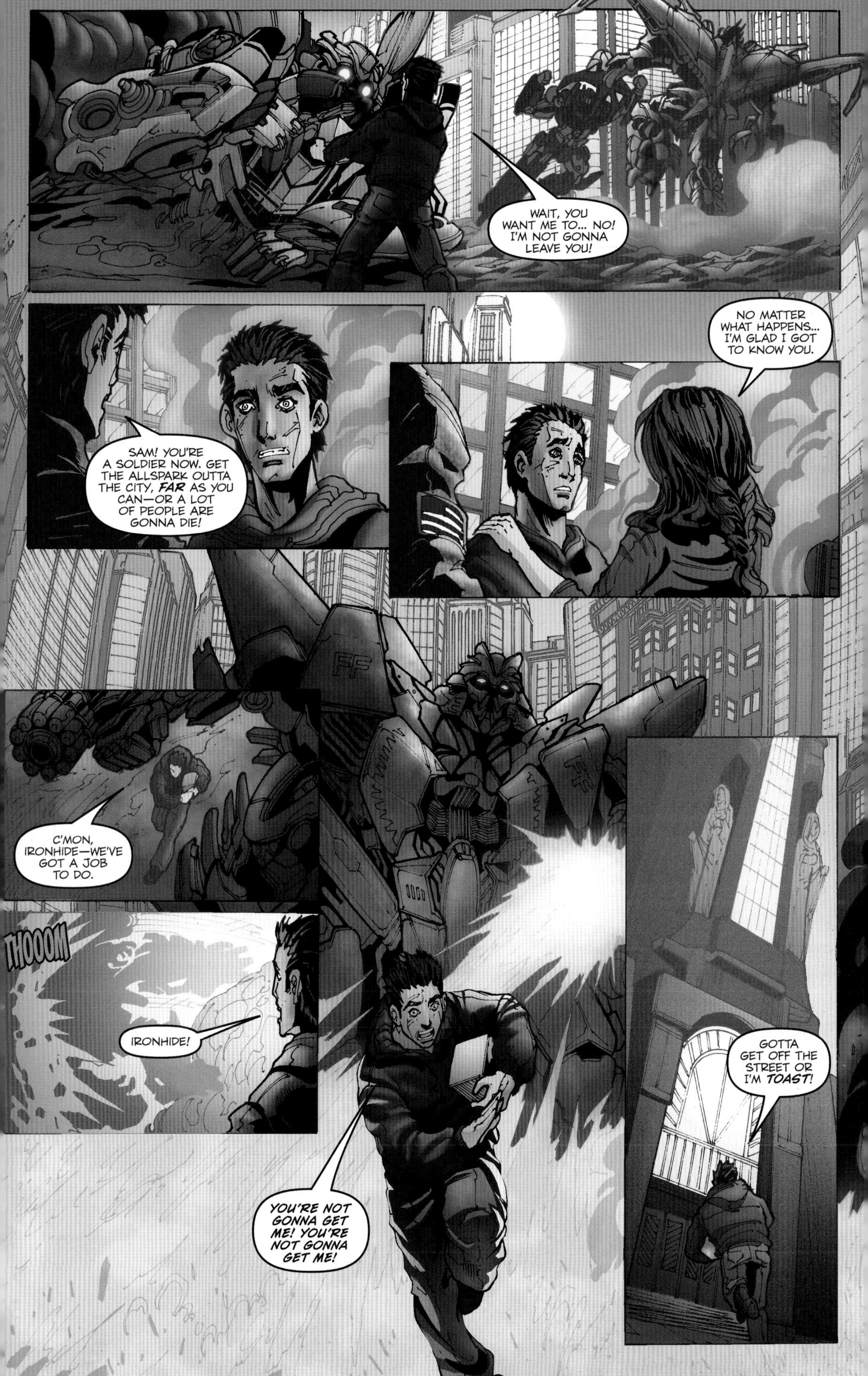
WAIT, YOU WANT ME TO... NO! I'M NOT GONNA LEAVE YOU!
SAM! YOU'RE A SOLDIER NOW. GET THE ALLSPARK OUTTA THE CITY, FAR AS YOU CAN—OR A LOT OF PEOPLE ARE GONNA DIE!
NO MATTER WHAT HAPPENS... I'M GLAD I GOT TO KNOW YOU.
C'MON, IRONHIDE—WE'VE GOT A JOB TO DO.
THOOOM
IRONHIDE!
YOU'RE NOT GONNA GET ME! YOU'RE NOT GONNA GET ME!
GOTTA GET OFF THE STREET OR I'M TOAST!

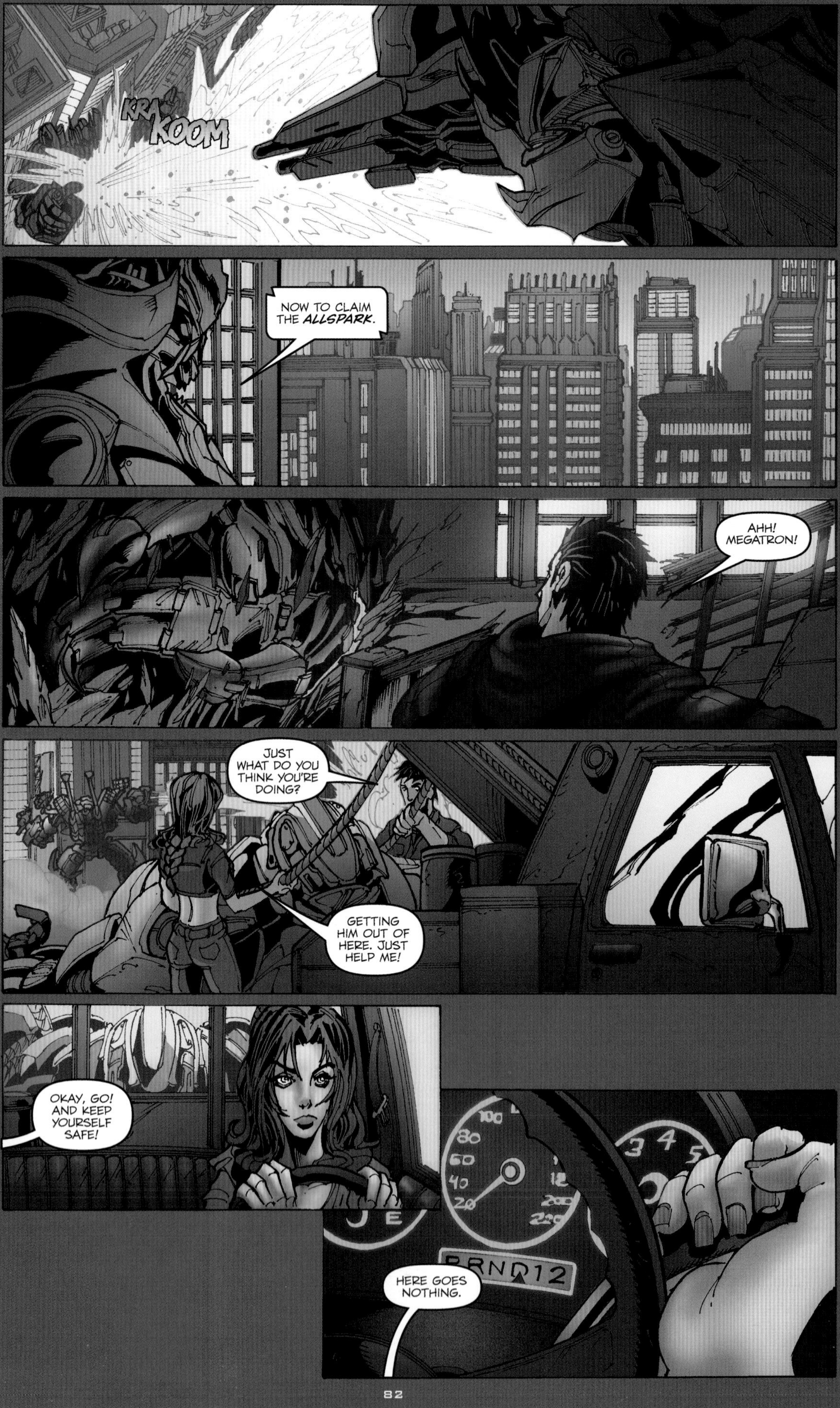
KRA-KOOM
NOW TO CLAIM THE *ALLSPARK*.
AHH! MEGATRON!
JUST WHAT DO YOU THINK YOU'RE DOING?
GETTING HIM OUT OF HERE. JUST HELP ME!
OKAY, GO! AND KEEP YOURSELF SAFE!
HERE GOES NOTHING.

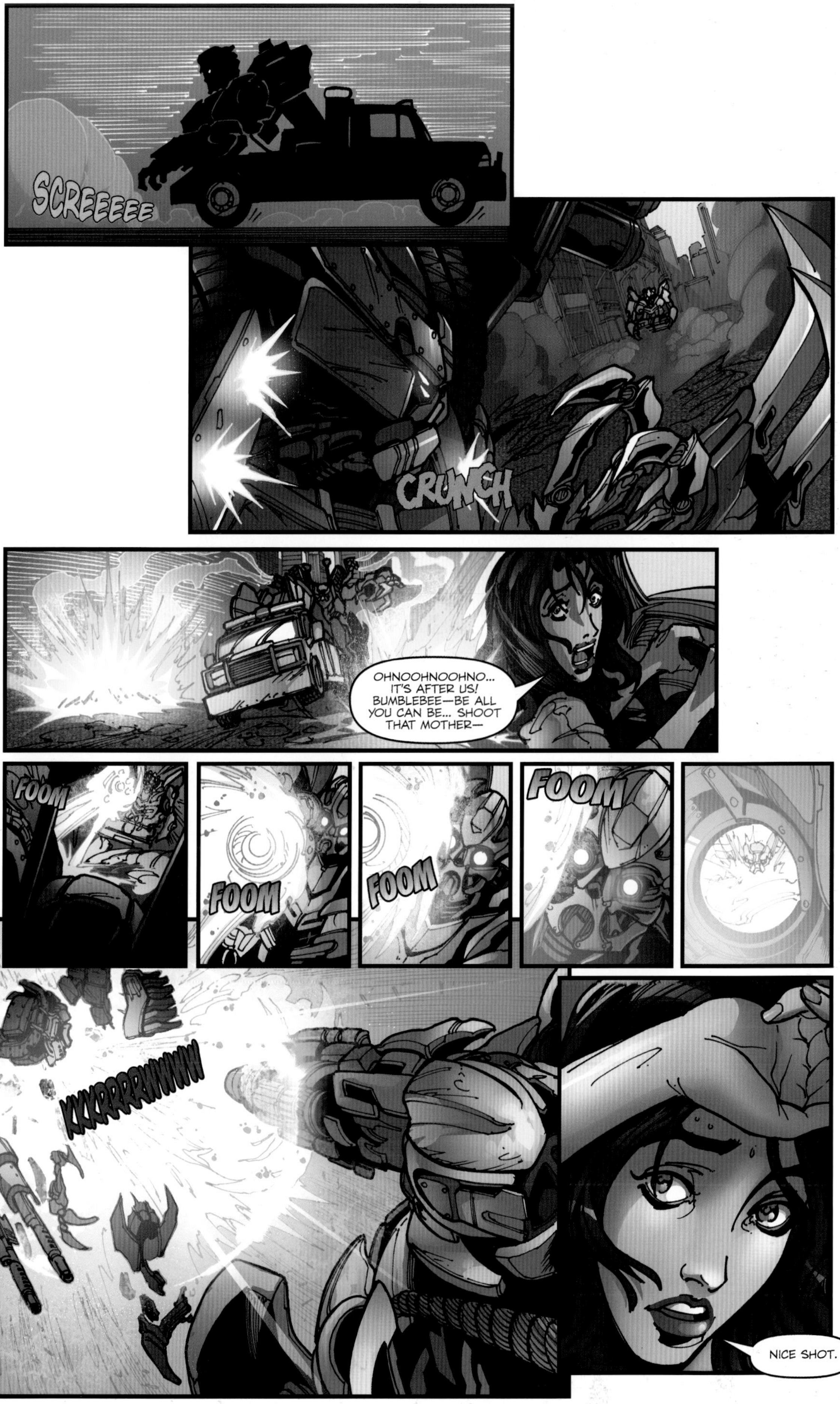
SCREEEEEE
CRUNCH
OHNOOHNOOHNO... IT'S AFTER US! BUMBLEBEE—BE ALL YOU CAN BE... SHOOT THAT MOTHER—
FOOM
FOOM
FOOM
FOOM
KKKRRRRNNNNN
NICE SHOT.

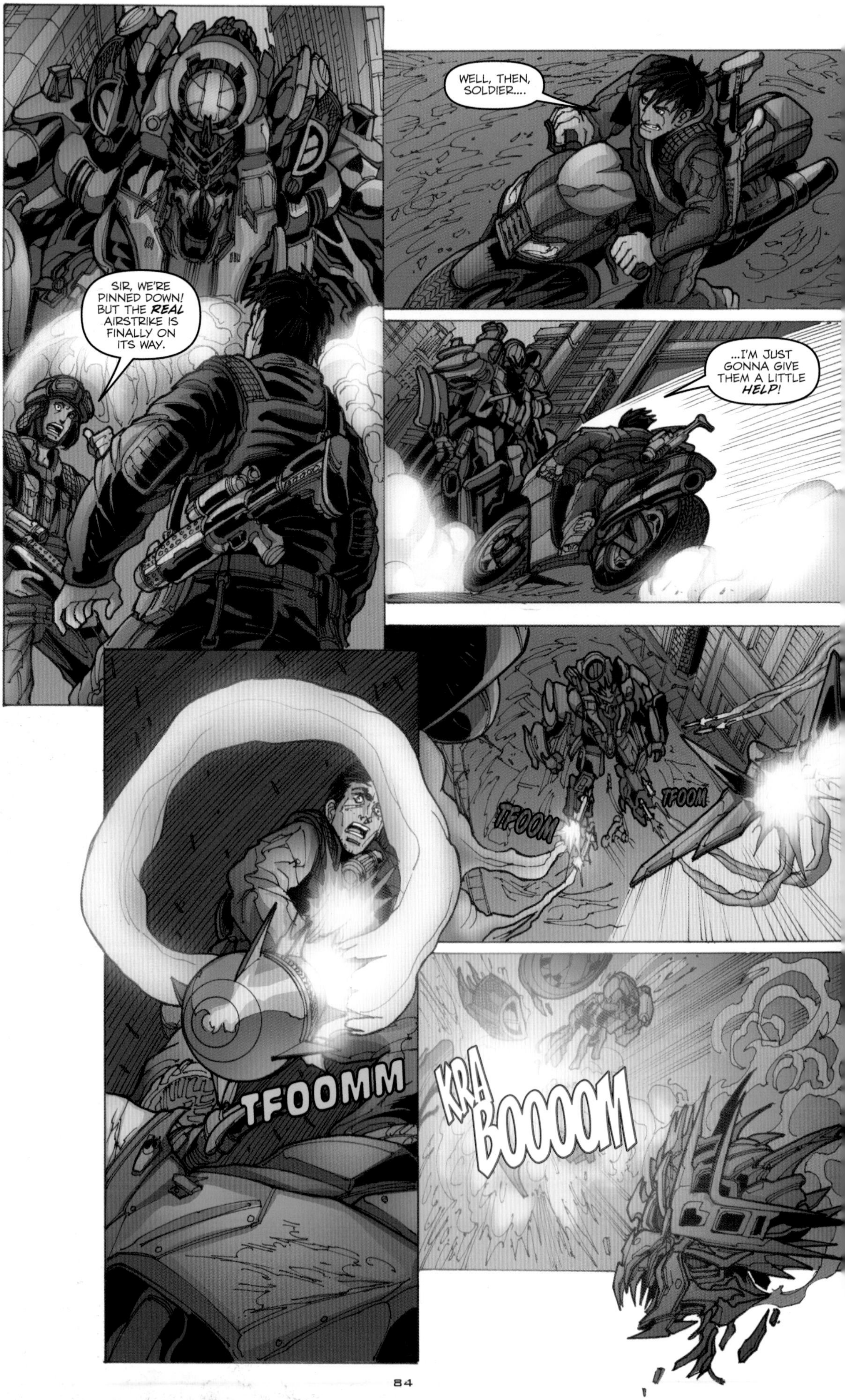
SIR, WE'RE PINNED DOWN! BUT THE REAL AIRSTRIKE IS FINALLY ON ITS WAY.
WELL, THEN, SOLDIER....
...I'M JUST GONNA GIVE THEM A LITTLE HELP!
TFOOM
TFOOM
TFOOMM
KRA BOOOOM

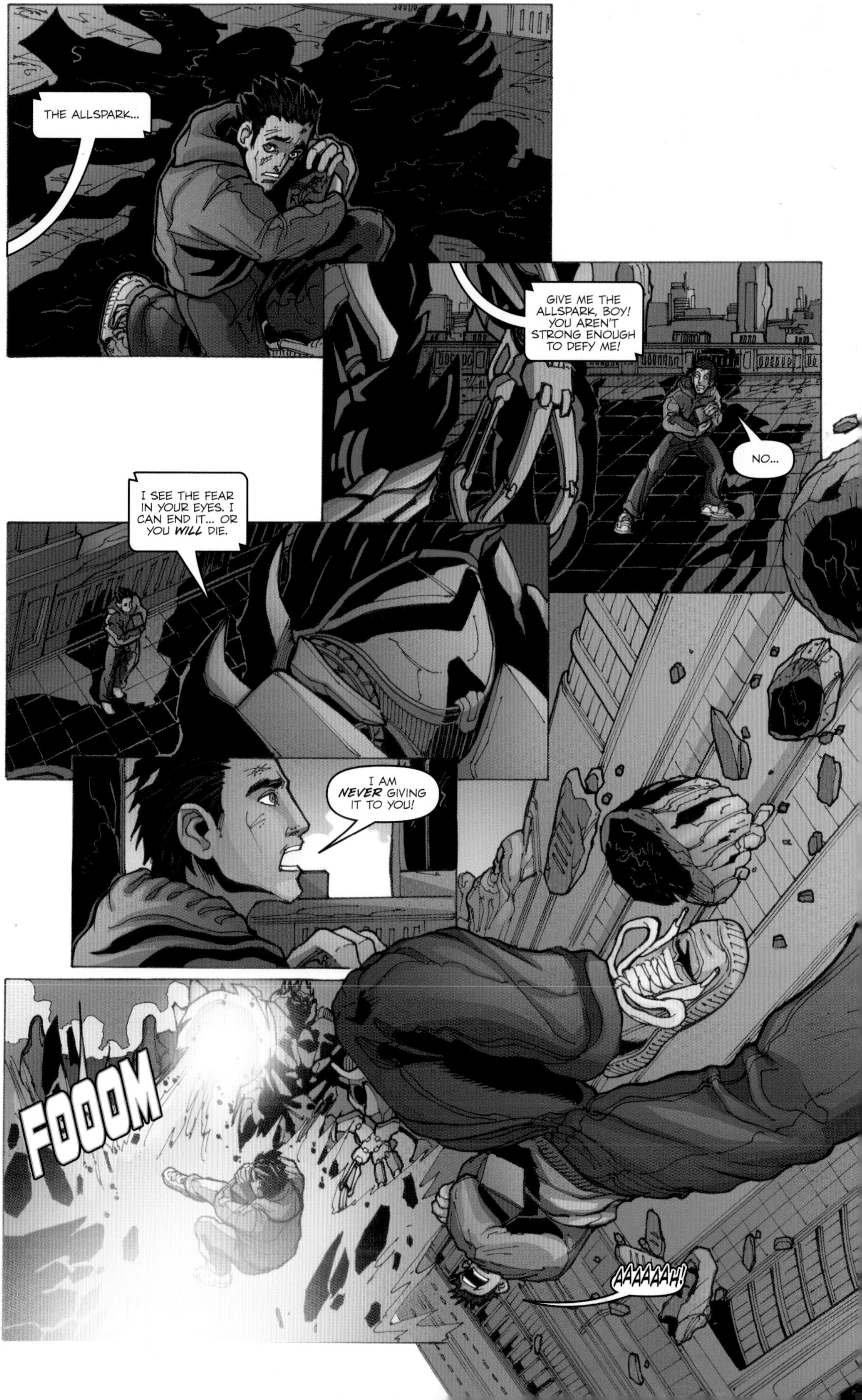
THE ALLSPARK...
GIVE ME THE ALLSPARK, BOY! YOU AREN'T STRONG ENOUGH TO DEFY ME!
NO...
I SEE THE FEAR IN YOUR EYES. I CAN END IT... OR YOU *WILL* DIE.
I AM *NEVER* GIVING IT TO YOU!
FOOOM
AAAAAAH!

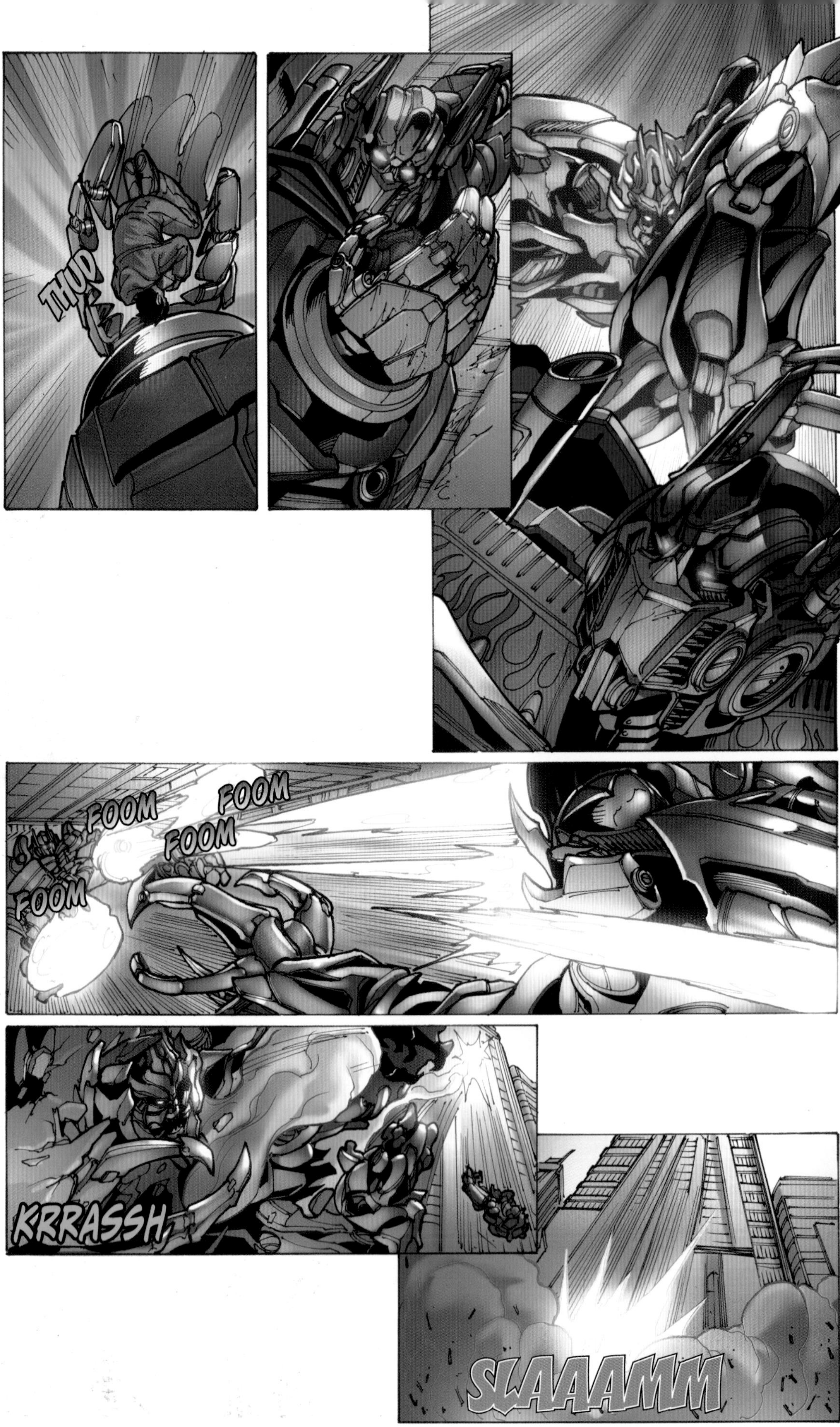
THUD
FOOM
FOOM
FOOM
FOOM
KRRASSH
SLAAAMM

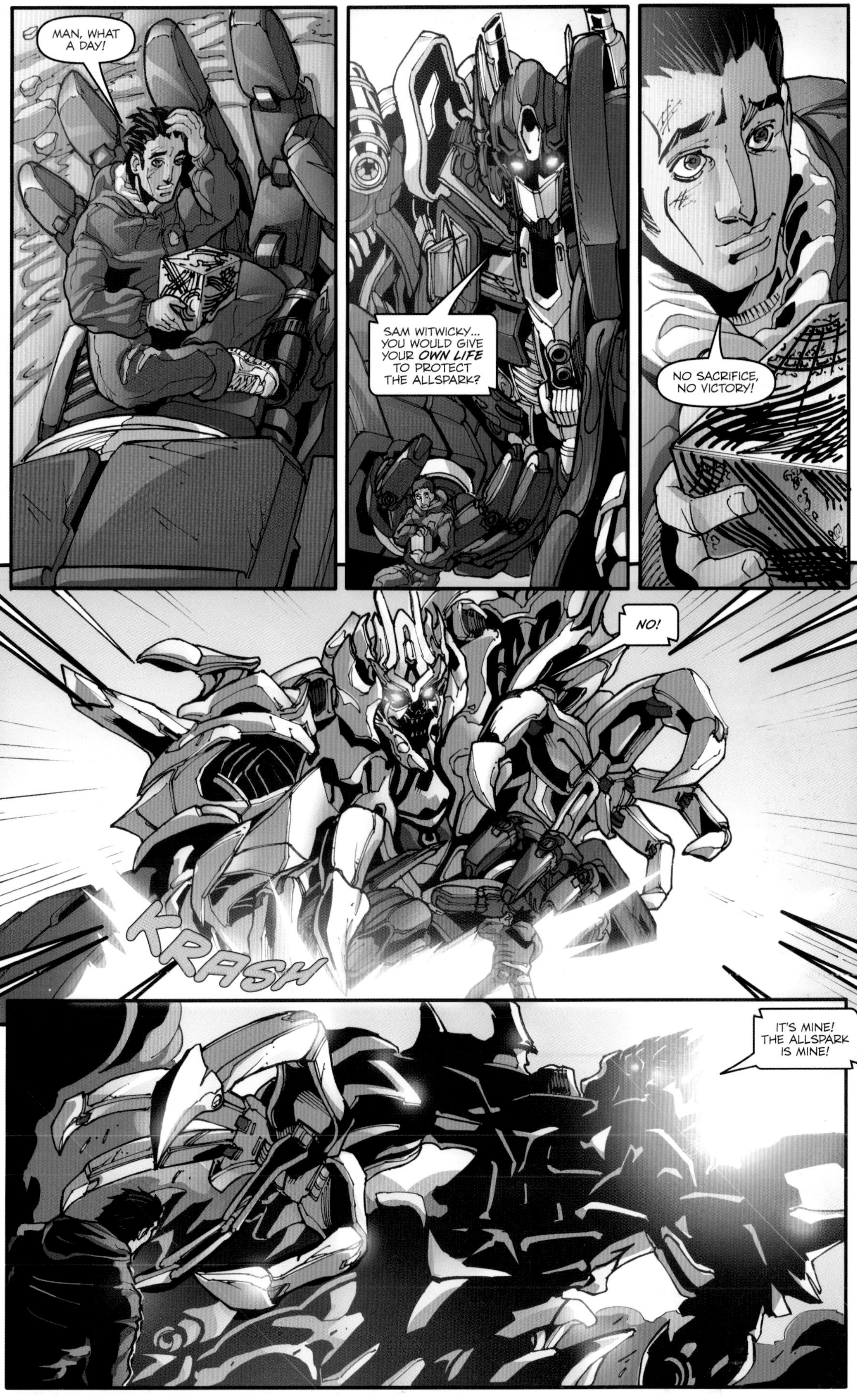
MAN, WHAT A DAY!
SAM WITWICKY... YOU WOULD GIVE YOUR OWN LIFE TO PROTECT THE ALLSPARK?
NO SACRIFICE, NO VICTORY!
NO!
KRASH
IT'S MINE! THE ALLSPARK IS MINE!

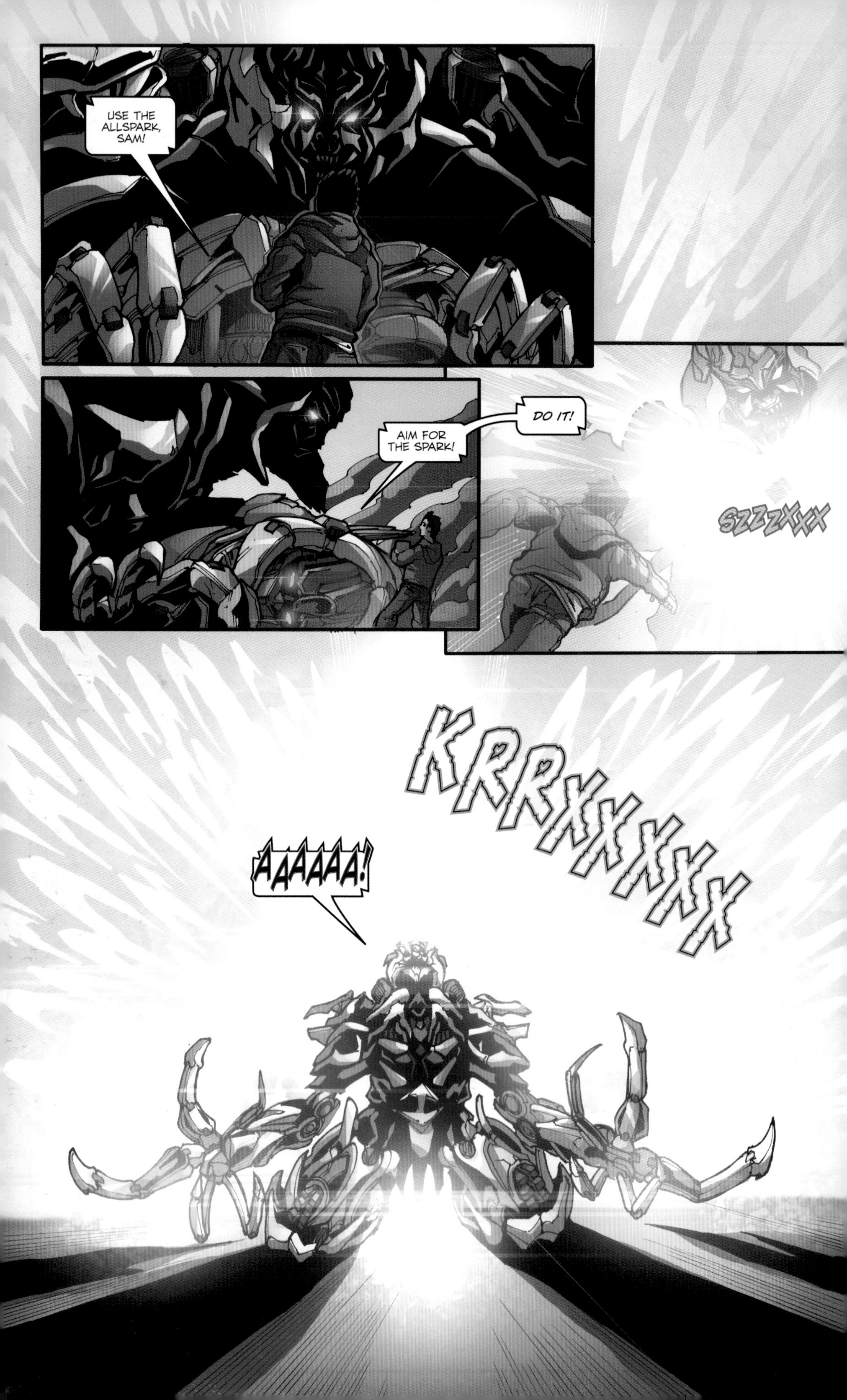
USE THE ALLSPARK, SAM!
AIM FOR THE SPARK!
DO IT!
SZZZXXX
KRRXXXXX
AAAAAA!

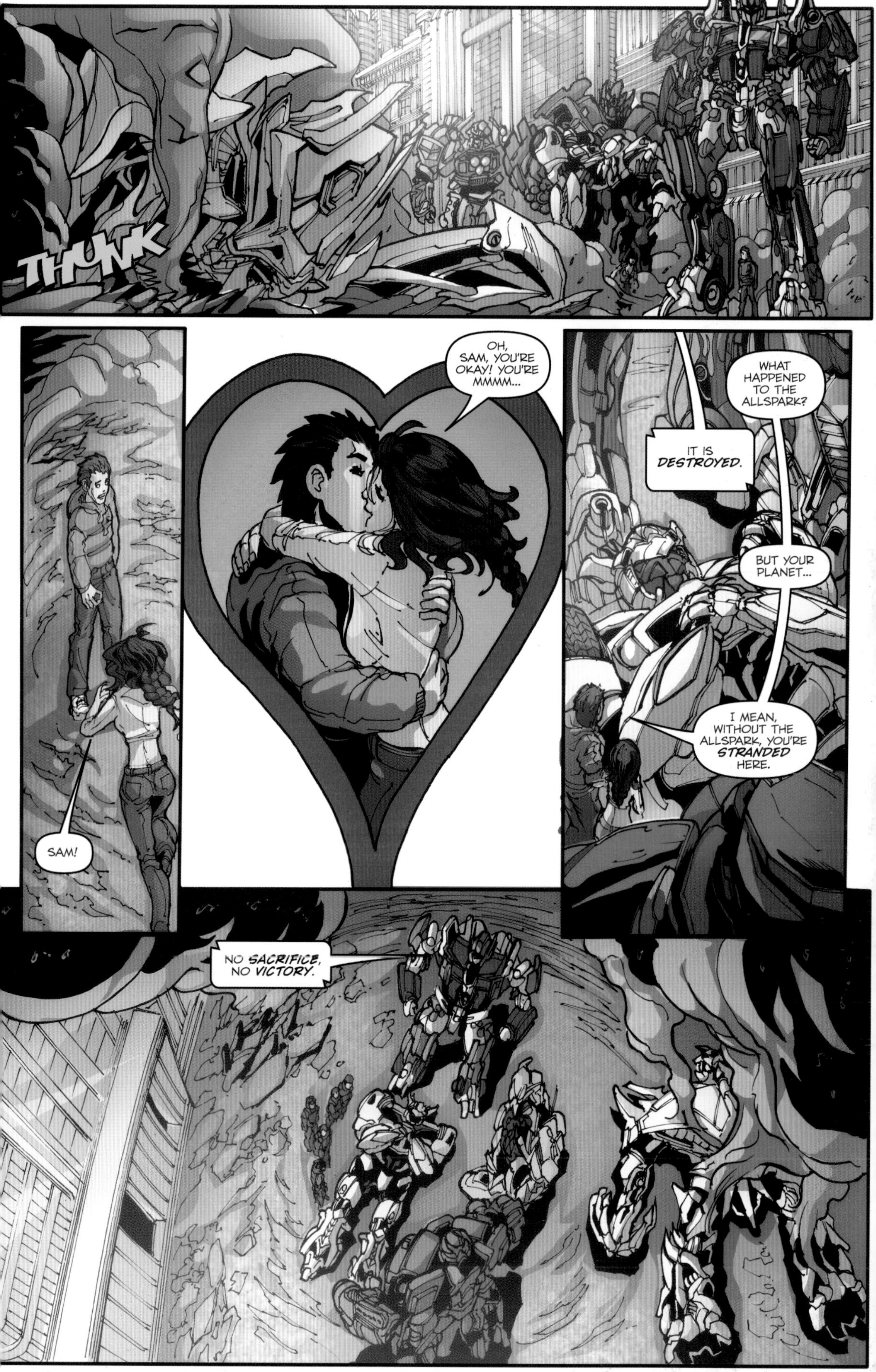
THUNK
SAM!
OH, SAM, YOU'RE OKAY! YOU'RE MMMM...
WHAT HAPPENED TO THE ALLSPARK?
IT IS DESTROYED.
BUT YOUR PLANET...
I MEAN, WITHOUT THE ALLSPARK, YOU'RE STRANDED HERE.
NO SACRIFICE, NO VICTORY.

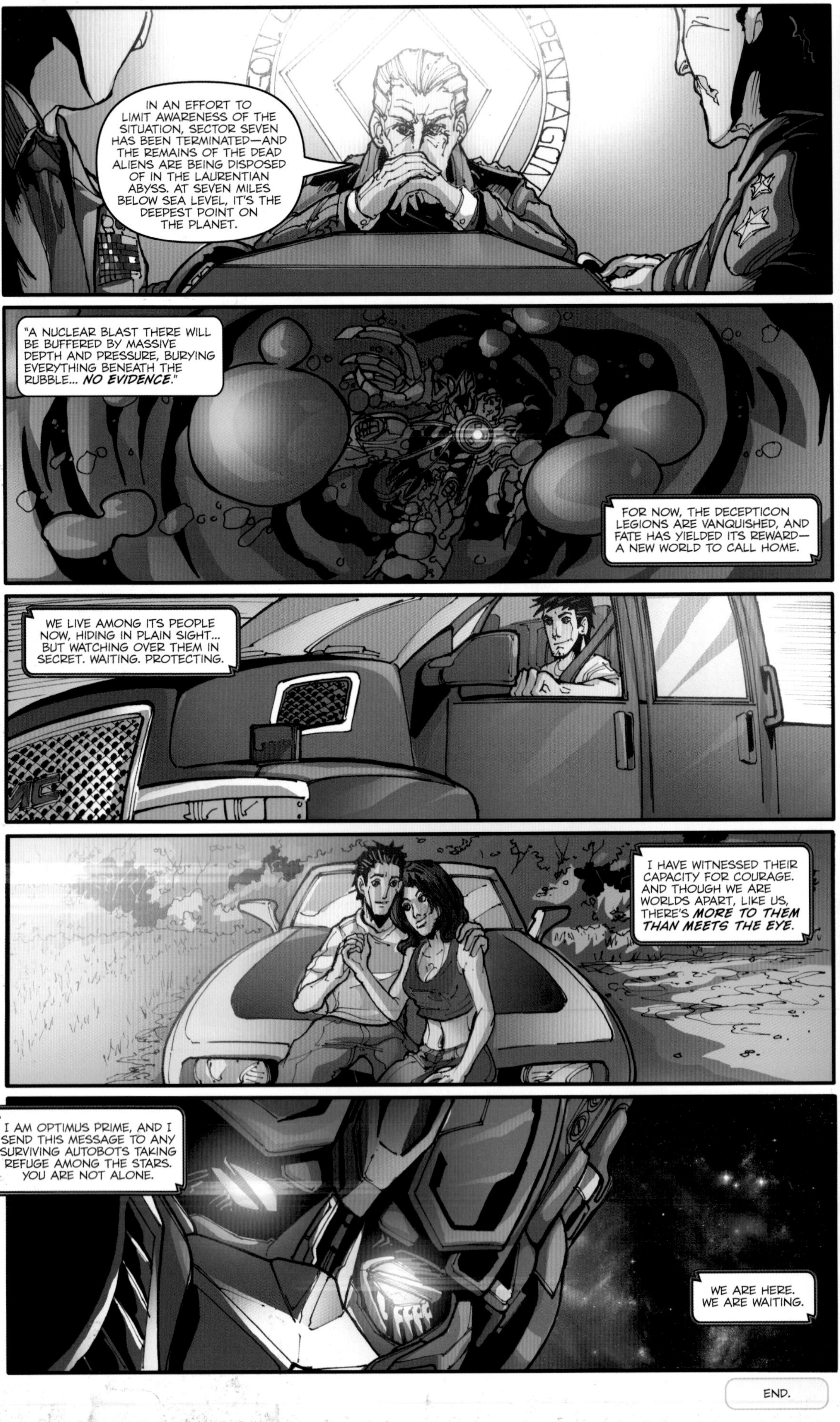
IN AN EFFORT TO LIMIT AWARENESS OF THE SITUATION, SECTOR SEVEN HAS BEEN TERMINATED—AND THE REMAINS OF THE DEAD ALIENS ARE BEING DISPOSED OF IN THE LAURENTIAN ABYSS. AT SEVEN MILES BELOW SEA LEVEL, IT'S THE DEEPEST POINT ON THE PLANET.
"A NUCLEAR BLAST THERE WILL BE BUFFERED BY MASSIVE DEPTH AND PRESSURE, BURYING EVERYTHING BENEATH THE RUBBLE... NO EVIDENCE."
FOR NOW, THE DECEPTICON LEGIONS ARE VANQUISHED, AND FATE HAS YIELDED ITS REWARD—A NEW WORLD TO CALL HOME.
WE LIVE AMONG ITS PEOPLE NOW, HIDING IN PLAIN SIGHT... BUT WATCHING OVER THEM IN SECRET. WAITING. PROTECTING.
I HAVE WITNESSED THEIR CAPACITY FOR COURAGE. AND THOUGH WE ARE WORLDS APART, LIKE US, THERE'S MORE TO THEM THAN MEETS THE EYE.
I AM OPTIMUS PRIME, AND I SEND THIS MESSAGE TO ANY SURVIVING AUTOBOTS TAKING REFUGE AMONG THE STARS. YOU ARE NOT ALONE.
WE ARE HERE. WE ARE WAITING.
END.

ART GALLERY

ARTWORK BY ALEX MILNE

COLORS BY JOSH PEREZ AND ESPEN GRUNDETJERN

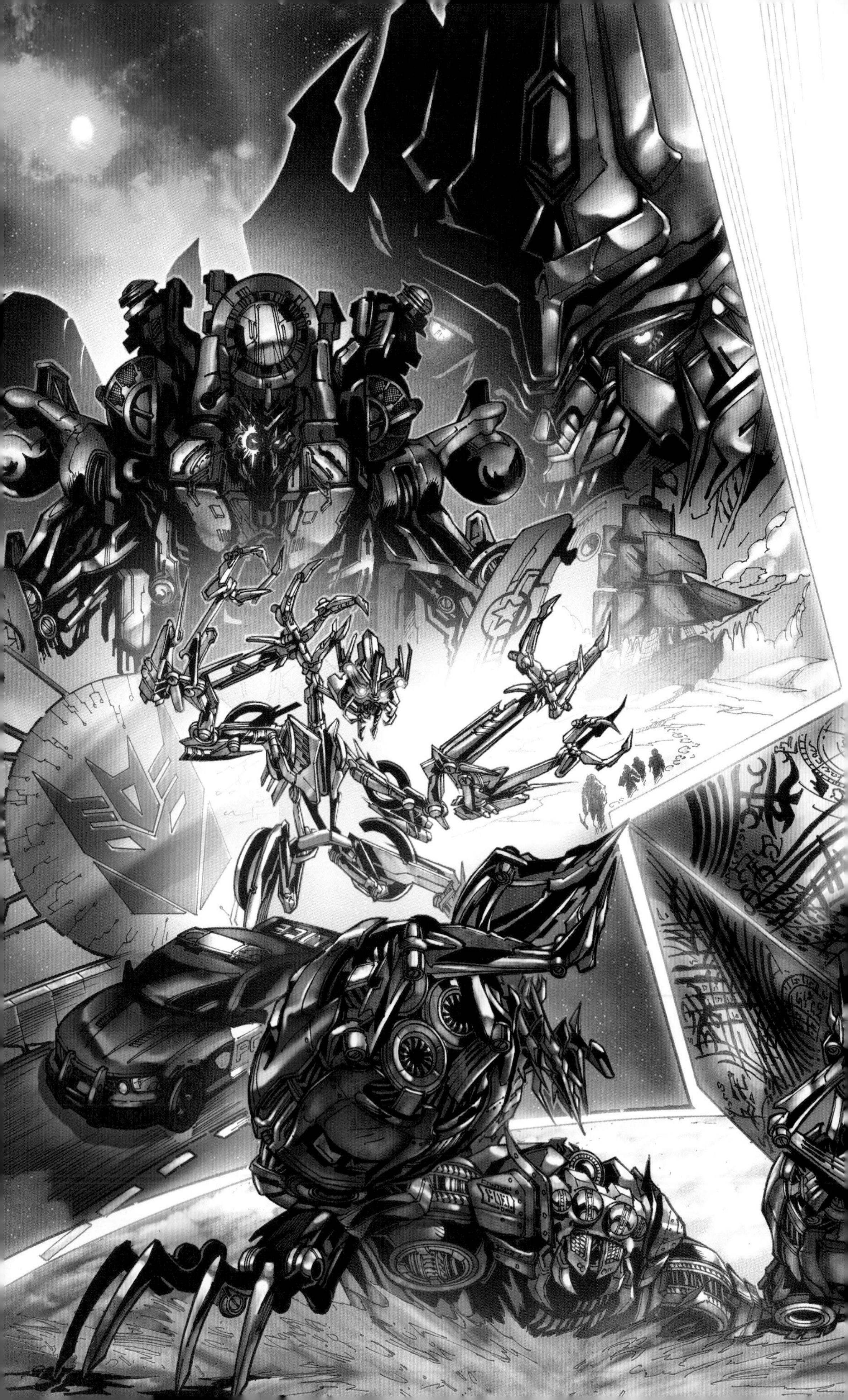

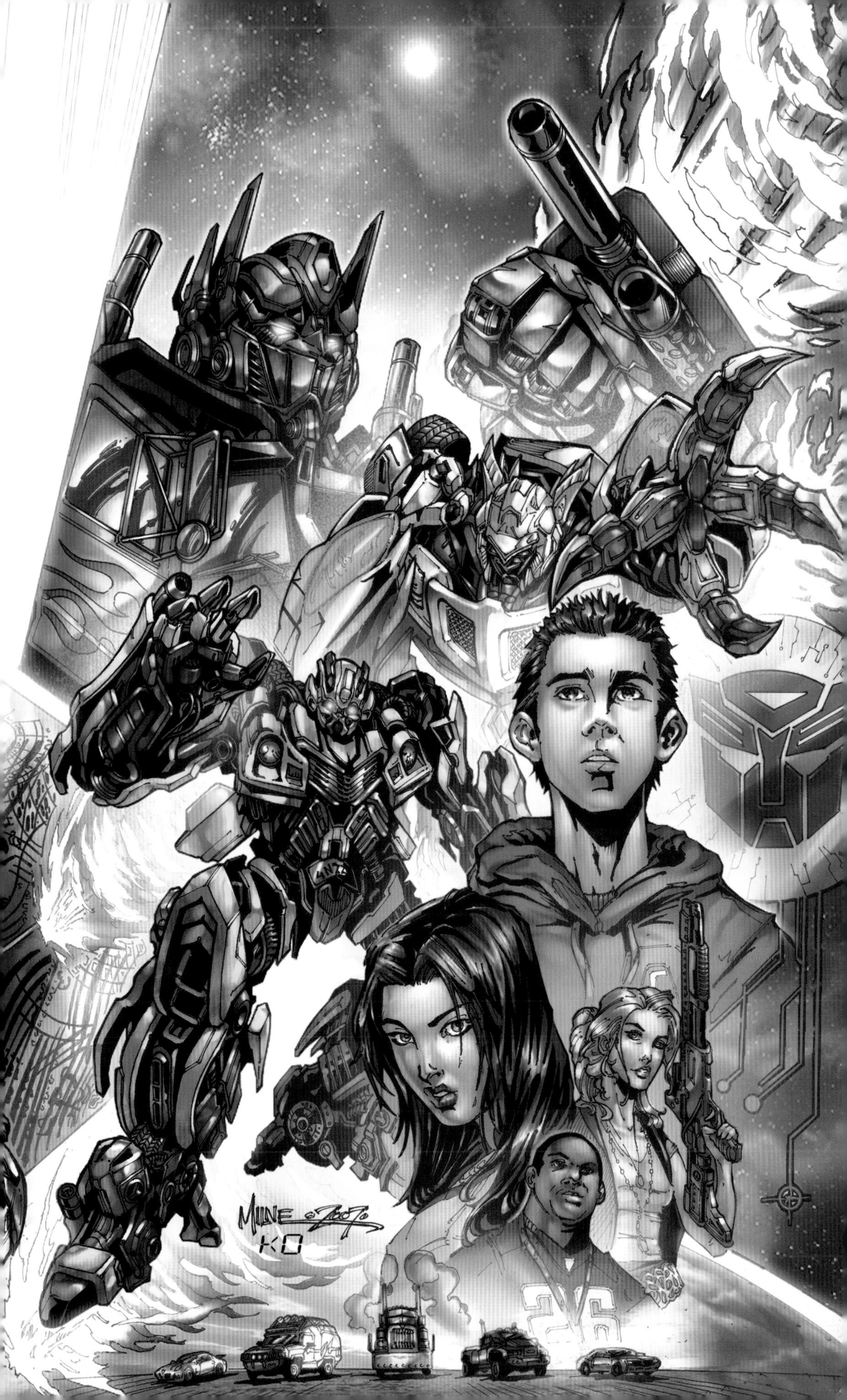
MILNE ©2007
KO

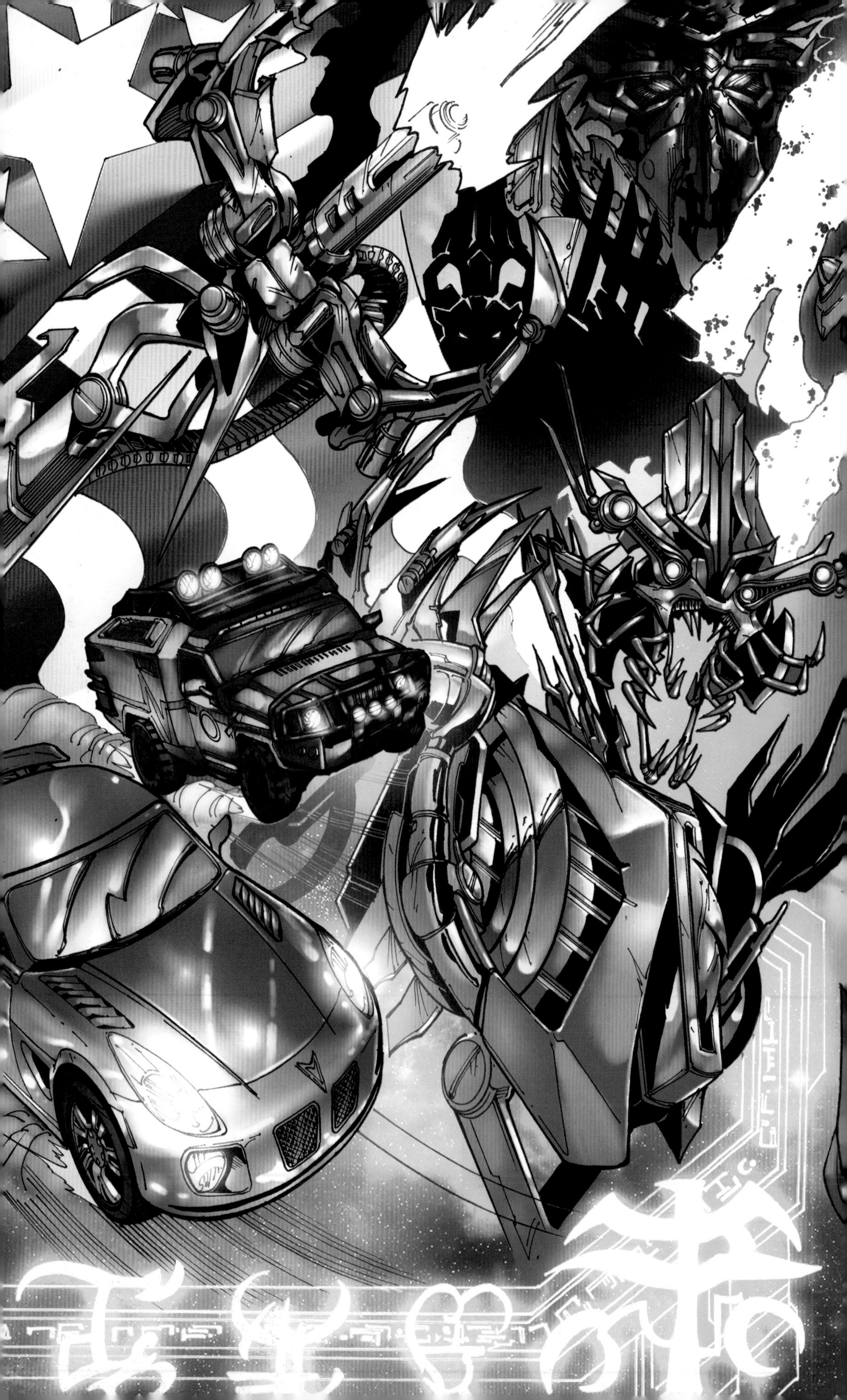

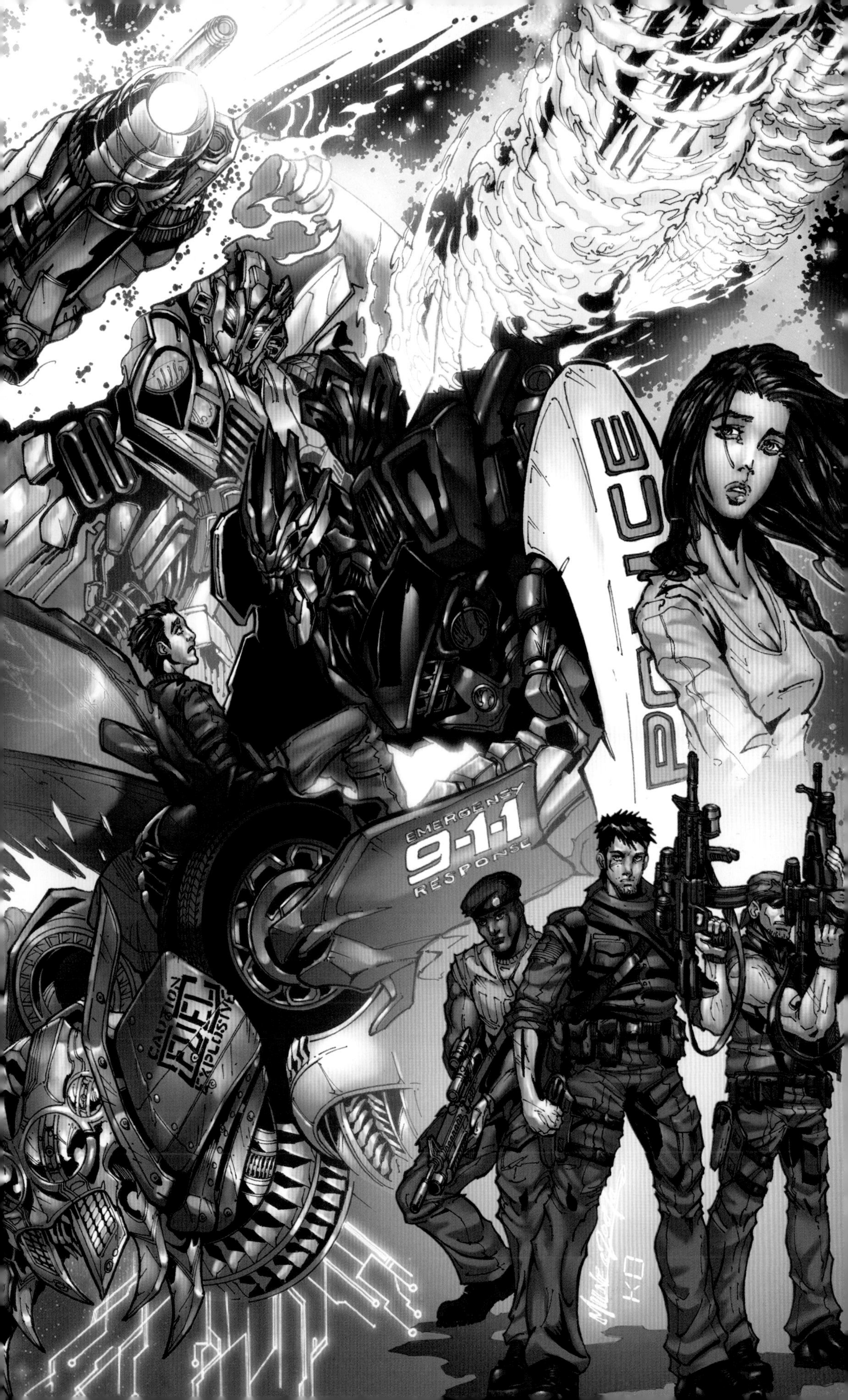
POLICE
EMERGENCY
9-1-1
RESPONSE
CAUTION
EXPLOSIVE

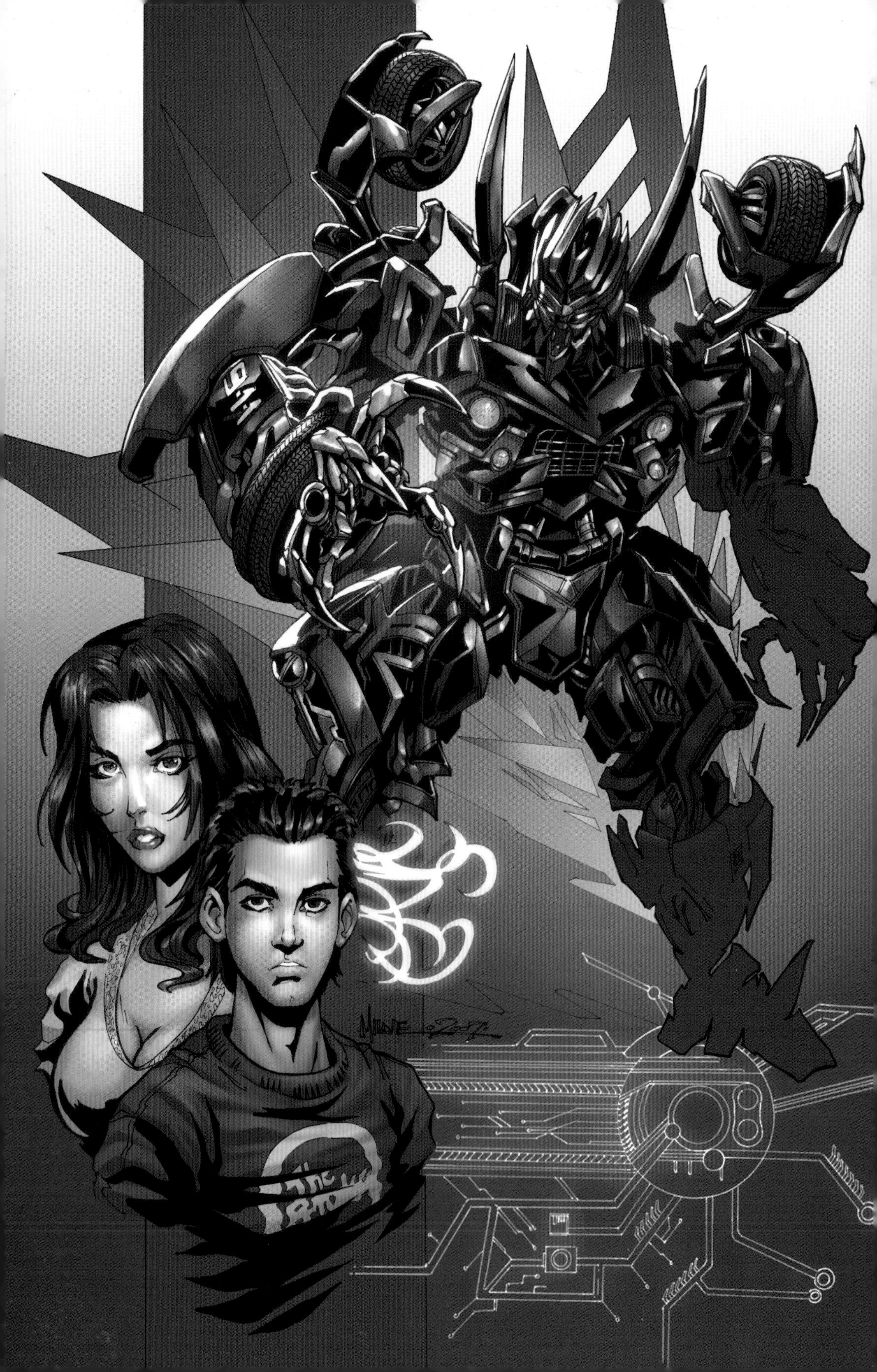

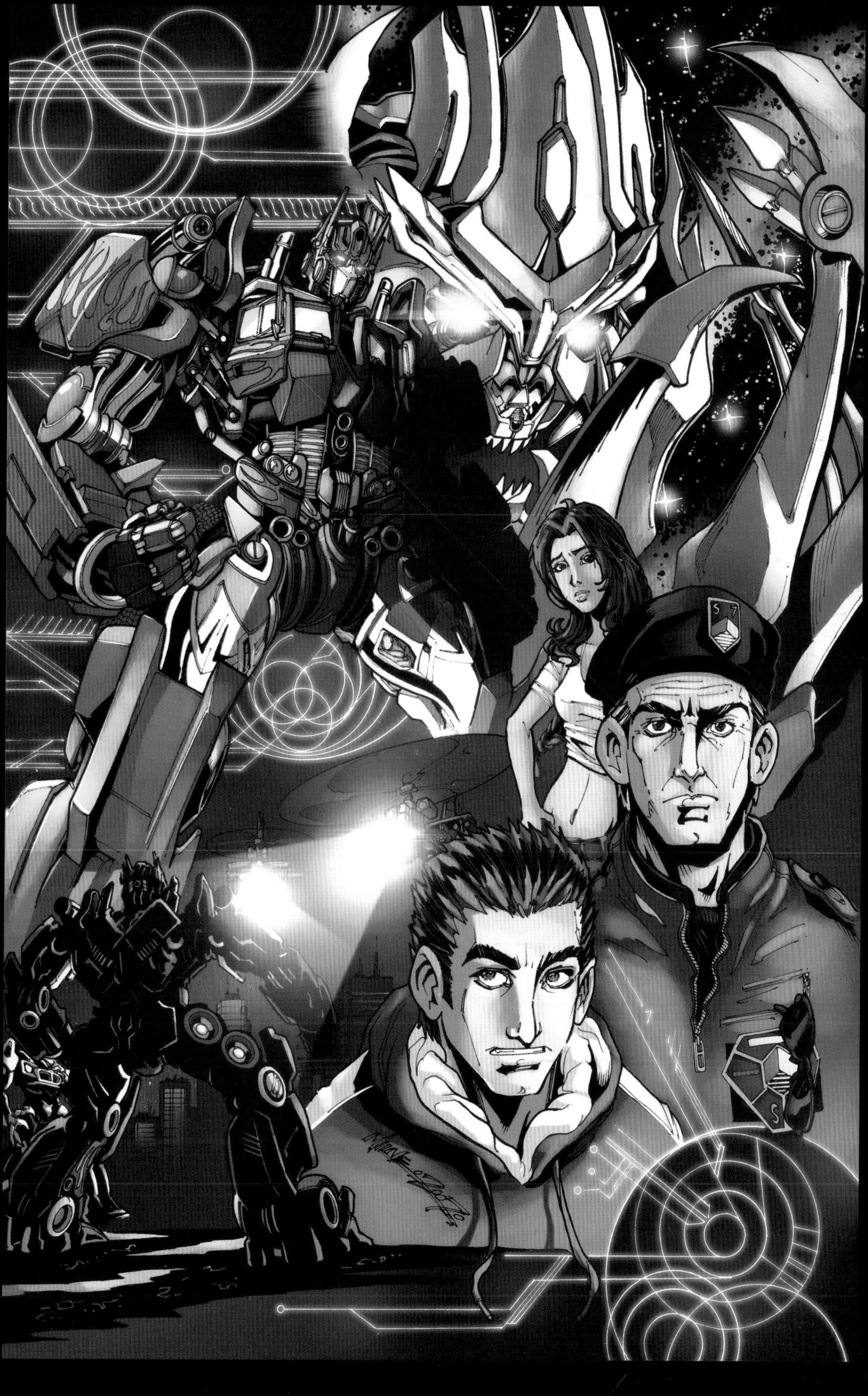

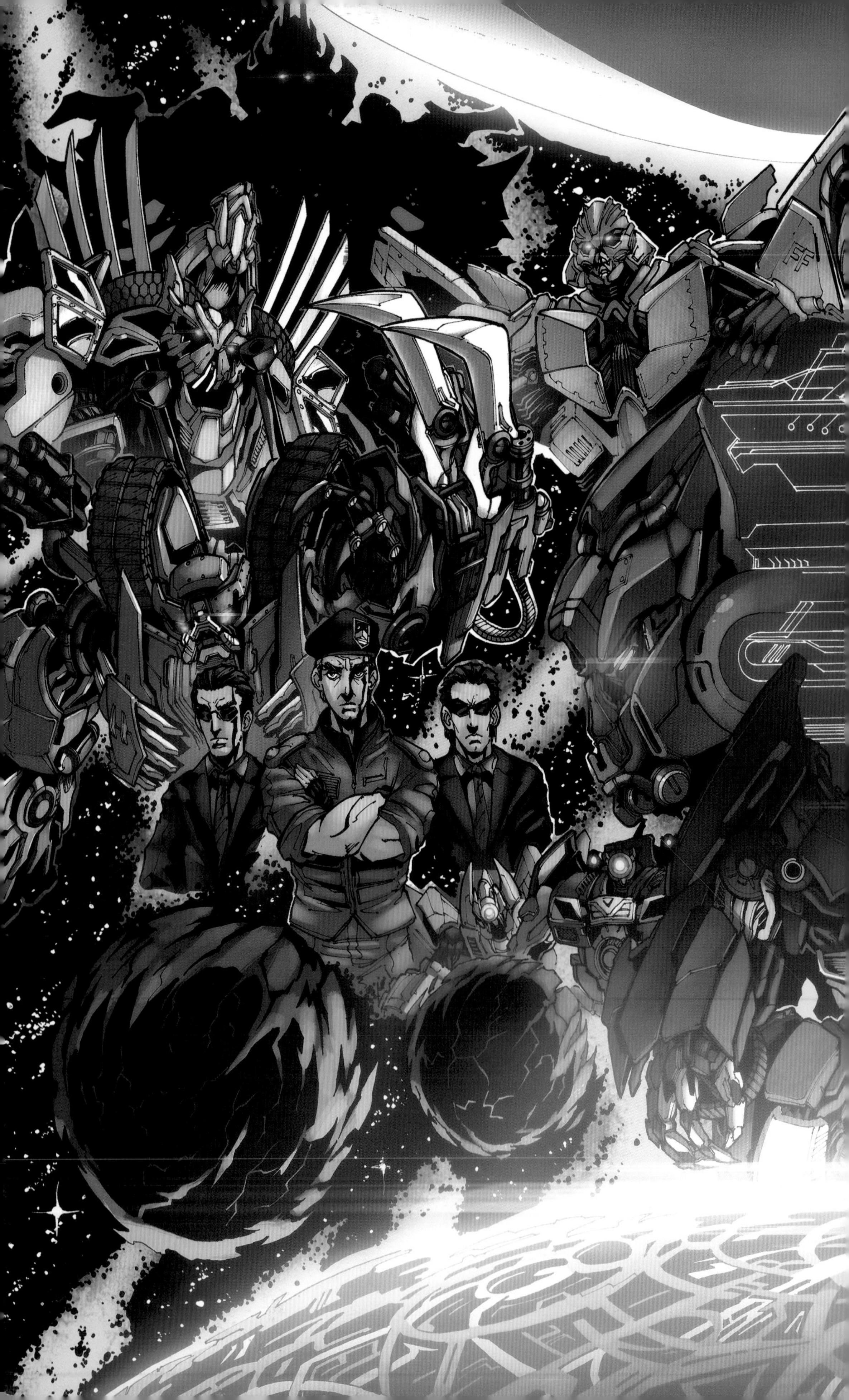

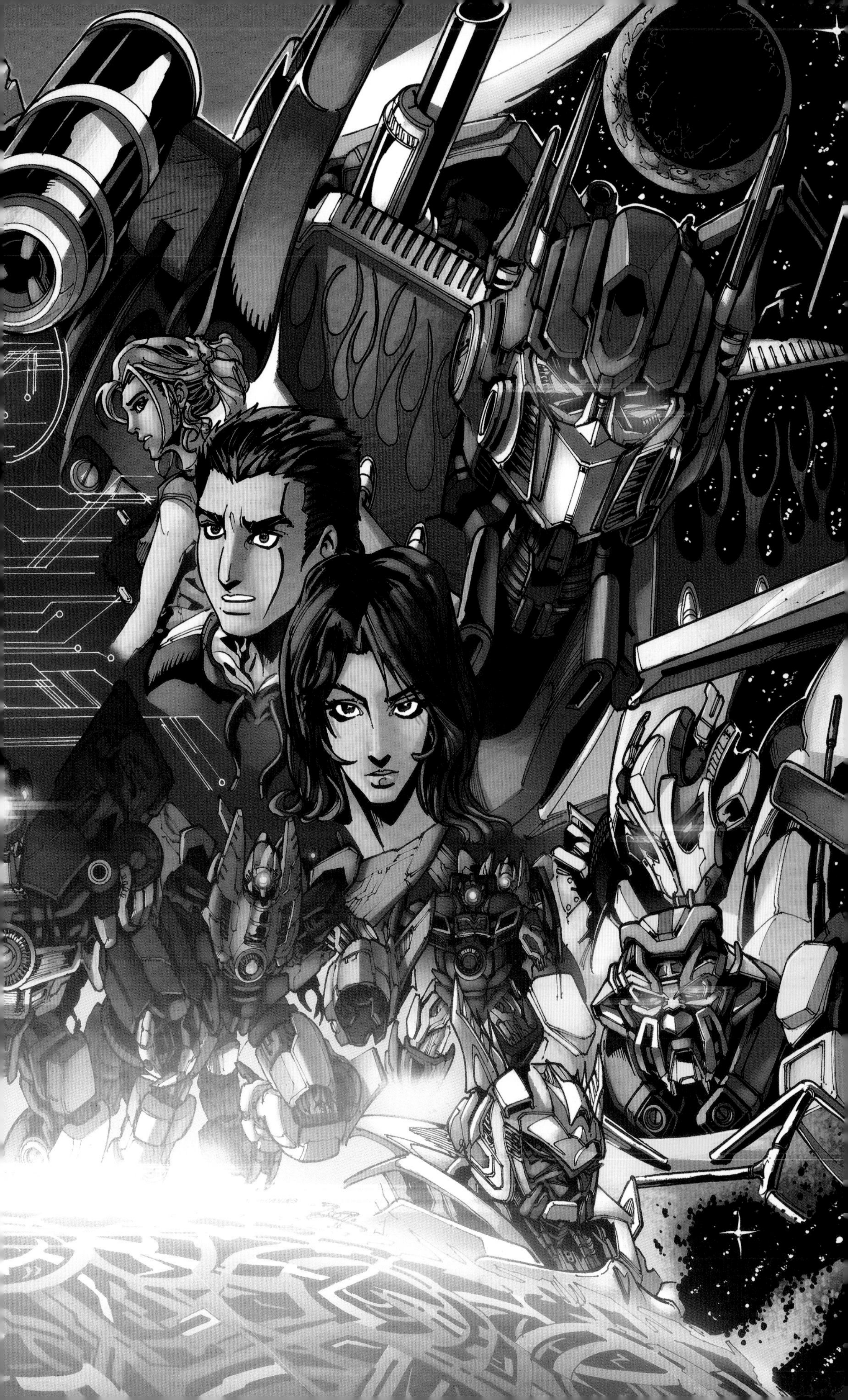

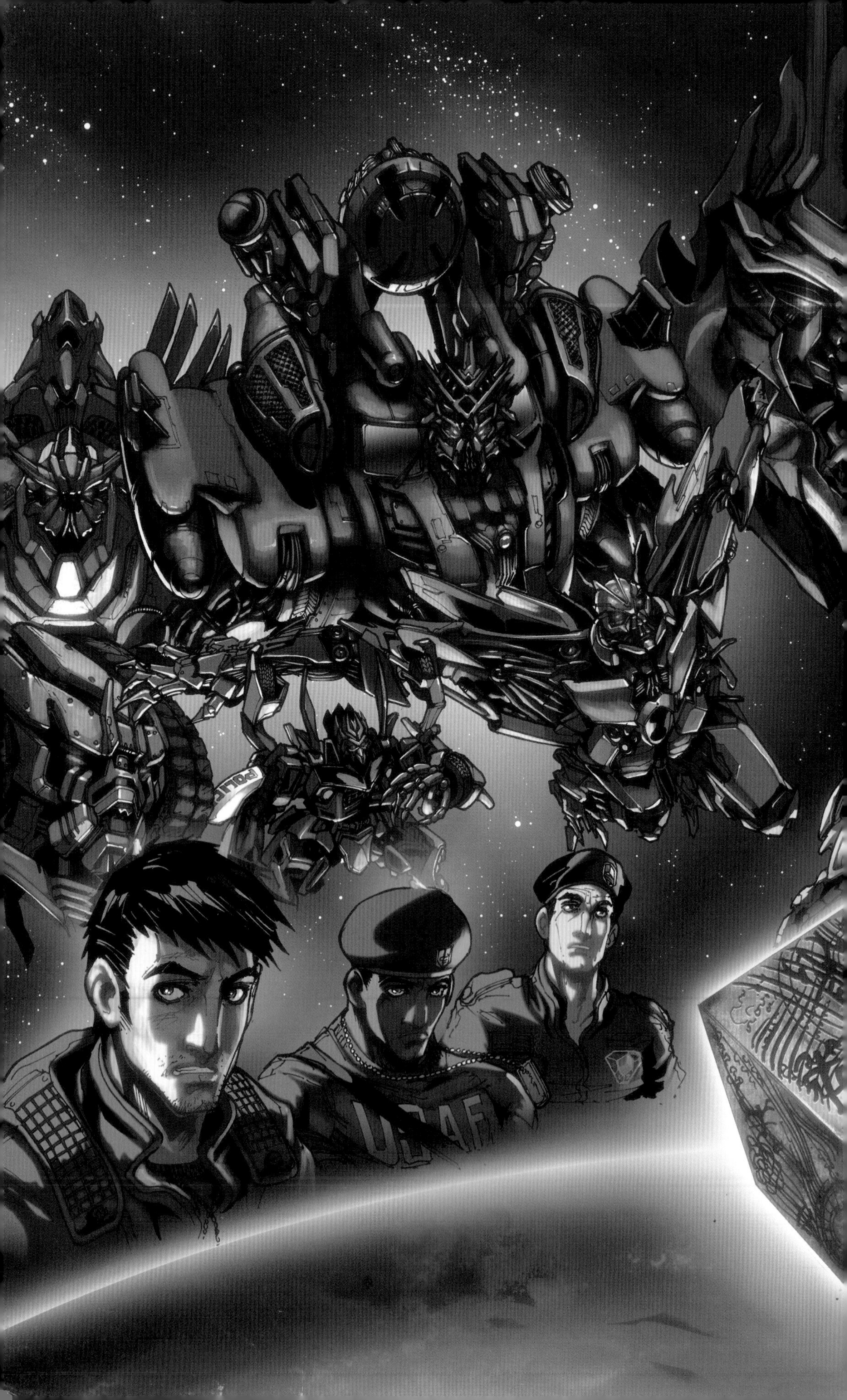

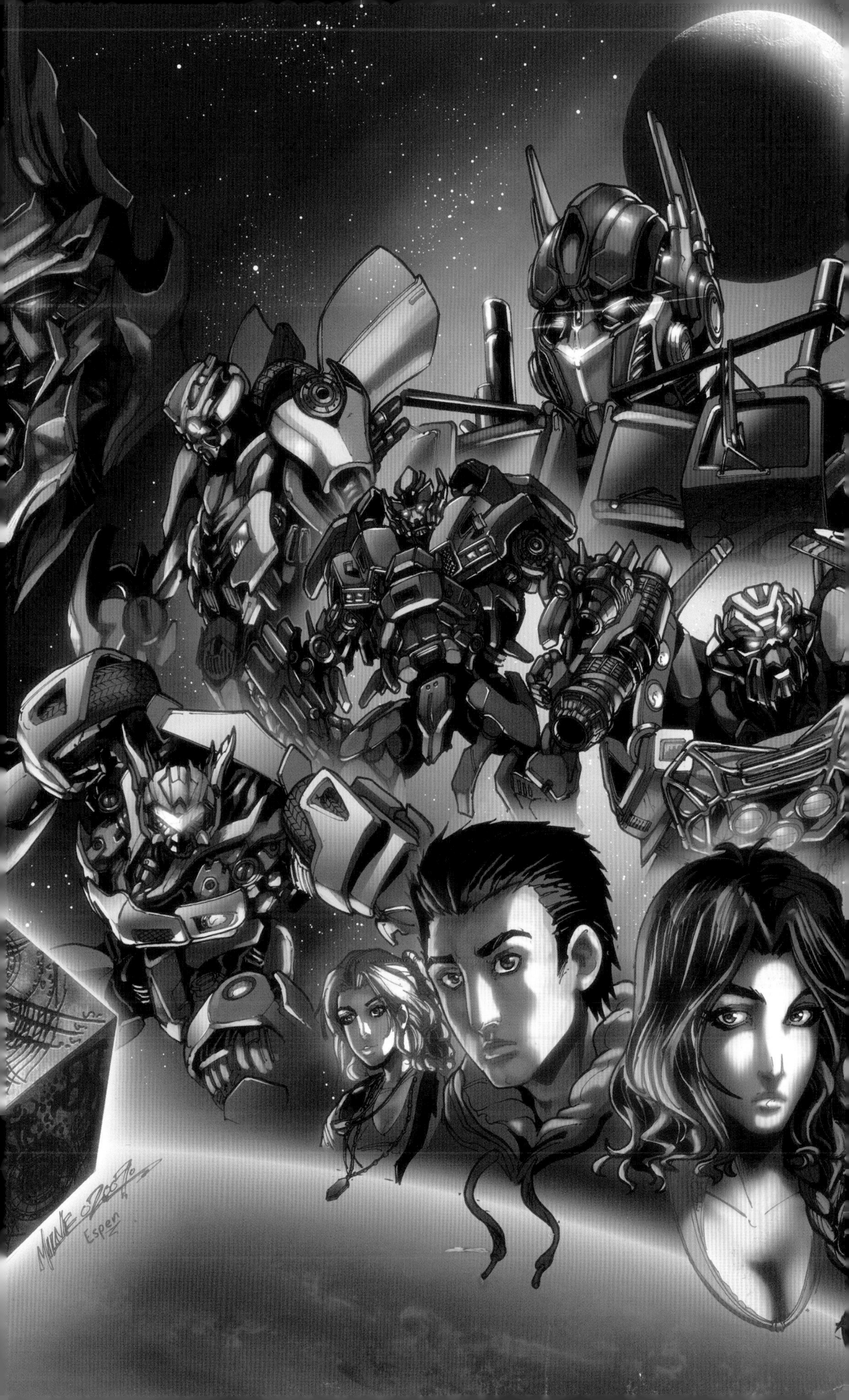
Espen

READY FOR MORE?

READ the official prequel
to the blockbuster film!

THE OFFICIAL PREQUEL TO THE
UPCOMING BLOCKBUSTER FILM!
TRANSFORMERS™
GHOSTS OF
YESTERDAY
ALAN DEAN FOSTER

And don't
miss the
official
TRANSFORMERS
movie
novelization!

OUR WORLD. THEIR WAR.

Available wherever books are sold.

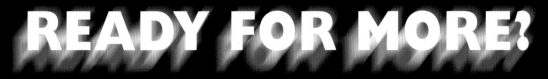

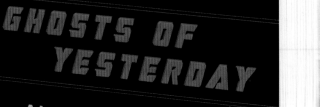

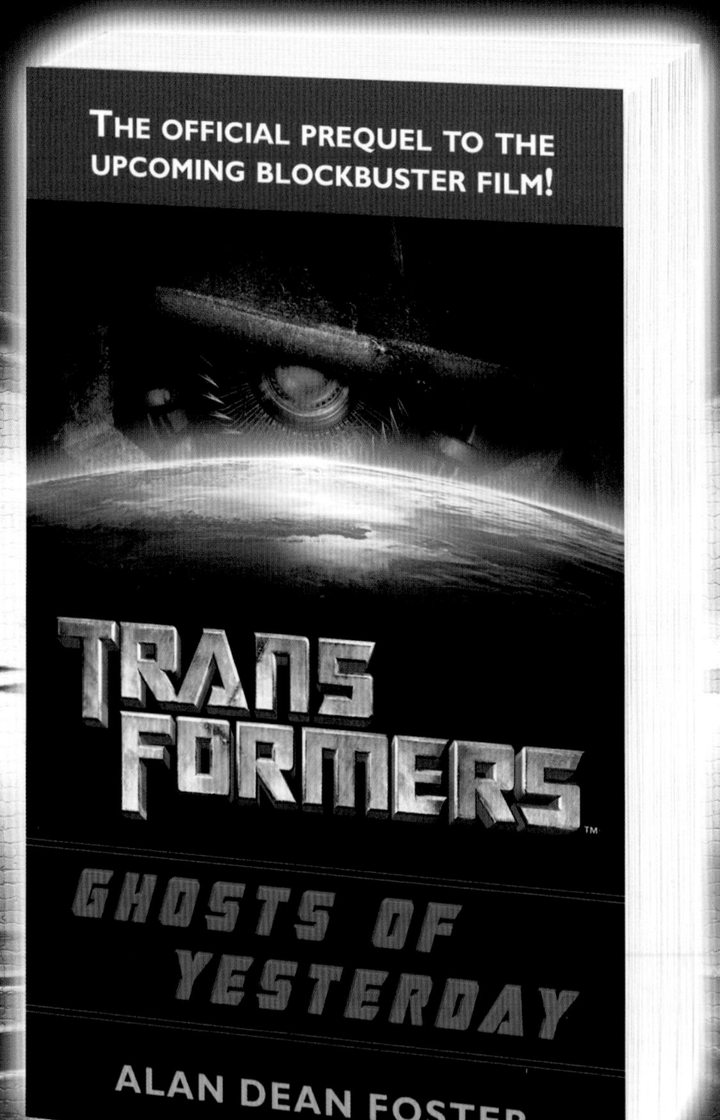

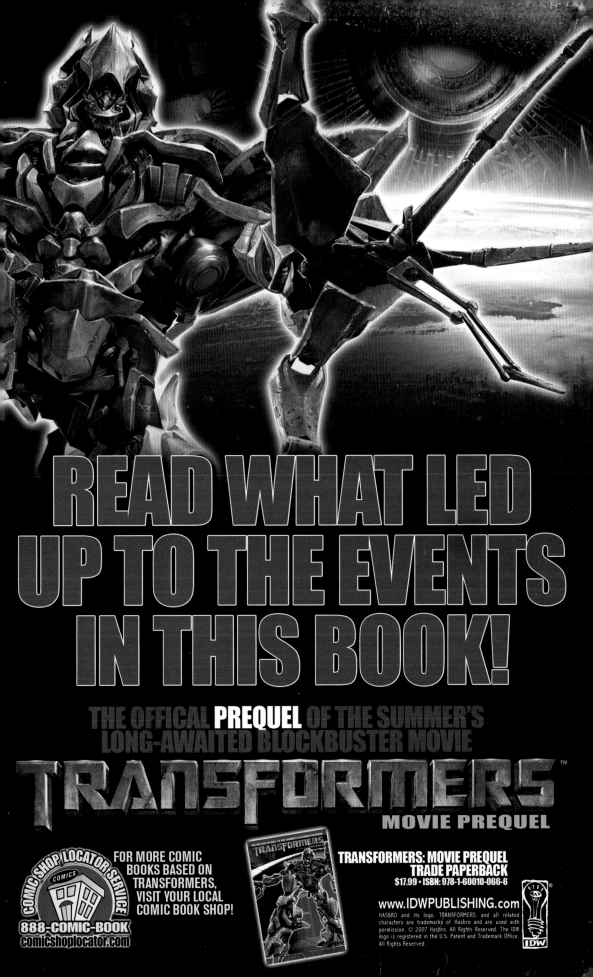

www.IDWPublishing.com

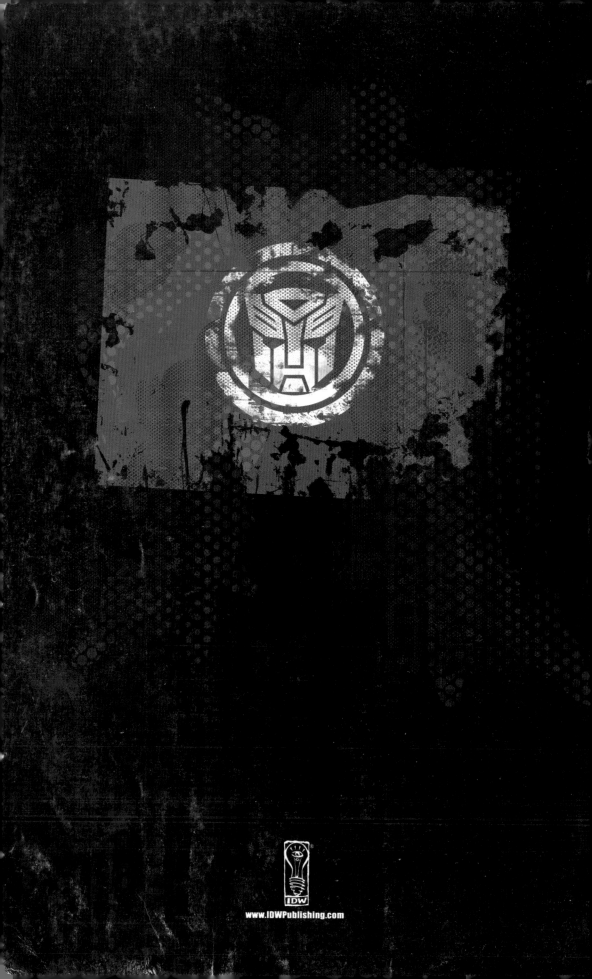